1507

1250

Greek Tragedy
on the American Stage

Jacqueline Kim as Electra in the Guthrie Theater's 1992 production of *Electra*. Photo Credit: Michael Daniel.

GREEK TRAGEDY ON THE __AMERICAN STAGE__

Ancient Drama in the Commercial Theater, 1882–1994

Karelisa V. Hartigan

Contributions in Drama and Theatre Studies,
Number 60

GREENWOOD PRESS
Westport, Connecticut • London

Library of Congress Cataloging-in-Publication Data

Hartigan, Karelisa.
    Greek tragedy on the American stage : ancient drama in the
commercial theater, 1882–1994 / Karelisa V. Hartigan.
        p.   cm.—(Contributions in drama and theatre studies, ISSN
0163–3821 ; no. 60)
    Includes bibliographical references and index.
    ISBN 0–313–29283–3 (alk. paper)
    1. Greek drama (Tragedy)—Presentation, Modern. 2. United States—
Civilization—Greek influences. 3. Theater—United States—
History. I. Title. II. Series.
PA3238.H37   1995
792.9′5′09730904—dc20   94–48016

British Library Cataloguing in Publication Data is available.

Library of Congress Catalog Card Number: 94–48016
ISBN: 0–313–29283–3
ISSN: 0163–3821

First published in 1995

Greenwood Press, 88 Post Road West, Westport, CT 06881
An imprint of Greenwood Publishing Group, Inc.

Printed in the United States of America

∞™

The paper used in this book complies with the
Permanent Paper Standard issued by the National
Information Standards Organization (Z39.48–1984).

10 9 8 7 6 5 4 3 2 1

For Kevin, with love

Contents

Preface

This book developed from the chapter on the history of Greek tragedy production I wrote at the request of Meyer Reinhold for the *Classical Tradition in the Americas* project. As I did the research for that multivolume, multiauthor series, I realized there existed a great wealth of material scattered in various collections and journals that might be brought together to give a more complete picture of how Greek tragedy has been staged in the United States. More interesting was the critical reception given these stagings of the ancient texts. Two themes soon became evident: first, a performance of a Greek play prompts the theater critics to wax philosophical; a production leads them to ponder the ideas learned (however imperfectly) in school and to debate the value of "the classics." Second, the texts that held appeal for directors and the American audience varied with the political tenor of the times. Thus *Trojan Women* was frequently staged during times of military conflict, but seldom during times of peace. Euripides' *The Bacchae* was not performed early in the century, but became the play of choice during the 1960s. While not every production of Greek tragedy was staged in response to social conditions, general trends are possible to identify.

The book has been arranged in chronological units that roughly correspond to the social history of this nation. To avoid a disjointed discussion of a text's performance history, I have blended the two possible methods of presentation: the plays that appealed during a specific time period are noted, and then a full production history of the most popular play (or plays) of that period is given. Thus while the discussion breaks the time frames of the chapters, the production histories are continuous. While Greek tragedy has long been a vibrant part of the repertoire of college and university theaters, I have limited the performance histories here to the shows done in commercial theaters, primarily those in New York, Chicago, and Minneapolis (at the Guthrie Theater), then to those on the West Coast, although Greek tragedy has earned less acclaim in the theaters of California.

The time covered spans about 112 years, from the famous production of *Oedipus Tyrannus* in New York in 1882 to that of *Medea* in 1994, although the 1845 staging of *Antigone* is noted. The information has been gleaned from the reviews penned by drama critics of the major newspapers, from programs, press releases, and magazine articles; in several instances the comments are based on my own observations of more recent productions.

The intent of this book is both to enlighten and to entertain the reader. The performance histories should serve the former, the critics' comments the latter. I consider it worth noting how these classical plays have been interpreted in such widely divergent ways while their texts have remained (apart from updated translations) fairly constant. My further aim has been to illustrate the continued vitality of the ancient texts, to show that the words of the Greek playwrights speak to issues of the modern world. Throughout the past century in America the plays of Aeschylus, Sophocles, and Euripides have regularly been, in the words of the ancient Athenian judges, "granted a chorus," and as in recent years the dramas have been performed even more often, I have no doubt they will continue to be accorded the opportunity to be staged.

ACKNOWLEDGMENTS

There are many people who have assisted me in this project. First I must recognize the excellent staff of the Billy Rose Theatre Collection at the Library of the Performing Arts of the New York Public Library in New York City. Without their help and without their collection this book would not have been possible. Second I must thank various colleagues around the nation who have sent me both texts and reviews; among these Jeffrey Wills of the University of Wisconsin at Madison deserves to be mentioned. Finally and most importantly in bibliographic help I must note the outstanding assistance given by Blake Landor and John Van Hook of the University of Florida Library, whose extensive electronic literature searches brought me numerous recent theater reviews.

Special thanks are due also to Dr. Fiona Macintosh of the University of Reading, to Dr. William Mould of the University of South Carolina, to Dr. Walter Forehand of Tallahassee, Florida, and to Dr. Robert Sonkowsky of the University of Minnesota for reading the manuscript in draft form. Several student assistants at the University of Florida deserve recognition: Douglas Band, Catherine O'Hanlon, and Carol Walker made my work much easier. Finally I recognize the assistance and patience of Peter Coveney and Lori Blackwell of the Greenwood Publishing Group during the final stages of manuscript preparation. I am grateful, also, to the National Endowment for the Humanities for a Summer Travel Grant to support one trip to the Billy Rose Theatre Collection in New York City.

Most especially I acknowledge my husband, Kevin McCarthy, first for guiding me in the type of research a book such as this required, second for his continued support and patience during the research and writing, and finally for his belief in my ability to complete the project. It has been a delight to share my interest in drama with him. Thus the book is dedicated to him.

Greek Tragedy
on the American Stage

I

Introduction

Greek tragedy has had a continuous appeal for the American commercial theater for the last hundred years. Although the tendency of our country is to hail the new and reject the old, the Greek dramas are still brought to the stage. The theme or message of the plays by Aeschylus, Sophocles, and Euripides has consistently been deemed important, because the issues addressed by the writers of fifth-century B.C. Athens continue to be current, continue to have a relevance for twentieth-century America. Only the form, not the content, of the texts has limited the number of productions: directors find the lengthy speeches and the lack of physical action too restricting, while the ever-present chorus is difficult to use effectively.

Whenever a director or producer determines to offer a Greek tragedy, or an actress wishes to portray one of the great figures of Athenian drama, the theater critics flock to the performance. Whether or not they finally acclaim the production, almost without fail they devote much of their review to the importance of the event, and reiterate to their readers a single theme: Greek drama is worth seeing. The passion displayed by these mythic characters lies at the heart of all our emotions, proclaim the critics; the choices the characters face and the decisions they make offer valuable examples to the modern audience. At times a Greek tragedy has been hailed as the best play of a contemporary theater season. But even when a show is panned, the negative reviews arise not from the play but from the production.

Over the years the interpretation of these ancient texts has varied. Directors and producers have seen different messages in the plays, and critical reception of the performances has also changed. Thus we find that although the basic texts of Aeschylus, Sophocles, or Euripides remain fairly constant, the meanings drawn from their plays do not. Certain plays, furthermore, have been more popular at one time or another during the past century. A script that played well during World War I, for example, earned scant praise during the 1950s; another tragedy never seen in the 1930s was frequently staged during the 1960s. A study such as I have made here also reveals that some Greek plays have been consistently popular, others are seldom—if ever—produced: the twentieth-century American audience has seen many performances of Sophocles' *Antigone*, but virtually none of the same playwright's *Women of Trachis*, few of his *Ajax*.

In this book I review the comments written by the drama critics about the productions of Greek tragedy on the American commercial stage for the past century, or, to be completely accurate, for the last 112 years, 1882–1994. The critics describe, often in much detail, the way the ancient plays have been staged as well as the quality of the acting. But we can glean more from their reviews: from the comments of contemporary critics we learn the temper of the times, for the plays are not produced in a social vacuum. In ancient Athens, the poet-playwrights were the teachers of their society, and their plays reflect their social context. The same holds true today. Although in the modern theater *ars gratia artis* may be a recognized principle, nevertheless the theater must cater to an audience, and a director or especially a producer must consider what might appeal to the paying public. Small theater troupes may have more room for the experimental, but even they must rely upon box office sales. Thus when the decision is made to stage a Greek tragedy in a commercial theater in modern America, this decision rests upon a belief in the viability of the text to reach a contemporary audience, and the reviewers for the various newspapers record for the American public the success of the venture. The words of the drama critics become a record of both a particular performance and the times in which it played.

In the following pages I discuss the productions of Greek tragedy on the American commercial stage from the first performance of Sophocles' *Oedipus Tyrannus* in New York City in 1882 to the Tony Award–winning production of Euripides' *Medea* on Broadway in 1994. My text has been divided into ten- to twenty-year periods according to the social and political history of the United States. With the possible exception of the last two decades, this nation was engaged in a major war about every twenty years, and these military conflicts made an impact upon theater as well as political history. During the more recent years of my study there has been a noticeable increase in the number of productions of Greek tragedy, and the reasons for this bear consideration.

Within each time frame I note key performances of Greek tragedies and then give the total record of those that earned special acclaim, tracing the history of that play's productions, for certain texts have had greater appeal during any given time. Euripides' *The Bacchae*, for example, was the Greek tragedy of the 1960s, while his *Trojan Women* is staged each time the United States goes to war. Furthermore, it seems that certain productions become the touchstone for an era and often remain the standard by which future performances are judged. Thus the critics likened any actress playing Medea in the 1920s to the interpretation by Margaret Anglin in 1918; any actress attempting to play the barbarian princess after the 1940s knew she would be compared to Judith Anderson, who dominated the role during the latter years of that decade.

Throughout this study it must be remembered that the scripts of Aeschylus, Sophocles, and Euripides have remained relatively unchanged. There have been, naturally, updated versions, and new methods of production have been introduced. Charles Mee's 1990s *Orestes* is an example of the former, while Andrei Serban's multilingual productions during the 1970s illustrate the latter. Nevertheless, the old legend shows through; the alteration lies in the interpretation. The varied reception accorded to the ancient Greek tragedies reflects contemporary American society and gives us a record both of a play's performance history and an artistic view of our nation.

While the origins of Greek drama are uncertain, the idea of a masked actor, impersonating a figure from traditional mythology and addressing a responsive chorus, is credited to Thespis in the late 500s B.C. His creation was developed further during the fifth century B.C. in Athens, when Aeschylus, Sophocles, and Euripides wrote their tragedies for the annual state-sponsored festival in honor of Dionysos Eleutherios in the springtime month of Elaphebolion. Each author entered into competition a set of three tragedies and a satyr play for production during the five-day City Dionysia.[1] From archaeology and vase paintings many aspects of the theater itself and the style of performance are familiar, while the actors' use of masks, stylized costumes, standardized sets and gestures is common knowledge. Also well known are the emphasis upon words, not staged action, and the ever-present twelve- to fifteen-member chorus. Knowing these characteristics of Greek drama, many modern directors hesitate to stage the ancient plays; they recognize that the themes are important, a part of the very fabric of Western culture, but find it difficult to make the texts come alive for an audience raised upon visual, not verbal action, an audience who prefers to see violence enacted, not merely hear what has taken place.[2] Thus if the plays are staged, they are often altered and "updated"; directors try to make them "more relevant" by changing the text, the setting, or even the plot itself.[3]

When an approximation of the ancient method is attempted, often the approximation is pushed to excess, with the new creation becoming something bizarre, perhaps interesting, but often failing to communicate the beauty and power of the classical text.[4] Other difficulties arise when conventions of the ancient stage are attempted; in the proper setting masks can be effective, but on the standard proscenium stage in an average-size theater, the masks often become too much an object of interest or amusement in themselves. Again, the deus ex machina, the god who suddenly appears on high to offer a closing solution for the dramatic action, is a difficult aspect of ancient drama for a modern audience to accept, and if the deity arrives awkwardly by crane, the divinity brings humor, not salvation.

Modern versions of the plays of Aeschylus, Sophocles, and Euripides are effective when they are performed in a manner that both respects the authors' texts and preserves such conventions from antiquity that are beyond dispute and accessible to a modern audience, i.e., a serious style and a chorus that participates and dances to a musical accompaniment.[5] Over the years, well-done productions of Greek tragedy which have approached the classical texts holding these considerations in mind have attained a considerable measure of success and have earned both critical acclaim and audience enthusiasm.

A NOTE ON METHODOLOGY AND SOURCES

This book records the performance history of Greek tragedy on the commercial stages of America. The histories are based on the comments of contemporary drama reviewers and critics, and thus naturally reflect the sentiments and the biases of those who make a living by judging theatrical productions.[6] The validity of my method rests on two primary assumptions. First, Greek drama is not an unknown quantity: the classics have long formed at least a part of formal education in this country. For better or for worse, "every schoolboy"—or girl—has at some time read a Sophoclean tragedy, usually *Oedipus Tyrannus* or *Antigone*; from time to time the texts of Euripides and even Aeschylus are part of the regular curriculum. Those who write from the drama desk have usually had broader training; some have worked at one time in the theater. Thus when Brooks Atkinson, Walter Kerr, Clive Barnes, Dan Sullivan, Sylvie Drake, or other familiar names on the drama pages of major newspapers attend a Greek show, they bring with them a basic knowledge of the play and the traditional method of presenting it. Their judgments are made from an educated point of view.[7]

Second, the drama critics pen their reviews after seeing the show. They are not writing of imagined productions, nor of performances remembered or culled from literary sources. As one scholar of the theater notes, the critics "have done their play-going in the theatre."[8] Thus the critical comments upon which I have based *my* judgments form an immediate record of what took place on a given night in the theater, when a tragedy by one of the three Athenian playwrights was performed on an American stage. Finally, no performance takes place in a social or cultural vacuum; each is part of the contemporary milieu. The critic reflects the society which comprises the audience. That audience and its point of view are a key element in the practice of live theater.

While ideally the critic should be better informed than the general audience, only the top newspapers hire a theater specialist. Here I have relied on the reviews of the better known theater critics, writing for the top newspapers, and thus the same names recur throughout my text. Nevertheless, perhaps a caveat is in order. In his history of the San Francisco stage, Dean Goodman suggests five points to consider when one reads a critic's review.[9] He elaborates; here I merely summarize. The theater critic must love all kinds of theater, and have knowledge of its history. He or she should strive for a blend of subjectivity and accuracy. The critic should also understand something about both acting and directing. Fourth, good criticism depends upon clear writing. Finally, and most important for me, those who write critical reviews should have a sense of "social and artistic responsibility." If the comments of those drama reviewers whom I have quoted here are considered with Goodman's criteria in mind, I think readers will receive an honest evaluation of the Greek tragedy performances staged during the past century in this country.[10] From their reviews the interface of theater and social history may also be known.

NOTES

1. The festival was celebrated 9–13 *Elaphebolion*, the ninth month of the Athenian year, which roughly corresponds to late March/early April today. On the eve of the event, a *proagon* took place, at which participants in the dramatic contests were introduced as an advance announcement of the persons to be featured. The three tragedies might have a connected theme, forming an equivalent of the three acts of a modern play (e.g., Aeschylus' *Oresteia*), or be three discrete dramas. These were followed by the satyr play, a burlesque version of a myth, often one related to the story told seriously in the tragedies.

Originally performances were offered on four days of the festival, but this was cut to three during the Peloponnesian War, with the comedies then being played in the evening; see H. W. Parke, *Festivals of the Athenians* (Ithaca, NY: 1977): 131, and Margarete Bieber, *The History of the Greek and Roman Theater* (Princeton, NJ: 1961): 3–5. For the staging of Greek drama, see Oliver Taplin, *Greek Tragedy in Action* (Berkeley, CA: 1978): 9–21, and J. Michael Walton, *Greek Theatre Production* (Westport, CT: 1980): 59–80.

2. We know that even in antiquity the ancient plays were performed less often than read; the ancients, who did not read silently, might well have had what we term "readings." Aristotle (*Poet.* 1453b14) was the first to suggest that the plays need not be seen to be appreciated; one could feel pity and fear merely by knowing the plot outline. Although Taplin (*Greek Tragedy in Action*: 2) states that "only a lunatic fringe of students of Greek drama" deny the primacy of performance, the reality is otherwise: far more scholars assert the primacy of text over performance.

3. I am not referring to those successful plays based on the ancient legends, O'Neill's *Mourning Becomes Electra*, for example, or the dramas of Giraudoux, Anouilh, or Cocteau. These scripts seek to express their message via the myths themselves and do not pretend to be re-creations of an Athenian original. For a

good discussion of this topic see Hugh Dickinson, *Myth on the Modern Stage* (Urbana, IL: 1969), and Angela Belli, *Ancient Greek Myths and Modern Drama. A Study in Continuity* (New York: 1969).

4. Examples of more bizarre productions would be Andrei Serban's *Agamemnon* or the Guthrie-Campbell *House of Atreus*; both are discussed in Chapter 6. While Serban's version of *Trojan Women, Fragments of a Trilogy*, wherein he used a mixture of ancient Greek, Latin, and unfamiliar African languages to convey the suffering of the captive women, received critical acclaim for the pathos the nonlanguage aroused, in his version of *Agamemnon* the so-called use of classical Greek was a mere pretense. In this production the absence of understandable language limits its impact.

5. While we lack sufficient knowledge of the music of classical Greece to be able to reproduce it, a musical accompaniment that responds to the conditions of an ancient production, i.e., simplicity and religious ritual, can and must be offered.

6. While actors and producers of necessity have a love-hate or, more usually, a hate-love relationship with the men and women who review their work, they recognize their importance.

In this study I have used the terms "critic" and "reviewer" interchangeably. Technically the critic is one who brings sufficient background to the position to be considered an authority; the comments of the critic form the longer and reflective articles of the Sunday editions. The daily reviewer, on the other hand, must make instantaneous decisions about the show just seen. Because of time, immediacy, and the size of readership, the latter has a greater influence on the public's perception of any given show.

7. A good discussion of the function of a review is given by Richard H. Palmer, *The Critics' Canon. Standards of Theatrical Reviewing in America* (Westport, CT: 1988): 5–17.

8. John Mason Brown, "Introduction," *The American Theatre as Seen by Its Critics. 1752–1934*, ed. by Montrose J. Moses (New York: 1967): 13.

9. Dean Goodman, *San Francisco Stages. A Concise History, 1849–1986* (San Francisco: 1986): 95–116.

10. Some might wish I had included at least thumbnail biographical sketches of the critics most often quoted here. The well-known figures are in the standard biographical dictionaries, *Who's Who in American Theater* and *Contemporary American Theater Critics*; many are featured in more specific studies, e.g., Lehman Engel, *The Critics* (New York: 1976). In my study, from their comments, the critics shall be known.

2

The Earliest Plays

SOPHOCLES: *OEDIPUS TYRANNUS*

"Oedipus in Greek is a beautiful example of the accomplishments of the ancient poets, but in English it is stupid, tedious, and utterly wanting in picturesqueness, two absolute essentials in modern play writing." Thus did the reviewer of the *New York Mirror*, of Saturday, 4 February 1882, react to the first commercial production of this Greek tragedy in the United States. It is startling to realize that nearly a full century passed from the days of the Founding Fathers, who were certainly schooled in the classics, until the plays of ancient Athens were, to use the Athenian term, "granted a chorus" for the American stage.[1]

The performance at the Booth Theater in the winter of 1882 was a venture undertaken after the success of the earlier staging of the Greek tragedy at Harvard in the spring of 1881. There, on an evening in May, George Riddle, class of '74, played Oedipus, and his supporting cast was drawn from the ranks of the undergraduate classes; all spoke their lines in classical Greek. The language may have been the only "authentic" aspect of the performance, however, for the set was lavish, the chorus large, and playing time was three and a half hours![2] The costumes, the reviewer of *Frank Leslie's Illustrated Newspaper* (4 June 1881) assures us, were authentic to fifth-century Athens, since "historical accuracy to the period of the mythical figures was not possible." From the pictures included in his article, however, one might guess that Julius Caesar would have found no problem in donning King Oedipus' attire, for the Greek cloaks, *himatia*, looked very like Roman togas. In any case, the production was a historic event and won wide acclaim, at least in the Northeast, and its success encouraged the idea of taking the Greek show to New York City.

Before opening in New York, however, a preview of the revised production was offered in Boston on a bitterly cold January night; but the chilling temperature did not deter the New York drama critics from attending the performance. The set had been elaborately refashioned to resemble even more closely an ancient Greek theater, upon which the curtain remained open the entire time, while costumes and music gave evidence of the care taken in preparation of this exceptional show.

The reviewer of the *New York Times* of 24 January 1882, while terming the show a "flattering success" and praising especially the dignified acting of Georgia Cayvan as Jocasta and Lewis Morrison as Creon, in addition to the excellent delivery of his lines in Greek by George Riddle, noted that the learned audience did find portions of the performance rather tedious. He cautioned, further, that the success of the play before a popular audience remained a question. As it turned out, his fears were well founded.

As the reviewer of the *Mirror* pointed out, it is a very different matter when the production is done in a commercial theater and the public is expected to pay a full $1.50 for a ticket. His reactions, and those of other contemporary critics, garner attention here as reflective of the times. First, however, should be noted the "polyglot fashion" in which the show was done: Riddle spoke the part of Oedipus in Greek, and the supporting cast gave their lines in English.

The production was, in the words of the *Mirror's* reviewer, "exquisitely mounted, admirably played, but not worth a ducat as a dramatic attraction." He continues:

The production of Sophocles' *Oedipus Tyrannus* at Booth's . . . was an event which was expected to create a deep interest among the *literati*, and a great curiosity among the general public, but anyone who scanned the unfilled auditorium before the play began discovered a very poor showing of either element.

Oedipus cannot justly be treated as a dramatic performance—there is nothing dramatic about it. [It is of literary interest] but to the average theater goer it is a decided bore.

Even more offensive to this reviewer was the translation used.

The name of the translator . . . was omitted from the bills for which we are sorry, for we should like to get at him. He has rendered the work into the most colloquial and commonplace form of English, often obscuring the meaning of the author, from sheer carelessness or ignorance of the Greek text, and oftener adding ideas of his own. It is the freest and vilest translation we ever saw.

He quotes a few lines form the scene he found best in the play, the messenger's report of Oedipus' blinding, and while the rendition is decidedly labored, "vilest" would seem to be hyperbole. But the performance could not have pleased this member of the audience in any way, for Sophocles' play itself earned the reviewer's derision.

The argument of the drama is brief, but overflowing with the most horrible and immoral incidents. . . . If Mr. Cazauran should write, and Manager Palmer produce, a piece with a plot like this . . . it is probable Anthony Comstock would close up the theater as a disorderly house in direct violation of the city's ordinances.

The critic from the *New York World* (31 January 1882) was equally displeased with the performance: "The work of a Greek player was a matter of mask and declamation. The task of really acting it was, therefore, an impossible undertaking, and the blood of bloody Oedipus is exceedingly repulsive, view it as one may."

The drama critic of the *New York Times* (31 January 1882) displayed a gentler despair with the entire production. For him, Sophocles' play was to be admired, studied, and cherished, but, he continues, it is with "regret and amusement" that one views the attempt to stage the drama: "To place the *Oedipus* of Sophocles upon the stage is like an attempt to paint a picture without perspective, or to stuff a large and brilliant canvas into a small portrait frame. . . . [His characters are ideals] which indifferent American actors render with little meaning and no impressiveness."[3]

The majority of reviewers, however, in spite of their disappointment in the play as drama and in its production as entertainment, praised the acting. While not pleased with the polyglot dialogue (which must have been somewhat disconcerting), the *Mirror*'s reviewer reported that George Riddle's Greek was "smooth, soft, elegant, musical, copious in gentle sibilants and marked by frequent aspirates," all of which earned him several rounds of applause. By all accounts, the hit of the play was Georgia Cayvan as Jocasta, who "fairly outdid herself in depicting the horror of the situation" when she learned the identity of Oedipus and her relationship with him. The other members of the cast also performed well, speaking their speeches with as much beauty "as the ridiculous travesty of the text made by the wretched translator allowed."[4]

All in all, the Booth staging of *Oedipus* was an event in theater history, if not a successful one. What is most interesting is that the play failed on its own merits, not in the actors' performance. Victorian New York was not ready for Greek drama.

The story of the king of Thebes who discovers that he has inadvertently committed the worst crimes society imagines, that he has stepped beyond the borders of the taboo, found no place of approval in late-nineteenth-century America. Many critics saw Oedipus only as the victim of the gods, and to watch a king brutally crushed by external forces against which he had no recourse was the antithesis to the philosophy of success, the American myth of universal opportunity in which each man achieves the realization of his goal by hard work, by his own personal endeavors.[5]

The less philosophical members of the audience took the events of the Greek myth at face value, regarding them in the same way as they would the stirring action of contemporary melodrama. But in melodrama, the victim is rescued in the nick of time, while in Greek drama, at least in *Oedipus Tyrannus,* no deus ex machina saves the king and queen from their destiny. Thus it is that the reviewer of the *Mirror* sarcastically notes, "In Sophocles' time, such trifling matters as a man's committing homicide, marrying his mother, and putting his eyes out afterwards was merely an indication of the culture, taste and artistic appreciation of the Athenian public to which his pen was devoted."

In spite of their hostility, most of the critics could not break free of the feeling that Sophocles was, after all, one of the classics, part of the canon every educated person should know. Thus while they could not refrain from noting that in the audience "the professors were out in full and college boys abounded," they urged their readers to see the show, at least to satisfy their curiosity. For that is what *Oedipus* was in Victorian New York: a curiosity but not a stage-worthy drama. The texts of Sophocles—Aeschylus and Euripides are not considered—were to be appreciated as relics of the past and glorious age of Greece, but they were unsuitable for the contemporary stage, both because of their static style and because their plots, although based on familiar myths, were not suitable for the audiences of late-nineteenth-century America. No Greek play was attempted again by an American company[6] in a commercial venue for nearly thirty years, and *Oedipus* would not be performed again until the 1920s, with the exception of two single evening performances in 1911 and 1913.

John Kellerd played the title role in both these shows. The reviewer of the *New York Times* of 4 February 1913 noted that his performance was "dignified and repressed" but that the rest of the cast was merely "adequate," while the pictorial aspect was "not impressive." However, the 1911 production, offered on a hot August evening, had earned higher praise. A review in *Theater Magazine* (October 1911) stated that the large audience at the Irving Place Theater were "well repaid for their physical inconvenience by the really intelligent, thoughtful and impressive performance" given by Kellerd and his associates. But the reviewer resented the continuous playing without a break that Kellerd elected to do; this member of the audience remembered the superb performance (in French) given by Mounet-Sully in 1894, in which the curtain fell several times.

The rather lengthy review is interesting in the clear evidence it gives of the critic's split emotions. He knows that he should praise a play by so great an author, and does praise Kellerd's enthusiasm in choosing Sophocles for a summer show. But nevertheless it is clear the reviewer did not enjoy the evening. Kellerd's acting, he finally reveals, was lacking in movement, while Lillian Kingbury's Jocasta was rather too modern. One wonders why the performance took two exhaustive hours, since "the so-to-speak editorial comments of the chorus were entrusted to two senators, [whose] dicta, be it said, was mercifully cut."

To this reviewer, the most notable fact about Kellerd's 1911 production was that it was the first to be performed in New York City in English. After these performances, *Oedipus Tyrannus* did not reappear in New York theaters again until 1923. This and future performances are discussed in Chapter 5.

SOPHOCLES: *ANTIGONE*

Even before *Oedipus* was staged in New York, an attempt to attract the general public to a Greek show had been made about forty years earlier. *Antigone* holds pride of place for being the very first Greek tragedy offered as a commercial venture in this country. In 1845 a New York businessman, hoping to inaugurate the production of serious drama in a city then delighting in melodrama and spectacle, chose to mount Sophocles' play as his initial offering. Thus did Mr. Dinneford rent Palmo's Opera House and open with *Antigone* on 7 April 1845.

There was much preshow publicity: Dinneford made sure that his venture was known. The *Albion* (5 April 1845) reports that the production would be done "with every accessory necessary for a faithful representation; among the most prominent of which will be the choral music of Mendelssohn." A box advertisement gave further information, in which Sophocles' play was labeled the chef d'oeuvre of his genius, and the enthusiastic reception given the play in Berlin, Paris, and London was noted. The stage was to be a model of a Grecian theater, with "scene, costumes, groupings, etc. [to be] in perfect keeping." George Vandenhoff was to be both the stage manager and the character of Creon; the advertisement box did not state who was to play the title role. The final inducement was that there was to be "an efficient Orchestra and powerful Chorus, capable of giving full effect to Mendelssohn's sublime music."[7]

In spite of the preshow publicity and anticipation, the play did not delight its audience. The *Albion's* reviewer, writing on 12 April 1845, could not hide the show's failure. Although done "in a style of classic elegance that should have insured the representation perfect success," the play was coldly received. The critic suggested first of all that the physical setting of the indoor chamber theater was not suited for Greek tragedy, which was created to be performed outside in vast open spaces. Second, he blamed both the actors, unused to speaking in the tragic style, and an audience, unused to hearing it, for the show's lack of popularity. Finally, Miss Clarendon, playing the title role, was disappointing. She was not able "to grasp the character of the noble and devoted Antigone." Thus despite Dinneford's reduction of the ticket price, the curtain fell on the production after barely two weeks. New York City was not to see another *Antigone* for well over a century.

The earliest stagings of Greek tragedy in the American commercial theater cannot be judged a success. *Antigone* failed on the quality of its production. *Oedipus Tyrannus*, however, failed on moral grounds: it was not the ineptitude of the actors that earned the critics' displeasure, it was the subject matter of the text. Sophocles' play touched no chord of understanding in the hearts of the American audience in the late years of the nineteenth century.

NOTES

1. In 1881, *Oedipus Tyrannus* had been staged to great acclaim in France, with Jean Mounet-Sully playing the title role. However, the popularity of the play on continental soil did not spread across the Channel: Sophocles' play did not escape the blue line of the British censor for a commercial production in London until 1910. This play, as well as a few others, had been staged at British universities nearly twenty years earlier. For a discussion of Greek tragedy performances at this time in England and Europe, see Fiona Macintosh, "Tragedy in Performance: Nineteenth and Twentieth Century Productions," in *The Cambridge Companion to Greek Tragedy*, edited by P. E. Easterling (Cambridge: forthcoming). I thank Dr. Macintosh for letting me read and cite her article in draft.

2. The length of time is unusual for a single play, for an entire trilogy could be performed in this amount of time, or perhaps a bit more; the satyr play would have added an extra half hour at most. I attended a continuous playing of Aeschylus' *Oresteia* at the Herod Atticus theater in Athens in 1985; the performance lasted just over three hours. For a scholarly discussion of the playing time of ancient dramas, see Peter Walcot, *Greek Drama in Its Theatrical and Social Context* (Cardiff: 1976): 11–21.

3. The reviewer continues with further speculation on the vagaries of time: "[Sophocles] could hardly have supposed, when he watched the growing popularity of his rival, Euripides, that *Oedipus Tyrannus* would be seen twenty centuries later in an American play-house, and would be gaudily advertised by startling lithographs displayed in Yankee grog shops."

4. In addition to those already named, the cast of this production included J. F. Hagan as Tiresias and the Corinthian Messenger, J. J. Hayes as the Priest and Shepherd, P. Charles Hagar was the Palace Messenger, Preston Wilcox was the Coryphaeus, the Misses Melville and Hill played Ismene and Antigone respectively and also served as attendants on Jocasta.

5. See Doris M. Alexander, "Oedipus in Victorian New York," *American Quarterly* 12 (1960): 417–421.

6. In late March 1894, the French troupe headed by J. Mounet-Sully brought his *Oedipus Tyrannus* and *Antigone* to New York. Performed at Abbey's Theater, the shows, so popular in France, played to an "audience that did not dangerously crowd the theater," according to the reviewer of the *New York Times* (28 March 1894). This critic praised the company as a whole, but did not find Mounet-Sully's acting in the second part of the tragedy fully satisfying, and considered the closing

scene overly long. To be noted, however, is that he did not condemn the play for its moral failings, stating rather: "Age has left no trace upon [the play]. In logic, as in emotion, there is nothing about this King and Queen that is not human, not the humanity of today." Later critics looked back to Mounet-Sully's performance as a touchstone against which to judge current actors—and found the more recent players wanting.

7. A full description of this music may be read in H. Rushton Fairclough, *Antigone. An Account of the Presentation of the Antigone of Sophocles.* (Performed [in Greek] at Stanford University in 1902) (San Francisco: 1903). Macintosh ("Tragedy in Performance": 5–7) discusses the European stagings of this version of *Antigone.* She points out that Mendelssohn's music was not particularly well received at the Covent Garden production in 1845, but that nevertheless the music remained popular for the next fifty years and was the main attraction in revivals at the end of the century.

3

Greek Tragedy Gains Recognition: 1900–1915

The first performance of Greek tragedy to garner attention as a statement relevant to the times took place in 1915, when Harley Granville Barker staged Euripides' *Trojan Women* (and *Iphigeneia at Tauris*) in an outdoor stadium in New York City and other stadia in the Northeast, and Maurice Browne took *Trojan Women* on tour from the Chicago Little Theatre. The reception accorded these productions inaugurates the connection between Greek drama and contemporary society in America.

EURIPIDES: *TROJAN WOMEN*

From the 1915 production to the present day, *Trojan Women* remains one of Euripides' most popular plays, staged, along with *Medea* and, in the recent past, *The Bacchae*, more frequently than any other. The continued appeal of this play is no mystery: *Trojan Women* is perceived to be the play from ancient Greece that most powerfully depicts the pain of warfare, and America has gone to war in nearly every decade of this century. Although some scholarly analysis of the drama tends to find it rather lacking in theme and characterization,[1] it usually plays to a receptive audience. The suffering of the women, all of whom we might call "brides of death," touches the hearts of any audience.[2] As long as mankind enters into armed combat, wherein one side must lose, the other triumph, *Trojan Women* will be returned to the stage. Euripides' play was first presented in America in 1915 during World War I, enjoyed several productions during World War II, and reached a height of popularity during the war-torn society of the 1960s.

Granville Barker's *Trojan Women* was performed outdoors on 29 May 1915, at the stadium of the City College of New York, to which some seven thousand came to see the show. Clayton Hamilton, writing in *Vogue* (July 1915), explained how the poet, who "had looked into the very mind of God," was "speaking with peculiar pertinence of the crisis which confronts the world today." The drama critic of the *Nation* (3 June 1915) noted that Granville Barker was wise to start "his experiment with Greek plays in America with the radical Euripides, whose dramatic use of the human emotions makes him nearer akin to Shakespeare . . . than to his own stately contemporary." The reviewer of the *New York Mirror* (2 June 1915) noted that Nature herself contributed to the play's theme with the gray skies assisting its tragic atmosphere. He closed his review with a strong affirmation: "The *Trojan Women* steps forth living, with the glory of a drama that has never, at any time, been dead."[3]

While the chorus chanted to the melodious music composed by Yale professor David Stanley, Lillah McCarthy as Hecuba and Edith Wynne Matthison as Andromache brought to life the suffering of these victims of war. Speaking the words of Gilbert Murray's translation, whose words, Francis Hackett claimed (*New Republic*, 5 June 1915), "made Greek tragedy possible on [the] contemporary stage," the cast of this performance held the audience enthralled. The *Mirror*'s reviewer was equally impressed with the "timely and suggestive performance" of the acclaimed cast.[4] Granville Barker's artistic direction made the drama acceptable both to the modern member of the audience and to the archaeologist, the critics asserted, for mask and cothurnus were avoided while music, dance, and costume (which pictures reveal to have been quite elaborate) enhanced the fine acting and helped bring the text to life. Even when seen from a distance the performance was appealing. As Montrose Moses, writing in *The Theatre* (July 1915) remarked, "From the farthest corner of the Stadium, this splotch of Greek Drama on the greensward must have looked like a picture; and it was the pictorial effect Mr. Barker wanted. . . . In that respect he succeeded."

In addition to the successful performance in New York, the show also played in stadia at Yale, Harvard, Princeton, and the University of Pennsylvania. Sometimes the atmosphere at these various arenas was closer to the circus than to the ancient theatre; at times the show was in conflict with surrounding events. At Harvard, Moses noted:

One could not hear Hecuba every time an undergraduate ball player made a two bagger on the diamond adjoining the Stadium. Still, Mr. Barker and his associate players rose above the incongruity of the National Game vs. Greek Drama. . . . Despite the humors of time and place, the force of Euripides struck the hearts of the spectators.

Granville Barker had brought Greek drama to acclaim because Euripides' *Trojan Women* told a tale relevant to the American audience of 1915.

But it was not only audiences in the Northeast who were to see and experience the pathos of Euripides' play. Another director, Maurice Browne, who believed in the power of poetic drama, had already staged *Trojan Women* three years earlier. Now in 1915 he revived the production as an antiwar script. For although the earlier production of the play had won local critical attention, it was the tour undertaken by the Chicago Little Theatre under Browne's direction that made this troupe and this play a part of America's theater history.

Maurice Browne and the Chicago Little Theatre

The Chicago Little Theatre was just that: a stage measuring fifteen by twenty feet and an auditorium seating ninety-one people on the fourth floor of the Fine Arts Building in Chicago. But the reputation of the troupe that started here in 1912 spread nationwide during the years of World War I, and its history is central to any discussion of the development of theater in America.

Gaining attention across the nation at this time was the idea of creating little theaters, playhouses more appropriate for the psychological dramas just then becoming popular, where in the small space a more intimate bond between actors and audience would develop. Financial as well as artistic demands contributed to the creation of the little theater: in a limited, affordable space a young company could offer plays too new to be well-known, too unusual to appeal to a larger audience.

Maurice Browne was an entrepreneur who had come from England to Chicago after falling instantly in love with Ellen Van Volkenburg (Nellie Van) in Italy in 1910 and following as her fiancé to her Midwestern home. There the two theater enthusiasts determined to open a playhouse devoted to poetic drama. Counseled by Lady Gregory during a visit of the Irish Players (of the Abbey Theatre) to Chicago, Browne and Van Volkenburg gathered together others equally in love with the theater and willing to work in it for experience, not money. As their first play they decided upon *Trojan Women*.

Euripides' script was not originally chosen as an antiwar play; only later would the Chicago Little Theatre's production gain fame as a protest against war. As Browne and "Nellie Van" assembled their troupe, those who first answered their call were all actresses, and thus necessity determined a text with a female cast.[5] Indeed, as the time approached to open the Little Theatre, the Greek play was postponed, and the first shows done by the company were W. W. Gibson's *Womankind* and W. B. Yeats' *On Baile's Strand*. Shortly thereafter, however, *Trojan Women* opened and would be played every season for the next five years.

Writing in *Harper's Weekly* (29 November 1913), Floyd Dell described the standard initial reaction to a performance of Greek tragedy:

Now it has been the unhappy lot of most people who are seriously interested in the theater to witness (one "witnesses" a crime, and the word is peculiarly appropriate here) a performance in English of some Greek tragedy. The effect cannot usually be described as being that spiritual catharsis to which Aeschylus [sic] (as every schoolboy knows) referred. . . . If we learn anything from such productions, it is that Greek tragedy is not performance-proof. Something more than dressing up in white nightgowns and reciting the lines is required.

Maurice Browne, in the words of this reviewer, knew that to make poetic drama successful he must create an appropriate atmosphere. He did this, and succeeded against all odds. Working with "a score of red, amber and blue electric lights, a few yards of colored cloth, a post-impressionistic canvas wall and a dozen amateurs," Browne put on what was termed by both Dell and scholars of Greek drama a miracle and the finest staging of a Greek drama ever seen. Dell quotes Dr. Richard Moulton of the University of Chicago as saying that the Chicago Little Theatre's production preserved "the real spirit of the ancient classical drama," i.e., "the harmony of all the arts, beauty of color, flowing draperies, statuesque figures and gliding movements . . . all united in lyric harmony." Dell admits that the production was not perfect, but nevertheless had the effect "to pierce the minds of the audience with a tragic beauty."[6] The long review closes with a statement quoted from Browne himself:

We have tried to prove that those people are wrong who say that the time for poetic drama is past. We think it is beginning. . . . We have found that by using the right methods, poetic drama can be made as *interesting* as any other kind of drama. That is our accomplishment. . . . Best of all, we are making Euripides a contemporary.

The decision to use the text to make a pacifist statement was born of the views held in Chicago in 1914 and by Browne's contemporaries elsewhere. Determined to share in the "stay out of war" mood high in the nation at that time, he decided to do his part on the stage: how better than by playing "The World's Greatest Peace Play."[7] Browne had learned that Granville Barker was about to open the play in New York; the two directors met and determined to divide up the country: Barker would play in the eastern states, Browne in Washington and all that lay west. Sponsored by the Woman's Peace Party, the Little Theatre's tour of *Trojan Women* began in Chicago's Blackstone Theater and then played for community groups, on college campuses, and in commercial theaters around the nation, and always to full houses. Browne records that they were in Washington, D.C., when the *Lusitania* sank, and they expected an empty house:

there was not a vacant seat. Usually I spoke before a performance. By now I had learned how to stir an audience. . . . But that day there was no spellbinding. . . . You sat motionless and silent, row after row of white numb faces; and I merely stepped in front of the curtain with an evening paper in my hand and held up the monstrous headline and said: "This play is about a deed like that." You and Euripides did the rest.[8]

By August 1915 the Chicago Little Theatre, for fifteen weeks under the auspices of the Woman's Peace Party, had presented Euripides' *Trojan Women* forty-two times in thirty-one cities to approximately thirty-three thousand people coast to coast.[9] Critical reception of Browne's productions was universally positive, indeed superlative, for his company's acting, especially the stellar performances by Nellie Van as Hecuba, made his pacifist message crystal clear. *Trojan Women* had become a part of the antiwar literature of twentieth-century America.

EURIPIDES: *IPHIGENEIA AT TAURIS*

Before leaving this early period one should note that Granville Barker's 1915 productions of Greek tragedy included a second play, *Iphigeneia at Tauris*.[10] Even at this early date, however, reviewers dismissed this script, as do more recent critics, as unworthy of serious consideration.[11] Thus little attention was given to the play's theme or message.

On the other hand, the visual impact of Granville Barker's production earned the show considerable praise. The drama critic of the *New York Times* devoted the greater part of his review of the performance held in the Yale Bowl to describing the actors' costumes. Other critics sustained his views, noting how Norman Wilkinson had paid no attention to archaeology but to how a modern audience might enjoy a colorful artistic creation. Thus the reviewer of the *New York Times* (16 May 1915) writes:

Certainly Norman Wilkinson . . . was not oppressed by the opportunity to be archaeological. He was just decorative, wildly decorative. He provided brilliant flashes to catch the warm sunlight, but neither in line or color was he particularly happy. Iphigenia in the earlier scenes before she donned an astonishing headdress, wore a costume exasperatingly suggestive of highly contemporary dishabille. . . . But it was when he came to trick out King Thoas and the warriors who attended him on the Friendless shore [*sic*] that Mr. Wilkinson seemed resolved to outdo in eccentricity anything he had achieved [earlier]. . . . There is simply no describing those soldiers with their union suits of black and white adorned with whisk-brooms of the hue of tomato bisque. There is no describing Thoas himself with his ornithological scepter, his checkered robe and his scarlet beard. It was a great reception accorded to this apparition.[12]

A group of twenty-one young ladies formed the chorus. These were costumed in "sweeping drapery of black and orange," which made a striking effect before the white facade of the stage temple and the gray oval of concrete that served as the modern equivalent of the ancient orchestra.[13]

Whatever the dramatic merits of the production, it definitely made a visual impact.

The cast of this production was headed by Lillah McCarthy as the princess and Ian Maclaren as Orestes, but the reviewers, who waxed eloquent about McCarthy's portrayal of Hecuba in *Trojan Women*, said nothing of her performance as Iphigeneia. Critics and commentators alike paid more attention to the issue of Greek drama production itself. While each recognized, albeit to differing degrees, the modernity and relevance of the antiwar play, *Iphigeneia* prompted questions: will the American audience, having "absorbed the oddity of the spectacle . . . secretly resolve to keep away from Greek drama in the future?" Or will it be discovered that, after the season has closed, once again the " 'uncommercial' drama" will have astonished and confuted the cynics?[14] If one may judge from the attention given to Granville Barker's dramatic experiment by contemporary drama critics, the ventures were more than modestly successful.

From 1915 on, Greek tragedy became part of the repertoire for those interested in serious and artistic productions in American theaters. As it turns out, for the next twenty years Sophocles and Euripides shared the commercial boards; Aeschylus had to wait longer for recognition in this country. It is worth noting, furthermore, that for the most part, it was the women created by these two playwrights who would speak most frequently to the American audience. A production history of ancient tragedies must focus upon the Greek plays that take their name from women, for in the early years these scripts were often used by leading actresses of the day as vehicles to display their acting abilities.[15]

EURIPIDES: *ELECTRA*

An early production that garnered only limited critical attention was the 1910 staging of Euripides' *Electra* by the Coburn players. A surprising detail in the production history of Greek tragedies in the United States is the virtual neglect of this play. Unlike Sophocles' drama sharing the same title and theme, Euripides' version has only rarely been brought to the commercial stage. This is strange, for Euripides' figure is the more psychologically interesting of the two tragic heroines. The reasons for her actions are more evident, if less appealing, to a modern audience than those of Sophocles' tormented princess. The Sophoclean Electra chose active grief as her weapon, a weapon she continually aimed at her mother and stepfather, but her lamentation over the urn wounds her disguised brother more deeply. Finally, at the end of the play, when vengeance has been done, Sophocles gives no real resolution; the audience, always somewhat uncomfortable with Electra's deliberate, yet unrestrained, mourning, leaves the theater still vaguely sensing that final issues have yet to be resolved.

The play may have been emotionally satisfying, but intellectually a gnawing uncertainty remains.

Euripides' heroine deceives only herself. From her first bitter cry to the night sky to her final complaint to the ex machina Dioscouroi, Electra is shown to be rooted in self-pity, twisted with the suffering she feels she endures. However, her lamentations for her murdered father ring hollow; it is all too evident that she has confused justice and jealousy, that she despises her mother not because she wielded the ax but because the queen lives in soft luxury while her daughter dwells in a peasant hut. Although this figure is not likable, she is certainly recognizable to an audience familiar with the bitter, tormented, and twisted women of the modern stage.

The Coburn Players, who first brought Euripides' *Electra* to the commercial stage, was a troupe at least persistent, if not always successful, in its attempts to offer the ancient texts to a modern audience. As they, like Margaret Anglin and Maurice Browne and his Chicago Little Theatre, are so much a part of the early theater history of this nation, a brief discussion of their company is in order.

The Coburn Players

Actor-manager Charles Coburn organized the company as the Coburn Players in 1905. They gained their reputation by extensive touring of college campuses, offering outdoor productions of serious drama, primarily Shakespeare and several of the Greek plays. Their summers were busy: in a typical season (between 1911 and 1917), the Coburn Players would visit nearly forty campuses and clubs, giving over one hundred performances. Their tour was wide-ranging, but they primarily played in the Midwest and South, at locations where they often offered the only performances of drama available. The popularity of their productions created an interest in outdoor theater, and other companies followed their lead.

While the Coburn Players were organized with the intent of doing away with the star system, Charles Coburn took most of the leading male parts himself, and his wife, Ivah Wills (always billed as Mrs. Coburn), played the female roles. The actors who joined them enjoyed the opportunity to perform the types of dramas not usually available in commercial theaters at that time. Although the members of his company were not particularly well paid, many returned year after year for the experience of working with him during the summers.

Their performances were praised "in direct proportion to the distance from Broadway theatre."[16] The New York critics usually found their performances rather amateurish in production, but "natural" in acting. Nevertheless, the company was invited to play *As You Like It* for President and Mrs. Taft on the White House Lawn in June 1910. That same year they added the *Electra* plays to their repertoire; *Iphigeneia at Tauris* was introduced four years later. After 1917 the Coburn Players closed their company so that Charles Coburn could devote himself to a Broadway career.

In late November 1910, then, the Coburn Players staged an earnest and elaborate Euripidean *Electra* in two matinees at the Hudson Theater. The set featured four towering Ionic columns, variously entwined with ivy. The cast included eight players in addition to Mrs. Coburn (Electra), Mr. Coburn (Orestes), John Kellerd (Messenger), and a chorus of fifteen. The translation was that of Gilbert Murray, whose rhyming verses preserved, according to the critic of *Theatre Magazine* (January 1911), "the bold, fluent, yet simple poetry of the great original . . . with marked distinction, vivid strength and graceful form." This reviewer summed up the entire production as "impressive," if not in all ways perfect, one that "satisfied the curious interest of the student, and conveyed the sense of consistency and perfect art in its form to all who witnessed it." He declared the highlight of the performance to be Kellerd's speech describing the death of Aegisthus "in splendid diction." Mrs. Coburn's Electra, he stated, was somewhat lacking in physical strength, but "eminently satisfying" in its plastic grace; she made the character so pitiful one could almost sympathize with her murder plans.

The greater part of the *Theatre Magazine* review was, however, devoted to the value of staging Greek drama at all. The writer honored the Coburns' purpose as sincere, then turned to his major theme, that since "interest in the production of a classic Greek play is necessarily academic," much scholarship and care must be taken in the venture. The limitations of stage and script, the almost inaccessible religious views and passionate violence of the ancient themes hinder even the most enthusiastic reader of Greek drama in the enjoyment of a modern performance. But since, the reviewer allows, "these plays were written to be acted, consequently something can be learned from a production which might escape one in the most studious reading of a play." The Coburn production, the critic finally confirms, was done in a "most highly satisfactory manner with reference to scholarship." He had some reservations about Euripides' version of the story; furthermore, for as to which an audience prefers, "it is safe to predict that Hofmannsthal's version of the Sophoclean play will always prevail." This prediction seems to have been correct, for Euripides' *Electra* did not reappear on the New York stage until the 1950s.

NOTES

1. It is but "one long lament" according to H.D.F. Kitto, *Greek Tragedy* (New York: 1950): 218–225, and although he does not fully denigrate the play, which he maintains must be viewed as tragic for the Greeks and "merely pathetic for the Trojans," he nevertheless asserts that "Euripides is not putting together a play but presenting a tragic idea." D. J. Conacher, *Euripidean Drama* (Toronto: 1967): 135–137, proposes that the play is a "mere chain of experience." More recent scholars, e.g., Shirley Barlow, in the introduction to her edition, translation, and commen-

tary of the text (Warminster, England: 1986): 30–35, considers it to be a powerful statement of the human suffering on both sides of the war.

2. The Greeks referred to a woman who died unmarried as a "bride of death," both because any woman in Greek society needed a master and as a consolation for dying still unwed. I use the term to describe the women of this play—Hecuba, Cassandra, Andromache, Helen, and the chorus—because each is in some way related to death: Hecuba is the mother whose son and grandson fall to Greek slaughter; Cassandra will cause the death of the Greek leader; Andromache is the embodiment of the term, as the death of her husband, Hector, has left her chamber empty, while Hector's greatness has doomed his son. Helen often earns this sobriquet, as she is the cause of the war itself. Finally the chorus represent all of the women who must go as "spear-won brides" to serve the beds of the men who slew their husbands.

3. Hamilton (*Vogue*, July 1915: 82) includes in his review of the play a discussion of Euripides' life and times; his comments are worth quoting:

> Euripides had served in the army for forty years, from the age of twenty to the age of sixty; he had fought for liberty, equality, fraternity, in hundreds of stirring combats, hand to hand; and with all this vast experience behind him, he realized the vanity of war and longed for universal peace. . . . [Athenians failed to listen to his message] and he was forced into exile, forced to break bread with the barbarians of Macedonia and, alone among their mountains, to write *The Bacchae* and die. Meanwhile, the expedition to Sicily set sail—and its sailing marked the doom of Athens.

4. In addition to Lillah McCarthy as Hecuba and Edith Wynne Matthison as Andromache, Chrystal Herne played Cassandra; Gladys Hansen, Helen; Philip Merrivale portrayed Menelaus; and Ian Maclaren, Talthybius. Alma Kruger led the chorus.

5. Eventually two men joined the lists, thus sparing Browne form having to play multiple roles and leaving him free to learn the art of directing. This and other details about Browne are recorded in his autobiography, *Too Late to Lament*, Book Two (1910–1917) (Bloomington, IN: 1956). For further information about the Chicago Little Theatre, see Cloyd Head, "The Chicago Little Theatre," *Theatre Arts Magazine* 1 (1917): 110–116.

6. Dell's review discusses the other plays Browne put onstage during his first season: Yeats' *On Baile's Strand* and Strindberg's *Creditors* and *The Stronger*, which were termed by Dell an unqualified success—especially since Strindberg had suggested his plays be done in the type of intimate setting the Chicago Little Theatre provided. The second season was to include, among others, Euripides' *Medea* ("in Gilbert Murray's wonderful verse translation"), and *Trojan Women* was to be repeated. As it would turn out, the latter was repeated more than once.

7. Browne records his thoughts and decision in *Too Late to Lament* (178):

> The Chicago to which we returned thought ill of war. . . . [Urged to join] I saw my duty elsewhere. Henry Ford was sending his Peace Ship to Europe; Jane Addams had organized the Woman's Peace Party; the Carnegie Peace Foundation was financing pacifist activities. The Chicago Little Theatre must play its part. How better than by touring *The Trojan Women*? We . . . were playing it at the moment. It was not merely the play which we loved most; in the city of The World's Largest Bookstore it was The World's Greatest Peace Play.

8. Browne, *Too Late to Lament*: 181. The remaining pages of Book Two record further events of the tour, which eventually traveled coast to coast, playing from

Baltimore to San Francisco. Within three years since its inception, three months since taking *Trojan Women* on the road, the Chicago Little Theatre had "expanded from a tiny stage to a huge one and from ninety to six thousand seats" (187).

9. Quoted by Browne from a letter by Nellie Van to an official of the Woman's Peace Party (*Too Late to Lament*: 188).

10. Granville Barker had created his *Iphigeneia* for the London stage in 1912, where Lillah McCarthy also played the title role. In London, as in New York, her interpretation was praised.

11. It is rather in vogue during the past twenty years to speak of *Iphigeneia in Tauris* as "Euripidean comedy"; cf., in particular, Bernard Knox, "Euripidean Comedy," in *The Rarer Action: Essays in Honor of Francis Ferguson*, ed. Alan Cheuse and Richard Koffler (New Brunswick, NJ: 1970), reprinted in Knox's *Word and Action. Essays on the Ancient Theater* (Baltimore: 1979): 250–274. While the very phrase would be an oxymoron to the ancient writers, it is true that such plays as *Iphigeneia in Tauris*, *Ion*, and *Helen* lack the more tragic message of, for example, *Heracles* or *Hecuba*. Nevertheless I share the view that these plays hold a serious message, that Euripides did not write merely to entertain, but intended his audiences to question the interaction of gods and mortals and the foundations upon which the latter rest their beliefs.

12. Another critic (*New York Times*, 1 June 1915), writing of the New York production, noted that "Norman Wilkinson's super-fantastic costuming for the luckless Taurian monarch and his attendants were received with hearty laughter at New Haven. The audience at the Stadium yesterday just grinned."

13. Quotation and set information from Harrison Smith, "The Revival of Greek Tragedy in America," *The Bookman* 41 (June 1915): 411–412.

14. Questions posed by Smith, "Revival of Greek Tragedy": 414–416.

15. More extant Greek tragedies are named for the female lead, of course, but with the exception of Oedipus in his play, other males from Attic drama are largely absent from the American stage. We do not find many productions of *Ajax*, *Hippolytus*, or *Philoctetes*; an interest in *Prometheus* or *Orestes* develops later.

16. This quotation and other information about the Coburn Players taken from the entry by Richard Palmer, "Coburn Players," in *American Theatre Companies 1888–1930*, ed. by Weldon B. Durham (Westport, CT: 1987): 86–90. I would dispute Palmer's text and repertory, however; it was Euripides' *Electra* that the Coburns performed in 1910; Sophocles' play may have entered their lists in 1913, but it did not play in New York.

4

Greek Tragedy Comes of Age: 1915–1935

During the period 1915–1935, Euripides' *Trojan Women* continued to be the text favored by those who rejected the idea of war. The more significant development in the understanding and appreciation of Greek tragedy lay in its acceptance as an exciting and viable art form for the contemporary stage, and thus Sophocles' *Oedipus Tyrannus* gained acceptance as a powerful and dramatic script in the 1920s. Furthermore, the ancient texts became the favorite plays for leading actresses of the day, and among the figures of Greek tragedy, it was Electra, as portrayed by Sophocles, who dominated the stage. Thus I have said that it was in the time period 1915–1935 that Greek tragedy came of age in the United States.

As it was Sophocles' *Electra* that was both popular and the new addition to the Greek tragedy repertoire, my discussion here focuses upon its production history.[1] For although the Coburn Players had performed Euripides' *Electra* in 1910, this text has remained in the shadows of Greek tragedy production in America, while Sophocles' drama has been consistently staged. The play might have been chosen as illustrative of a way to endure hardship, to remain true to one's cause in the face of adversity, to be ready to act at whatever cost—all themes which may be gleaned from this play—but its appeal lay in the role of Electra herself. The lament of the princess over the urn of her brother's (supposed, but spurious) ashes appealed to any aspiring actress, for this scene is one of the fine moments of drama, as great sorrow plays well on stage.

SOPHOCLES: *ELECTRA*

Margaret Anglin was the actress who brought Sophocles' *Electra* to the commercial theater of New York, where she performed the play in 1918 and again in 1927. In the winter of 1918 some three thousand people gathered at Carnegie Hall to see Margaret Anglin perform Sophocles' drama in a way that rendered it fresh and vital. John Corbin, writing in the *New York Times* (7 February 1918), asserted that the actress proved that the ancient text was "a thing of rich, human vitality and gorgeous color." Through her acting "the play lived again in all its deep splendor, its intensity of passion. . . . Miss Anglin gave the greatest performance of its kind . . . since the heyday of Bernhardt." Enhanced by the music of Walter Damrosch, the production was hailed as a venture deserving of highest praise.

For the drama critics to give this accolade, however, meant that they had to overcome the difficulties of the play's theme. "The play is somewhat removed from modern moods and ways of thinking," mused a second reviewer of the *New York Times* (7 February 1918), "revenge as a religious duty does not easily command our sympathy." Corbin, too, believed that in this play Anglin was facing a theme alien to the modern mind. "Revenge, even for the murder of a father," he asserted, "does not strike us as weightily tragic." After hailing every aspect of the show, the *Times* critic reported on its effect on the audience: "The audience yesterday was held breathless throughout and, at the climaxes, was swayed by the most powerful emotion. The performance left one stunned and limp, yet with the sense of having for once been privileged to live on the pinnacles of dramatic art."

Margaret Anglin and her performance of Sophocles' *Electra* had taken New York by storm, a feat she was to repeat several times during the next decade. She and her company had made the play and its "alien theme" acceptable to the American audience of the period.

Margaret Anglin

Margaret Anglin had already made a name for herself in California as an actress excelling in Greek drama. The Canadian-born actress had determined by age fifteen that she wanted to be on the stage; with the secret assistance of her mother she went to New York and was one of the first pupils to enter Nelson Wheatcroft's Empire Dramatic School. She was soon playing major roles with recognized companies and moved from the New York area to San Francisco, where she attracted the attention of directors and drama critics alike. Anglin's first major engagement was as Ruth Jordan in Vaughan Moody's *The Great Divide*; playing opposite Henry Miller she charmed New York audiences from 1906 to 1908.

When the following year she announced she was tired of tragic melodrama, she immediately proved her ability as a comic actress as well, but soon she moved on to what would be her major contribution to American theater history. Becoming an actress-manager in 1913, she began to present serious drama in repertory; Shakespearean tragedies initiated her program. In 1915 her career in Greek drama began, when she produced and starred in Sophocles' *Antigone* and *Electra*, then *Iphigeneia at Aulis* and *Medea* at the Greek Theater of the University of California at Berkeley. Critics proclaimed that her enactments of these roles brought Greek dramas alive in the proper way. She brought a personal tradition of fine acting to the New York stage, where her appearance immediately attracted attention.[2] She was equally acclaimed when she returned in the role some nine years later.

"When the Shuberts announced Miss Anglin's *Electra* last week as a regular theatrical 'attraction,' Sophocles came close to being the leading dramatist of the Spring season." So does Brooks Atkinson open his review[3] of Anglin's performance in *Electra* in May 1927. The show played to a packed house at the Metropolitan Opera House, but ran for only two nights. Anglin decided the strain of doing the lead role eight times a week would be too great, and so *Electra* vanished from the boards and "the Spring stage slump[ed] into mediocrity."

What interests us here is Atkinson's declaration that Sophocles' play was far better than others currently on Broadway. Even though, as the reviewer continues, Greek tragedy "is not the true expression of American civilization in the year 1927" and should not be compared to the "dramatic pablum" of the time, one can praise the "sublime beauties" of *Electra*: "contact with *Electra*, as Miss Anglin plays it, is contact with majesty." She knew the style necessary for this type of play: her speaking "must have echoed the style that was employed in the classic theatre of Dionysus."

Atkinson found most of the production excellent. Those who played Clytemnestra, Orestes, and Aegisthus, he asserted, showed their comprehension of the tragic style.[4] Mr. Platt's set in its massive severity evoked well the palace of ancient Mycenae. The chorus wove the play together, while the colorful ceremonies accompanying prayers and the offstage "pleading of Phrygean themes" made the entire evening an experience of true "theatre."

In one hour and forty minutes *Electra* moved "with dignity and deliberation to its final climax." Atkinson's comments on the murders committed at the play's end are an indication of the temper of the 1920s, an age clearly different from the more recent years of this century, years that in artistic expectation might be termed "post-*Godfather*":

As moderns we would shudder at the sword-thrusts and groans if any of the characters involved had been portrayed as individuals. They are kept so high above personality, however, that the murders are sublimations of inexorable justice: They are not violence, but the restoration of order in the stricken house of Atreus.[5]

Atkinson concluded his review by noting that Anglin's decision not to play *Electra* regularly was met with widespread regret. But within four years the play opened in Boston and the performances once again roused the reviewer(s) to praise Sophocles' text, if not all the acting as well.

Later Productions

In May 1931, Boston audiences saw Blanche Yurka portray the title role in Sophocles' *Electra*. The production was on its way to open a dramatic festival in Ann Arbor, Michigan, but played first at Jordon Hall in Boston. There was some expectation that *Electra* might open on Broadway, but that hope was termed a long chance by Boston area reviewer H. T. Parker, for he found little to like in this production. His comments, written for the *New York Times* (24 May 1931) are worth attention.

First he describes in full detail the set—which he did not like—for it "less suggested the Cyclopean architecture of prehistoric Greece than a mid-nineteenth-century 'academy' in a New England town." The chorus, made up of five members identified not as Argive maidens but as "a servant," "a peasant mother," and so on, performed their designated parts poorly. Of those playing the "secondary parts" (Orestes, Pylades, Paedagogue, and Chrysothemis), only Amy Loomis, as Electra's "gentle sister, had any notion of clear, poised and rhythmed speech." Especially misguided, it seemed to Parker, was the decision to have Miss Graham "illuminate" the play: "Miss Graham undertook to extra-illustrate . . . a masterpiece of Sophocles. Through two thousand years there has been rather general agreement that it is self-contained. To extra-illustrate *Electra* suggests a singular obtuseness to the art of poetry and the arts of the theatre." Parker did, however, enjoy some moments of Blanche Yurka's acting: "By instinct, practice and environment, Miss Yurka is drawn toward a quasi-realistic Electra." In the first part of the drama, her enactment of the mourning heroine missed the poetry and pathos of Sophocles, but then the audience saw:

Of a sudden, the cleared mind, the enlightened spirit, the return from Hofmannsthal to Sophocles, the works not of realism but of purified imagination. [As Miss Yurka receives the urn of ashes, she] touches the Sophoclean tenderness, the beauty that is called classic. . . . In Miss Yurka's cry, her speech, her action, is the Sophoclean exaltation, the deep-measured, classic beauty. Not in a frenzy of vengeance, but in sacrificial fulfillment, the priestess by the altar reared within her spirit, such an Electra waits the slaying of Clytemnestra.

Parker's comments tell us much about his view of ancient drama, but they also indicate what the public expected to see in any performance of Sophocles' dramas. The director's choice to play the Greek text in a more "realistic" fashion was not appreciated. Even if we allow that the acting in the "secondary parts" was not up to standard, Parker vents his displeasure upon the entire conception of the production. We are left to imagine how Blanche Yurka elevated the play to its classic beauty and thus became "the theatrical news of the week in Boston"; it would seem that she played Electra in the grand tragic mode familiar to audiences for the past fifty years. For those who wished to perform Greek tragedy in a way that would be relevant to a contemporary audience, a difficult task lay ahead.

In spite of Parker's doubts and negative review, Sophocles' *Electra* opened the following January in New York at the Selwyn Theatre. Again Blanche Yurka played the lead role, but for all other parts, with the exception of Robert Henderson's Aegisthus, there was a new cast. Nevertheless, the production again failed to please its audience or reviewer Brooks Atkinson. He found time during the show "to meditate quietly on the uses of Greek tragedy in the modern American theatre." He suggests (*New York Times*, 9 January 1932) some possible reasons for staging the ancient texts:

The Greek fables are not our fables, nor is fable a part of our culture. To understand the history of the drama it is good to have Greek tragedies staged occasionally. If it does nothing else it reminds us of the theatre's heritage. Not being votaries of Greek fable, however, we cannot bring to Sophocles' *Electra* the faith the Greeks carried into their festival theatres. . . . The nobility of the characters is a matter of scholarly instruction rather than emotional recognition.

Atkinson found that the rituals added to the production properly evoked the tragic spirit: "Spectacle and sound are the instruments that can give Greek tragedy life in the modern theatre." He, like Parker, objected to the nonheroic style the director had chosen for the players. Blanche Yurka seemed to him to be not the daughter of a king but "a weeping peasant maid."[6] Indeed, she was "crumpled, disarrayed like a witch on the heath." For Atkinson, it was the memory of Margaret Anglin's Electra that guided his appreciation of Greek tragedy—her interpretation of 1927 remains, he asserted, "still unchallenged."

Among the critics crying "woe," one voice was raised in praise of Yurka's performance. Richard Dana Skinner, writing in *Commonweal* (27 January 1932), disagreed with those who denigrated this actress in comparison with Anglin. He suggests that in the earlier production the actress, while good, was assisted by the size of the theater, the time of the show, and a rather weak supporting cast (a view that seems to be singularly his own). While granting that Margaret Anglin brought to the part the grandeur we expect of Sophocles, Skinner wanted to recognize Yurka's interpretation as deliberately more intimate. This actress, he declared, "has presented Sophocles in the humanized and realistic fashion of Euripides." The absence of the grand style was, to his way of thinking, better suited to the small modern theater, and critics should understand the validity of such presentations. But for most of the drama critics and the audience of 1932, Greek tragedy demanded exalted acting and heroic staging to be successful on the modern stage. Sophocles' *Electra* as performed by Blanche Yurka in 1932 failed to touch an audience desiring to see Greek drama done in the "classic" mode.

Thus perhaps it is not surprising that twenty years passed before *Electra* opened again in New York. This time it was performed in modern Greek by the National Theatre of Greece on tour to the United States and Canada. In the 1953 production at the Mark Hellinger Theatre, under the direction of Dimitri Rondiris, Katina Paxinou played the title role. The published photographs of this performance indicate the company preferred the formal and traditional mode for Greek tragedy, and so did the theater critics—except for the limitation imposed by the Greek language.

Atkinson (*New York Times*, 20 November 1952) urged anyone wanting to know "how Sophocles' *Electra* should be acted" to see this performance. He found everything "dramatically imposing," but especially fine were the musical score and the chorus. The score gave the performance "depth and eloquence," while the chorus was "drawn straight into the heart of the performance as counsel on one hand and audience on the other": "Remove the chorus from the stage and this *Electra* would lose its spiritual magnificence. No doubt the ancient Greek dramatist regarded the chorus as an integral part of the whole tragic experience . . . [as it is here]." Atkinson praised individual members of the cast, giving special attention to Paxinou's powerful acting and A. Raftopoulou's royal Clytemnestra. He closed his review by asserting that "now we know Sophocles' *Electra* is more than a schoolbook myth." Under the skillful acting of Rondiris' troupe, Atkinson apparently learned that the ancient fables are more than "a matter of scholarly instruction."

William Hawkins was equally impressed. Writing in the *New York World-Telegram and the Sun* (20 November 1952), he proclaimed Katina Paxinou an "Electric Electra," and the performance as a "rare and astonishing experience." He, too, waxed eloquent about the chorus, "certainly the second most important character of the play," but he paid homage to Paxinou's shattering power, a power that draws the viewer "into the whirlpool of her emotions."

Other theater critics found the acting powerful, but the language a difficult barrier. Thus John McClain of the *New York Journal American* (20 November 1952) warned that although this was a magnificently acted production it would have limited appeal. Robert Coleman of the *Daily Mirror* (20 November 1952) assured his audiences that *Electra* was worth seeing as the performance looked more interesting than it sounded. Walter Kerr (*New York Herald Tribune*, 20 November 1952) was perhaps the least charmed by the National Theatre of Greece and Katina Paxinou, but even he gave praise to the chorus. They, he asserts, give to this *Electra* "genuine theatrical excitement." Kerr, like the other critics, expresses a final satisfaction that "this impressive modern work, born of a magnificent earlier tradition, should be brought to these shores."[7]

Nine years later, another theater company from Greece brought the ancient texts to New York. The Piraikon Theatron, again under the direction of Dimitrios Rondiris, staged *Electra* at the City Center for a two-week run, September 19–October 1, 1961. The show played in repertory with

Choephoroi and *Eumenides*. The press photos indicate Rondiris still preferred the classic style; *Time's* critic, parading his knowledge of Greece, said the brown costumes of the chorus resembled the Caryatids of the Acropolis' Erechtheum.

Again the majority of the New York drama critics found the perform-ance—even though done in modern Greek—to be exciting; most, indeed, said that the translation provided by transistors was not really necessary; the power of the acting carried the play's meaning. Howard Taubman (*New York Times*, 30 September 1961) led the ovations, opening his laudatory review thusly:

> The intense, concentrated passion of a towering Greek classic was unleashed at the City Center last night. With Piraikon Theatron offering its splendidly orchestrated version of *Electra* by Sophocles, New Yorkers had a golden opportunity to see and hear an ancient masterpiece brought to vibrant life.

John Beaufort (*Christian Science Monitor*, 23 September 1961) asserted, "A classic worthily revived reasserts the capacity of art to span the ages."[8] Richard P. Cooke (*Wall Street Journal*, 21 September 1961) stated that the production by the Piraikon Theatron was "the most important recent event artistically" of the early 1961 season. He thought that to see the chorus itself was worth the evening, for "the use of the chorus is so far removed from present theater technique that it might seem very avant garde to minds interested in that." Robert Coleman, too, writing in the *New York Mirror* (20 September 1961), could not resist emphasizing the value of the ancient dramas or displaying his knowledge of the classic theater: the Greek tragedies were "heroic, [and] moved with compelling inevitability toward their climaxes and their ends." He closed his review by urging his readers to the theater to see something more than "tepid slices of life."

Aspassia Papathanassiou's performance in the title role earned her much praise; Leighton Kerner, writing in the *Village Voice* (28 September 1961), was more than eloquent as he described her performance:

> Yes, [Electra] could blaze in her rage at Chrysothemis' inaction, hold up a mirror of guilt in front of Clytemnestra, spit sulphuric sarcasm at the doomed Aegisthus, and moan like a thing inhuman to make the gods shudder. But . . . the Electra of Sophocles and of Miss Papathanassiou was an Electra who touched your heart ever so gently in the way she laid aside all her righteous fury in front of the chorus and became only a daughter and sister wrapped in despair, or in the way she would not give up to the unrecognized Orestes the urn supposedly containing his ashes.

For the New York drama critics, the only difficulty encountered with this performance lay in finding sufficient superlatives to describe the Piraikon Theatron's *Electra*.

The same troupe when playing on the West Coast, on the other hand, did not garner similar praise. Philip Scheuer, writing in the *Los Angeles Times* (7 September 1961), was able to overcome the Greek language barrier only with difficulty. He did have high praise for Papathanassiou in the title role: to see her was to thrill at her "supernal skill and beauty." But despite her acting ability, the applause at the finish was "all but stifled in the stampede toward the exits." Jack Smith, cynical reviewer also of the *Los Angeles Times*, spent the greater part of his review (13 September 1961) titled "Electra Needed the Old Switcheroo," railing against foreign-language productions while he pondered how to make the ancient Greek tragedy a modern musical comedy.[9]

Their success in New York earned for the Piraikon Theatron a return visit to the United States in the late summer of 1964. This time they offered *Electra* in alternation with *Medea*, with Aspassia Papathanassiou and Elsa Vergi alternating in the title roles. Papathanassiou again received acclaim. Paul Gardner, writing in the *New York Times* (8 September 1964), praised the range of emotions flitting across the actress' face. He also admired the performances by Titika Nikiforaki (Clytemnestra) and Nidos Chadziskos (Orestes) as well as the gracefully moving fourteen-member chorus.

The year 1964, indeed, might be termed the year of *Electra*. In addition to the Piraikon Theatron offering the play in Greek at the City Center, during the three weeks prior to their opening on 31 August, the New York audience could see Sophocles' play at the Delacorte Theatre in Central Park, where Lee Grant and Olympia Dukakis played Electra and Chrysothemis respectively in a translation by H.D.F. Kitto. Reviewer Lewis Funke, writing in the *New York Times* of 12 August 1964, found much to praise about this production.

The outdoor setting was the initial pleasure of the show: the amphitheater in Central Park is "not too dissimilar in ambiance from those that dotted the Grecian countryside." After a brief synopsis of the myth, Funke offers praise of Lee Grant's interpretation of the title role:

An actress of intelligence, energy and grace, she makes Electra a truly poignant figure in this drama. [Although her voice is not strong] she more than meets the requirements of the role. [Taking the urn] she talks to [it], embraces it, caresses it, cradles it as if it were an infant, always evoking the pathos inherent in the moment.

Florence Stanley offered a Clytemnestra full of majesty and power; as she learns the final truth, "her bitter hysterical laughter fills the space of the theater and beyond." The other players, with the possible exception of Michael Baseleon as Orestes, did their parts well. All in all, the *Times* critic found the performance to be worthy and worth seeing, and applauded Joseph Papp for adding Greek tragedy to his Shakespeare in the Park idea. Greek tragedy had earned a place on the American commercial stage for it was now performed for "citizenry at large" as well as for the scholarly audience.

Before the decade ended, *Electra* was staged one more time in New York City. On 5 August 1969, the Mobile theater, working again with the New York Shakespeare Festival, opened Sophocles' play for a limited run in Washington Square Park. The cast of African-American players featured Olivia Cole in the title role and Josephine Premice as Clytemnestra. Director Gerald Freedman chose costumes reflecting an Egyptian and African influence, heavy with beads and a head-covering hat for a crown. The production was among the first to suggest the non-Western appeal of the Greek texts: the universality of the plays' appeal will become evident in the later pages of this study.

Electra returned to the boards in the summer of 1984 in a production at the Old Globe Theatre in San Diego, where Sophocles' text played in repertory with Shakespeare's *The Merry Wives of Windsor*, *Stage Struck* (by Simon Gray), Steinbeck's *Of Mice and Men*, and *The Torch-Bearers* (by George Kelly). Now the ancient plays were part of a season's regular offerings, staged in succession with the most contemporary scripts. As we shall see below, from the 1980s to the present, Greek dramas are often considered to be viable texts for a repertory company; they are no longer done as an unusual experiment.[10]

According to the review by Lloyd Rose (*Washington Post*, 1 February 1992) the Round House Theatre's 1992 production of Sophocles' *Electra*, rewritten by Ezra Pound and Rudd Fleming, was "slapstick tragedy of the broadest, most disorienting order . . . and, in its whacked-out way, pretty fabulous." Here director Tom Prewitt and his cast had apparently decided—against much evidence to the contrary—that Greek tragedy just doesn't play well in today's theaters; in his attempt to make the text more accessible, he created a play that was "advertently hilarious." Hap Erstein of the *Washington Times* asked whether this rewriting of Sophocles' text was intended to reveal "long-overlooked comic potential in Sophocles."[11]

The set portrayed "a typical urban dystopia" of brick and metal, with signposts that said we are "Here and Now," an atmosphere most audiences now associate with a "twilight zone of bad science fiction."[12] According to Rose, however, the performances offered by the actors in this updated version were sufficiently powerful to overcome the negative reactions generated by set and text. Sarah Marshall's Electra was driven mad by her obsession with her father's death: she played "madness in all its ludicrousness and weirdness," playing the extremes of emotion while remaining in control. Others in the cast supported Electra's passions well: Marty Lodge became a menacing Orestes and Kaia Calhoun gave Clytemnestra a "self-satisfied bitchery." Erstein could not match Rose's praise; for him, the bad text overpowered the fine acting—he agreed that it was well acted—for "every few minutes with a well-earned wave of guffaws" the words shattered the dramatic mood.

Rose catalogues Prewitt's almost precious absurdity which "mixes the 'theatrical' with the realistic [and] combines ritual scenes with images from old movies." He closes his critique of this unusual production with language we recognize as typical of those reviewing Greek drama: "[This] *Electra* is, like life, simultaneously horrific and farcical. . . . The only traditional thing about it is that, in spite of yourself, it thrusts you toward pity and terror." To Erstein, however, the show's eighty minutes seemed a very long journey toward that pity and terror.

In the summer of 1992, *Electra* played at the South-of-Market Theatre in San Francisco. Steven Winn, writing in the *San Francisco Chronicle* (23 June 1992), found the production staged by Tony Kelly "a kind of three-dimensional map of the tragedy." He also considered the later scenes to be "out of balance." Played in street clothes and with gender-blind casting, this performance would seem to have mixed too many media to be fully effective. Still, in whatever production style, Sophocles' play has had difficulty in winning affirmative reviews in California.[13]

Chicago was the setting for a new *Electra* in 1993. In a modern translation by Nicholas Rudall and as directed by Mikhail Mokeiev, Sophocles' ancient play was given a modern treatment that set new standards for Greek tragedy production. In a preopening review Lawrence Bommer (*Chicago Tribune*, 26 February 1993) termed the play "an ancient and modern domestic tragedy," "a universal tale of grief and revenge." Sid Smith, writing for the same paper, proclaimed the play a Greek tragedy that should be seen, especially for the astonishing turn the play takes at its close. He revealed nothing more about the new ending other than that Mokeiev achieved a gutsy "electrifying, final, indelible moment." The culture-blind casting aided the play's power. Jacqueline Williams, giving a riveting interpretation of the title role, was "an African-American signpost in a deliberate kaleidoscope, playing opposite a fairy-tale princely Orestes." Others in the cast brought East European and Latin accents to the performance. The contrasts provided by the cast were echoed in the costumes and set, which juxtaposed satin drapes, black-hooded raincoats, and dark metallic panels. Electra's story was updated and made universal in a way the drama critics of the 1920s and 1930s could never have imagined.[14]

Sophocles' *Electra* has appeared with regularity throughout the twentieth century. The drama critics consistently praise the leading actresses in particular, but also the play itself. The ancient text seems to speak to audiences in nearly every decade: the pathos of Electra's ode with the urn, always a fine vehicle for a powerful actress, reaches across the centuries and touches those attending a Greek tragedy in an American commercial theater. Of all the drama critics writing of this passage, *Time*'s critic gives the most powerful description of why this play continues to move an audience.

Referring to the Piraikon Theatron's 1961 production, he writes (29 September 1961):

[The play] has one of those scenes of naked emotional intensity that have been missing on stage since Olivier gave his howl of self-recognition as Oedipus. . . . [As Electra sees the urn] she drops where she stands with a wild animal cry; she clutches at the urn, cradles it and rocks it in entwining arms [and] the strangulated sobs of a soul bereft. She is an open wound bleeding passion and the spectator sees what is almost too shameless to see, grief at the pitch of human endurance.

When a drama confronts an audience with such emotion, its continued popularity is no mystery. We now accept the theme earlier critics found alien to their time; we have also come to realize the universality of the play's message can be clear whether the cast is in robes or raincoats. The power of the ancient drama lies in the text no matter how it is staged—as long as it is honestly acted.

SOPHOCLES: *OEDIPUS TYRANNUS*

It was also during the 1920s that *Oedipus Tyrannus* finally came of age. In Berlin in 1911 and then at Covent Garden in London in 1912, Max Reinhardt had created a massive set upon which several hundred plague-ridden citizens of Thebes assembled to hear the words of Oedipus, played by Sir John Martin Harvey. In 1923, Harvey brought his interpretation of the King of Thebes to New York City, including in the production "some touches" of the Reinhardt version.

By this time America's theater critics had come of age and become more familiar with Greek drama. Thus the reviews of the 1923 production commented on the *Oedipus* as drama, not as a bizarre conception of a distant and incomprehensible culture. Mr. Hornblow, who commented on both "the novelty of the occasion" of seeing Sophoclean drama and the power required of an actor attempting "this tremendously exacting role,"[15] determined that Sir John Harvey lacked the "fire and majestic sweep of great acting." The play, a powerful picture of a king facing a dire fate, was well mounted but not well acted. Far more condemning of Harvey's show, yet far more understanding of Sophocles' text, was Stark Young, writing in the *New Republic* (7 November 1923). This critic found nothing to praise in the performance: actors, chorus, set, costumes—upon all he vented his ire. For the Athenian playwright alone did Young have a positive evaluation. Thus did he sum up Sophocles' *Oedipus Tyrannus*:

The whole of Sophocles' play is a line, splendidly held, modulated with superb emotion, balanced and ordered with due cause and effect, driven with the pressure of a fatal and splendid truth. . . . There is no play whose art is so taken out of the depth and not the tumult of the soul; . . . no play that contrives to mount and descend with such security, discovering for its climax the greatest image in all drama.

Just forty years previous *Oedipus* had been considered shocking and immoral, a play of no dramatic value, not worth the price of admission.[16] Sophocles' script remained unchanged, but it was understood with a great difference. Members of this audience had participated in the Great War and had learned that even for the victorious the path of progress is not always an unbroken ascent. Furthermore, the writings of Sigmund Freud had recently appeared, and under the influence of his ideas thought patterns would never be the same again.

Although both *Oedipus* and the American audience had come of age by 1923, it was during the next decade that Sophocles' most famous play became the Greek tragedy most frequently performed in the commercial theaters of the United States. Its production history is discussed in the following chapter.

NOTES

1. The initial performance of Sophocles' play in English was given by the students of the American Academy of Dramatic Arts in 1889. However, the first showing of the play in a commercial New York theater, the Garden, was in the winter of 1908; this was an English translation (by Arthur Symons) of Hugo von Hofmannsthal's version, and starred Mrs. Patrick Campbell in the title role. Critical reception was not entirely favorable. The reviewer of *Theatre Magazine* (March 1908) praised Mrs. Campbell's acting, but wondered as to the purpose of doing Greek drama at all. The critic of the *New York Times* (12 February 1908) also found the acting to be good, but the performance overall weak. He properly rejected the idea that Hofmannsthal's script was based on that of Sophocles, recognizing that Hofmannsthal's play parallels that of Sophocles in form, but the interpretation of Electra echoes Euripides' drama. In 1909 Richard Strauss made Hofmannsthal's *Elektra* the libretto for his opera, and in this form the German script became familiar to both European and American audiences.

2. Margaret Anglin's name appears frequently in the performance histories of Greek tragedies in the early decades of this century, but she broadened her career to play many roles; during the forty years she spent in the theater she performed in at least eighty plays. Her last Broadway appearance was in *Fresh Fields* in 1936; her final appearance was in a road company production of *Watch on the Rhine* in 1943. Anglin died in Toronto in 1958.

3. Brooks Atkinson (*New York Times*, 15 May 1927); in addition to discussing this performance, he compared *Electra* to *Hamlet*, finding the latter very different: "*Electra* holds up to our human eyes the thoughts, passions, and responsibilities of superhumans in contrast with *Hamlet*'s dissection of the human soul. *Electra* has the brilliance of a perfect winter day."

4. Miss Boucicault played Clytemnestra, Mr. Roeder and Mr. Dalton played Orestes and Aegisthus, respectively. The other characters "had not shaken off the habits of the modern stage."

5. See in Chapter 5, for instance, the comments of Anthony Burgess when he decided to have Oedipus blind himself onstage because the modern audience expects to see violence.

6. *Theatre Arts Monthly* also roundly denounced the production, declaring that Greek tragedy was "better left in the grandeur of its distance than brought back in a fashion so mixed, so lacking in the rudiments of . . . formal style as to be 'heroic melodrama.' " Yurka, the review continued, "was satisfied to mumble into the earth as she swayed to and fro in her realistic private grief."

7. Coleman, Kerr, and Watts all note the international aspect of the 1952 Broadway season, with the French company of Jean-Louis Barrault playing at the Ziegfield Theater at the same time the National Theatre of Greece opened at the Mark Hellinger.

8. Beaufort praises each and every member of the cast as well as the production's overall style; worth quoting is this comment: "In a style of heroic realism, the company . . . transformed the City Center stage into a meeting ground between the figures of little-known or half-forgotten myth and spectators of the gadget age."

9. Even Cecil Smith, whose review in the *Los Angeles Times* was more favorable, felt it necessary to comment on the difficulty of the language. All three critics spend more of their review on their own thoughts than on the Piraikon Theatron's performance.

10. Other performances of Sophocles' play include that done by the Greek Theater of New York, which inaugurated its new home at 120 West 28th Street with a production in 1981; in the spring of 1988, the Pearl Theatre Company of New York offered *Electra* starring Donnah Welby in the title role. A "work-in-progress" production was presented to invited audiences by Joseph Chaikin in 1974, wherein he and playwright Robert Montgomery created a new version of the Electra story. According to Mel Gussow (*New York Times*, 24 May 1974) the work abounded with animal images, and most effective were such innovations as Electra encouraging Orestes to the matricide by playacting the deed.

11. Erstein (*Washington Times*, 1 February 1992) quotes several "howlers": Electra's cry, "God, where the hell are you?" and "Nothing stinks more than bad advice." Pound's use of "inappropriately informal expressions," Erstein claims, "injects comedy that is wholly counterproductive."

12. This dystopia, however, is intended to be the nation's capital. Thus does Prewitt try to make the ancient tale "relevant": both set and costumes make clear the wide gulf between those who have and those who do not, a situation very evident in Washington, DC.

13. Also in 1992, Sophocles' *Electra* was made the closing act of the Guthrie's "Clytemnestra Project," where it was powerfully performed; at various times the play has been included as a part of longer tellings of the House of Atreus story. Discussion of these versions is included in Chapter 6.

14. In the summer of 1994, the New Jersey Shakespeare Festival, playing on the campus of Drew University, gave other new twists to the play. Here Novella Nelson as Clytemnestra dominated the action, so much so that there really was no contest between mother and daughter. According to Alvin Klein (*New York Times*, 26 June 1994), the incestuous attraction between Electra and her brother far outweighed any suggested between the princess and her father. Otherwise, he con-

cluded, apart from some mood-inspiring music there was little that "pierced the routine."

15. Cited from *Theatre Magazine* (December 1923). In case there should be doubt about his familiarity with the demands of the role, Hornblow reminds his readers that "only three actors have personated in this country the fate persecuted Theban king—George Riddle, Mounet-Sully and John E. Kellerd."

16. One critic remained who clung to the old ideas about this play. Ludwig Lewisohn (*The Nation*, 7 November 1923) proclaimed that it was time to speak the truth about *Oedipus*: the play was bad melodrama. No one could believe that the king and queen would not have talked of their past, he asserted; no one should be surprised that the hero turns out to be the villain. Even he, however, could not deny the poetic power of the Greek play.

5

Greek Tragedy Achieves Status:
1935–1950

From 1935 to 1950, three Greek tragedies achieved status on the American commercial stage. *Trojan Women* responded to the emotional tenor of the times during World War II, for Euripides' tragedy, as noted above, is the text from the archives of Western literary culture that best illustrates the suffering of women in war waged by men. The text is a powerful indictment of the callous and cruel nature of political war. But the playwright's vision is broad, and *Trojan Women* suggests that the victims of military conflicts include the men who fight them, that both innocent bystanders and the perpetrators of war suffer, for the deities at the play's beginning warn that ruin lies ahead for the victors as well.

Sophocles *Oedipus Tyrannus* continued to be staged, and again, this preference is not surprising. Sophocles' play portrays a man facing with courage the knowledge that he has transgressed society's sternest taboos, that he has innocently inherited mankind's worst curse. Oedipus stands at the beginning of Western literature as the paradigm for one who seeks and accepts the truth at all costs; he stands at the beginning of Freudian psychology as the ultimate example of self-awareness. What better figure from ancient myth to exemplify the dilemma of mortal men during the dark days of the late 1930s and opening years of the 1940s?

The third Greek play to capture attention at this time was Euripides' *Medea*. Few directors chose to stage Greek tragedies during the last years of the 1940s, for it was not the time to mourn and lament ruin, but to rebuild and look to a brighter future. But one poet-playwright still found power in the ancient myths and turned his hand to writing modern versions of the old plays, versions in which psychological insights played a greater part, and in which those who rejected society stood free. Robinson Jeffers brought

Greek myth to the modern stage in several plays; *Tower Beyond Tragedy*, for example, retells the Orestes story. Only one of his dramas, however, became popular, but the unrivaled success of that single play outweighed by far the few productions of his other retold legends. Jeffers' *Medea* took the audiences of the late 1940s by storm. Thus in this chapter I review the history of commercial productions of Sophocles' *Oedipus Tyrannus*, Euripides' *Trojan Women*, and Jeffers' *Medea*.

SOPHOCLES: *OEDIPUS TYRANNUS*

The most successful production of *Oedipus Tyrannus* in the first half of the twentieth century (if we consider Harvey's 1923 performance limited in its appeal) was that of the Old Vic Theatre Company on tour in May 1946, with Laurence Olivier in the starring role. Olivier was joined on stage at New York's Century Theatre by Eva Burrill as Jocasta, Harry Andrews as Creon, and Ralph Richardson as Tiresias, plus an effective and attractively garbed chorus of twelve. The reviews were mixed, but the favorable outnumbered the negative. Lewis Nichols of the *New York Times* (21 May 1946) commented that Olivier was excellent and at the height of his playing power; "Oedipus can be mangled," he wrote, "but Mr. Olivier instead has offered a model." Stated Herrick Brown of the *New York Sun* (21 May 1946): "In the hands of the Old Vic, the grim story of the ill-starred King of ancient Thebes becomes lively and intensely exciting theatre. If all productions [of Greek tragedy] were like this, the public would be clamoring for more." Robert Coleman of the *New York Daily Mirror* (22 May 1946) wrote, "*Oedipus* . . . is to our way of thinking the greatest whodunit yet penned"; while Kronenberg of *PM* magazine (22 May 1946) summed up the general reaction to Sophocles' play in 1946:

[This was] a truly great experience in the theatre. What Sophocles wrote with perfect art remains something that the stage, after 2500 years, can perfectly contain and project. [The play is] intense, as befits a tragic kingly figure and a primitive and passionate age. . . . Oedipus is a naked drama of crushing knowledge, and naked tragedy of crushing guilt.

Such words are far removed from the censure given to the text by the New York critics some sixty years earlier. Olivier's acting also drew acclaim. His exclamation when he learned the truth of his identity became a standard for tragic expression, a template against which future performances of this role would be judged: a passionate and bitter cry that echoed through the decades.[1]

The Old Vic used Sophocles' play as a vehicle for Olivier, for the evening had a double bill: *Oedipus Tyrannus* shared the program with Richard Sheridan's *The Critic*. Olivier drew praise for his skillful portrayal of both the tragic king and the ridiculous Mr. Puff. Although several reviewers did not see the need for doing the juxtaposition, most agreed it was successful, since Sophocles' play "is one of the goriest" and *The Critic* is one of the funniest.[2] What the critics did not realize was that the idea of following a tragic text with a comic play was not original with the London company (although its purpose was surely to showcase Olivier). At the Athenian drama festival after the performance of three tragedies the satyr play appeared: a bawdy burlesque of a familiar myth, often one told seriously in a preceding tragedy. The fifty-century B.C. Greek audience left the Theater of Dionysus laughing, not in tears.[3]

The Greek National Theatre Company came to the United States in 1952, including in their schedule a performance of *Oedipus* at New York's Mark Hellinger Theatre. Here Alexis Minotis and Katina Paxinou played the lead roles. This performance was, according to Wolcott Gibbs (*New Yorker*, 6 December 1952), "one of the most impressive events of the season." He allowed that Minotis' portrayal probably could not be compared to Olivier's, but the rest of the cast, and especially the chorus, succeeded brilliantly. Richard Hayes (*Commonweal*, 19 December 1952) thought that, even if Minotis was not as powerful as he might have been, the moment when he grasped his fate and "stands on an elevated stage, girded about by a chanting, dancing chorus . . . , one felt something of that prerational awe before the splendor and terror of life which is the essential classic quality." Brooks Atkinson (*New York Times*, 25 November 1952) also commented on the classic style the Greek National Theatre evoked. Despite the incomprehensible language, the acting displayed by the company was "illuminating and exalting." Praising all elements of the production, Atkinson affirmed the event as special, because "most of us have never had a chance to look so deep into the heart of a Greek classical drama." Following this all-Greek production, there was a lull in the performances of Sophocles' famous play. The king who suffered undeservedly at the cruel hand of fate had as little appeal to the audiences of the 1950s as it did to those at the beginning of the century. During the happy days of the 1950s audiences found little pleasure in the Greek tragedies.

Sophocles' famous play was staged again on the West Coast at the Geary Theatre by the American Conservatory Theatre (A.C.T.) as part of their rotating repertory in 1970. Director William Ball chose to do the play in traditional style. Robert Fletcher created a massive Greek palace with a door that looked to be ripped off a Mycenaean citadel, while for the costumes he eschewed the assorted rags style so often favored and created robes that reflected the grandeur we associate with ancient Greece, whatever the truth may be. Paul Shenar offered an empassioned performance in the title role, while Carol Jenkins supported her husband/son well. Ken Ruta portrayed Teiresias with power: Ball's direction gave him sufficient stature to command respect; the audience could realize that Oedipus' anger sprang from a genuine fear that the seer might know the truth. It was unusual for the

A.C.T. to offer a Greek play, for Ball preferred to stage more contemporary playwrights. His decision to include the classic play within the 1970 repertory showed his belief in its validity for a contemporary audience.

Oedipus Tyrannus reappeared in New York City in the spring of 1970 in an unusual version offered by the Roundabout Theatre. In this adaptation by Anthony Sloan/Gene Feist, the story was transferred to a Caribbean island and the presidential palace of a Central American nation. Gordon Heath offered a masterful Oedipus. Although the idea that an ancient Greek rite of passage could be understood through the more contemporary rituals of a bullfight was interesting, all critics found the adaptation poor and the overall performance vulgar. The main theme Sloan/Feist wished to put forward was that "a fact is not a truth until that truth has been brought into the open." Thus in this version Oedipus, Jocasta, indeed everyone in the palace knows the relationship between the king and queen, but until it is acknowledged no one acts upon its implications. And when the fact is made public, far from becoming a truth or a discovery of self, it is, as the reviewer in *Time* (9 March 1970) put it, "but an unveiling of the rottenness of self." This writer also noted that "America can now understand Greek drama better, since fate may not be in one's own hands but at one's throat." While Jocasta's scream, "Oh, listen to me, I am your mother!" can only be termed vulgar, there is one moment of tragic terror in the play. At the close of this *Oedipus*, the king speaks: "You will live, Jocasta. That is my sentence upon all of you, you will live."

It was the staging of *Oedipus Tyrannus* at the Guthrie Theater that received the most critical attention, when Sir Tyrone Guthrie mounted Anthony Burgess' translation at his Minneapolis theater in 1972. Mystery unexplained marked this staging of the ancient tragedy. It was a fine show for all its darkening of Sophocles' light. This *Oedipus Tyrannus* was more traditional and more restrained than Guthrie's *Atreus* of 1966 (see Chapter 7), but, nevertheless, translator and director felt compelled to alter Sophocles' text. Interest in sacrificial ritual had begun in the late 1960s, and the probability that human sacrifice had been part of early Greek cult had been put forth by several scholars of myth and anthropology.[4] Thus the opening scene of *Oedipus* at the Guthrie was a freely created ritual sacrifice, carried out in a smoky semidarkness that both evoked the mysterious and masked its reality.[5] By the time Oedipus, "whom all men call great," appeared (*OT*.8), the citizen chorus had already attempted to gain release by the ultimate ritual of human sacrifice. It was up to the king to find a solution.

The second major alteration Burgess made in his adaptation of the script lay in the king's self-blinding. Sophocles properly left that action to be done in the royal bedchamber and its description to a crazed messenger. Burgess, however, had Oedipus blind himself onstage. This startling gesture, appearing in all press photographs and causing shock in the audience, was effective for its violence although perhaps slightly artificial in motivation (e.g., why did the king walk around with the brooches in his hands as he told of Jocasta's death?). When questioned about this alteration, the translator replied that it was appropriate for a modern audience to see the king's act of self-mutilation because they expect to see violence.[6]

A further change introduced by Burgess concerned the riddle of the sphinx. In addition to an elder who gave a complete spelling out of the riddle Sophocles assumed known to his audience, Burgess penned a mysterious exchange between a child and the chorus leader at the end of the play:

Chorus leader: Perhaps it was better to be killed by it.
The riddle was not meant to be answered.
Child: But he answered it. He saved us.
That's the story we're told.
Chorus leader: It is dangerous to answer riddles,
But some men are born to answer them.
It is the gods' doing. They hide themselves in riddles.
We must not try to understand too much.
Child: Why?

His question is left unanswered;[7] the mystery is allowed to remain.[8]

In the 1972 production, both Len Cariou as Oedipus and Patricia Conolly as Jocasta gave masterful performances.[9] The earlier scenes made clear their self-pride and their enjoyment of each other; as the play progressed, their fear became more manifest. They acted in a world of grays and browns: brown rags for the citizens crowding around the king, gray drapery for Jocasta's costume, gray fur and brown leather for the king's. The set was of rusted metal in massive shapes. All of this was a deliberate attempt to evoke the primitive, the atavistic, the archetypal tragic story.

After nearly a century of production, Sophocles' text had attained success in the American commercial theater. Now *Oedipus Tyrannus* was interpreted as illustrating the essential quest of a brave individual for both truth and identity, a quest that lay at the very beginning of mortal existence. Furthermore, through his quest the king became the savior of his society; through him it would be cured of its ills. Far from representing a moral failure, Oedipus' search in the later years of the 1900s was an exemplar of a moral victory.

EURIPIDES: *TROJAN WOMEN*

As we have seen, *Trojan Women* was first staged by Granville Barker in 1915 in outdoor settings in the Northeast, while the message of *Trojan Women* was kept alive in other parts of the nation by the devoted work of Maurice Browne and the Chicago Little Theatre. After these initial performances during World War I, the play languished on the shelf until the time of World War II.

Trojan Women appeared on the New York stage twice in 1938, at the St. James and Roerich Institute Theatres. The production at the St. James, done by the Federal Theatre Project, was panned for its arrangement which featured Tamiris "the ideological dancer." Brooks Atkinson (*New York Times*, 22 April 1938) said the message put forth was more like "workers of the world unite" than the ideas of Euripides' play. He doubted if Greek drama was able to be acted in the modern theater anyway. He was alone in his doubts, however, for a well-produced *Trojan Women* inspired most reviewers to note how timely was the message of Euripides' play. The second staging of 1938, this time in Edith Hamilton's translation, and starring Mildred Dunnock as Hecuba (a role she was to re-create twenty-five years later; see below), earned critical praise. Of this performance John Mason Brown (*New York Post*, 28 January 1938) wrote that although "the play was propaganda, it was also art, art with beauty, brutality, and majesty."

For her 1941 production at the Cort Theatre, Margaret Webster added to Euripides' play an opening scene set in a modern city during an air raid. Several critics found this blitzkrieg prologue unnecessary, for the power of the ancient text was evident without such anachronistic additions. Euripides' script again garnered praise. The message of *Trojan Women*, termed "a lament for the vanquished" by Richard Watts (*New York Herald*, 9 April 1941), was considered clear and, in the words of Sidney Whipple (*New York World-Telegram*, 9 April 1941), "gloomily impressive, exhausting, and all of it sadly true."

D Day (6 June 1944) marked the victorious landing of the American forces on the shores of France, and with this successful assault the final year of World War II began; the long military conflict would end the following year. And with the arrival of peace the appeal of Euripides' lament for the victims of war waned. From 1947 until 1963 a single performance of Euripides' tragedy opened on the commercial stage, and it received very poor notices indeed. Only one time during the last eighty years has *Trojan Women* found no favor in the United States: during the 1950s.

The production staged at the Theatre Marquee in 1957 brought these comments from Walter Kerr of the *New York Herald Tribune* (18 March 1957): "Everything is against these poor girls. As Euripides, the gods, and the production at the Theatre Marquee have arranged it, the women of Troy must stand idly by while atrocities are done." All of the reviewers panned what was, apparently, a poorly conceived production; Brooks Atkinson (*New York Times*, 19 March 1957) asserted that this was not the way to do Greek drama in the modern theater. But the point of interest lies in the fact that Euripides' play itself was as unpopular as was the acting and dramatic conception.

Times changed and the happy days of the 1950s gave way to the turbulent years of the 1960s. In the winter of 1963, Michael Cacoyannis staged *Trojan Women* at the Circle in the Square in New York City. The production featured Mildred Dunnock as Hecuba, with a strong supporting cast.[10] Walter Kerr, who had found this play so tedious in 1957, had different words six years later. Writing in the *Herald Tribune* (24 December 1963), he expressed how deeply the performance moved him: "The production catches hold and grows and comes to a point of exhaustion that is firmly satisfying—because one whole all-absorbing cry has been sounded to the full and then completed utterly." His judgment was echoed by the *Village Voice* (26 December 1963), which termed the show "tragedy incarnate," while Richard Watts (*New York Post*, 24 December 1963) asserted there was "no more striking protest against the cruelty of war."

The staging at the Circle in the Square in 1963 was the direct antithesis of the 1915 production, for in the off-Broadway theater the only similarity between the classical Greek stage and the modern arena was the round playing space. There the audience was physically close to the actors, and the power of the play rested in the careful gestures of Dunnock as Hecuba, in the silence of her pain between her words of grief.[11] Whether or not this performance was the initiating cause, from this date onward during the 1960s *Trojan Women* played both on campus and commercial stages around the United States. Its recognition as an antiwar statement, however, had begun in America with that initial performance staged under the gray-clouded skies of New York City in the summer of 1915.

For the opening of La Mama Annex in 1974, Andrei Serban staged a version of this antiwar play which was to become famous. Titled *Fragments of a Trilogy*, Serban combined into a single dramatic story *Medea, Trojan Women*, and *Electra*. This show was not the first directed by Serban for La Mama; he had staged *Medea* as a single play there two years earlier. La Mama, which plays a significant role in American theater history, was started by Ellen Stewart in 1961 in a basement at 321 East Ninth Street. Over the years the Buildings Department forced her to move La Mama Experimental Theater Club many times until in 1969 it settled on East Fourth Street, playing only there until the Annex, a much larger space, opened with Serban's *Trilogy* five years later. La Mama productions have always been devoted to the new and experimental, but Stewart believed firmly in the primacy of text. Thus she could include Greek drama within her repertoire of new plays by contemporary authors.

Andrei Serban, Romanian born and internationally trained, met Ellen Stewart in 1966 when the company was playing at a festival in Zagreb. She was so entranced with his abilities that she enabled him to come to America as part of her company three years later. He soon established himself as a director who believed in the primacy of language over text, of emotion expressed through sound and action alone. In 1972 Serban's *Medea* at La Mama was a success; his *Trilogy* capped that achievement.

Clive Barnes (*New York Times*, 20 October 1974) described *Trilogy* as "non-verbal theater of aural communication." Serban's actors spoke ancient Greek, Latin, and in Barnes' words, "a touch of this and a touch of that and guttural dirty. A linguist couldn't understand it, but, like anyone else, a linguist would just know what they [were] acting." Mel Gussow, writing in the *New York Times* (25 June 1974), was equally impressed with Serban's innovative theater. He focused upon the minimal lighting provided by flickering candles and the occasional spotlight: for Gussow the experience was both visual and aural, but still "voice pieces," not dance pieces. Through the incomprehensible language the mythic names rang out; emotions were transmitted by sound and movement.

Serban's use of movement as symbol carried the parts of the trilogy along while tying them together. Gussow recalls in detail the women's wailing protest before they are led off to captivity. Barnes describes how each part of the whole differs: *Medea* dark and tight, *Trojan Women* genuinely erotic in its grief, *Electra* "a ritual of fulfillment complete with a live snake and a live dove." Julius Novick, writing in the *New York Times* (17 November 1974), summed up Serban's *Trilogy* thusly:

> Plot, character, the thrust of argument, are all diminished or missing in these productions. Instead, the plays are turned toward their ritual origins, resolved into a series of ceremonials: of grief, of anger, of preparation, of sacrifice, of triumph. And these ceremonials are magnificently presented.... [The trilogy] offers awe and wonder—gasping, open-mouthed, fascinated wonder.

Euripides' play under Serban's interpretation took on symbolic dimensions beyond those evident in the richly symbolic text itself. And with the production of *Fragments of a Trilogy* at La Mama, the performance history of this text closes for a decade.

Trojan Women next appeared on the American commercial stage in a version staged by Tadashi Suzuki and his Little Theater, Waseda Sho-Gekijo.[12] Suzuki used Euripides' play as a takeoff point for a show set in postwar Japan. Kayoko Shiraishi portrayed Hecuba, Cassandra, and an old woman who suffered in the bombing of Tokyo. Suzuki's version played at the Japan Society in New York in 1982, but he earned most acclaim for the production mounted at the Olympic Art Festivals before and during the games themselves in Los Angeles.

Robert J. Fitzpatrick, director of the Olympic Arts Festival, asserted that as the Greeks believed art and sport to be inseparable, so the production of music and drama was appropriate for the modern games. He made sure the arts performed were as international in representation as were the athletic contests: thirty companies representing fourteen countries offered in eight languages a total of thirty-eight shows, or 305 performances, during the festival. He also dared to engage troupes that were avant-garde by any standard. Thus was the Japanese *Trojan Women* a part of the festival program.

Fitzpatrick himself took this very foreign performance in stride: "At first there's panic. But after ten minutes you forget you don't speak Japanese."[13] Suzuki's *Trojan Women* fused both classical Japanese theatrical forms and ancient Greek themes, both bound together with contemporary (i.e., post–World War II) allusions. As Welton Jones points out in his review (*San Diego Union*, 8 April 1985), the adaptation used the ideas, not the form of the Greek original. It seems, he opines, that the Japanese prefer "to receive their drama through filters of style complex enough to fulfill their culture's need for emotional density." Jones thought the well-tuned precision style—rehearsed for nearly a decade—soon overwhelmed the emotional impact of the play; "the final effect," he states, "is that of an antique lacquer bowl . . . briefly fascinating, [but] probably not worth the effort." Dan Sullivan (*Los Angeles Times*, 20 June 1984) was intrigued by the apparent importation of Western elements into the clearly Eastern staging, but was uncertain as to whether the final effect was successful. He did, however, praise Kayoko Shiraishi's acting, noting both the powerful range of her voice and her unique blending of burning rage and physical stillness.

All in all, Suzuki's *Trojan Women* received critical attention for its extraordinary style, but whether or not the power of the Greek tragedy endured was a matter of debate.

The most recent staging of *Trojan Women* was also on the West Coast, a production by the L.A. Rep Company in the summer of 1992. According to *Los Angeles Times* writer Ray Lloyd, John Neville's direction brought to the stage a "moody, stinging" show. This version modernized the tragedy without updating the text, thus maintaining the impact of Euripides' original. The entire cast, asserts Lloyd, offered stellar performances. Kimberly Chase portrayed Hecuba's suffering and rage with her burning eyes; Kendall Hailey brought a "maniacal focus" to the role of Cassandra; while Joy Kilpatrick's Helen was a "bedazzling, coiled vixen . . . haughty and sensual." Having opened with the caveat that Greek tragedies are usually both intimidating and demanding, the critic offers this summation: "Seldom will you see a Greek classic staged better than this."

Euripides' drama was originally staged in America as a protest against the suffering of World War I; in its most recent production the performance was not tied to any specific event in this country, but rather railed against the vanity of military conflict itself. In the decade of the 1990s, the post–Cold War period, the world is fraught with armed combat arising from causes that seem, to many observers, no better founded than that quest for Helen wherein so many men fell because one woman strayed from home. The emotional impact of Euripides' *Trojan Women* remains and shines through, whether the text is played straight, blended with other cultural traditions,

or deprived of intelligible language. Few dramas could sustain such alteration, but the power of this play endures.

EURIPIDES: *MEDEA*

When Robinson Jeffers determined to write his new version of Euripides'
play of 431 B.C., he took his cue, perhaps, from French playwrights of that
time who composed a drama for a specific actress. Thus he rewrote
Euripides' *Medea*, which opened in October of 1947, for his favorite leading
lady, Judith Anderson. Over the next three years Miss Anderson would play
the barbarian princess from Colchis, wronged by the politically eager Jason,
for 214 performances. She toured worldwide with Jeffers' play, and each
time she took the stage, critics and audiences alike hailed her performance.
Anderson's interpretation of *Medea* has dominated American theater history, but it should be noted that while Judith Anderson stands at the center,
she shares the limelight with two other fine actresses who brought the role
alive, Margaret Anglin in the 1920s and Zoe Caldwell in the 1980s.

Medea has remained one of the most popular plays from antiquity to be
brought to the modern American stage. The desire to produce this one of
Euripides' dramas must rest, ultimately, on its theatricality and the strong
character of Medea herself: her great scenes are a challenge for any actress.
Its appeal is somewhat mysterious, however, for any character analysis of
Medea reveals some very troubling ideas: we are prepared to sympathize
with the woman scorned, but not ready to condone her violent deed; it is
one thing to applaud revenge taken upon the deserting husband, but quite
another to sanction a mother's deliberate slaughter of her own children.

Critical discussion of the play among classical scholars has long revealed
this ambivalence. Jason is easy to understand. He comes off very badly in
the play, for no one doubts he is wrong to use Medea's skills in advancing
his career and then choose a new, young wife for further political advantage.
A modern audience can immediately recognize Jason; he serves as the
archetype for the man who allows his wife to assist him in his early career,
then displaces her for what has recently been termed a "trophy" wife. But
Jason is foolish not to realize that the princess of Colchis has powers he
should not arouse, a temper he should not cross.

But what are we to make of Medea, this foreign woman removed to
Greek soil and there abandoned? Some scholars have suggested that
Euripides intended her to be a paradigm warning against women in general, foreign women in particular. Others have taken her at face value and
argued that she is in the right because Jason broke his oath to her, and thus
she illustrates the dangers that follow those who do so. Another view
removes her from the mortal realm altogether; as the granddaughter of the
sun, her access to magical powers exonerates her of blame: she acts as does
any Greek deity when wronged. This view gathers strength from the play's

ending, when Helios' chariot comes and whisks her away to safety, a mother still stained from the blood of her children. All of these interpretations have some validity.

Whatever the Greek view may have been, modern producers want the audience to side with Medea, while actresses find in her strong character a role to covet. Few great women of the stage can resist the opportunity to proclaim Medea's famous lines (250–251): "I would rather stand forth in battle three times than once to bear a single child." Thus the performance history of *Medea* reveals that great actresses in the title role have dominated the interpretation of the play on the twentieth-century American stage. This was true in the 1920s, the 1950s, and the 1980s; that the play's attraction rests on a leading actress is equally true in the 1990s, for Diana Rigg's interpretation in 1994 earned her international recognition: the 1994 Tony Award went to an actress bringing to life a play nearly 2,500 years old.

One of the earliest interpretations of Medea was that given by Margaret Anglin at Carnegie Hall in February 1918. As Anglin won acclaim for her portrayal of Electra during the same billing, so she did for her performance in *Medea*. "The barbaric heroine of Euripides rendered with true classic intensity and fire," headlines the *New York Times* (21 February 1918) review. While in his plot summary the (anonymous) reviewer shows some sympathy for Jason—"poor man, her husband and at once the cause of her fury and the chief object of it"—he admits that it is to Medea that Euripides directs his (and our) concern:

[She is] a very moving figure—splendid, too, caught as she is in a vortex of elemental feminine passions, richly colored by her barbaric soul. . . . She has all the primitive woman's love for her children, yet . . . she kills them both. . . . [Thus does she] leave Jason without bride, kingdom or child.

The role itself permitted Anglin to display her talents in portraying two very different sides of the heroine. While the reviewer concedes that there were perhaps depths to Medea's character that the young actress could not reach, he admits that she was "consummate" both in tenderness toward her children and violence in her rage. *Theatre Magazine*'s reviewer Mr. Hornblow agreed:

Most lavish praise [should] be paid to Miss Anglin for the vividly varied reading she gave of the daughter of the Barbarian queen[14]. . . . As a declamatory *tour de force* it was remarkable, aided by pantomimic intelligence and plastic grace that gave its varying words and eloquence tremendous [power] in its onrushing sweep of tragic significance.

The translation used for the 1921 performance was that of Gilbert Murray, termed by the *New York Times* "crisply vernacular" in its phrasing and "made even more modern by the strong outcroppings of feminism in the discourse of this legendary barbarian." The combined efforts of Anglin, Murray's translation, and Walter Damrosch's music offered (according to the *New York Times*) a theatrical success to a house "crowded to the doors" with an audience who "followed the performance with breathless interest, lingering after the final curtain for prolonged applause," or, to quote Hornblow, "[The show proved that] more than eighteen thousand metropolitans exist who can still derive pleasure and entertainment from the classics." The closing line of the *Times* review is also worth quoting: "In a season mainly devoted to trivialities, Miss Anglin's classical productions come somewhat in the nature of a benefaction." A play featuring such deeds of horror seems an odd candidate to be a theatrical "benefaction." But as a play to which a fine actress can bring vitality as well as emotion, *Medea* might well be the text to grace a drama season.

Two years later, however, the reviewers were somewhat less tolerant of the ancient Greek classic. Maurice Browne's Little Theatre troupe came east from Chicago to play *Medea* at the Garrick and earned less glowing comments. Several reviewers were distressed as much by the text as by the acting; this time, indeed, Hornblow himself (*Theatre Magazine*, 20 May 1920) complained that it was "a fearful strain to sit still for two hours" of Euripides. But while this critic had only praise for Maurice Browne's "artistic intelligence" and "physical grasp of stage opportunities," others were impressed more with Browne's *intent* than his *result*: the former was admirable, but the latter less successful; the production was artistic but not vital.[15]

Ellen Van Volkenburg did not rival Margaret Anglin in her portrayal of the wronged queen; the theater critics praised her as an "elocutionist" but not as a tragic actress. J. Ranken Towse (*New York Evening Post*, 23 March 1920) asserted she lacked the "skill, pathos and passion" of Anglin. The 1918 performance by Margaret Anglin had become the standard by which to judge any actress playing the title role.[16]

Maurice Browne's use of mood lighting had become his trademark. This time he darkened the stage when the tragedy was most dire, then lit Medea brilliantly at her moments of resolution. The *Theatre Magazine* reviewer found the lights in this production "a most convincing adjunct," but the writer in the *World* (23 March 1920) complained at length that the " 'art' of the production was always too obvious, that the lighting doubled the number of performers on stage"; the writer of the *New York Sun-Herald* (23 March 1920) thought the lights changed too much as if by clockwork, while J. Ranken Towse declared that there was "something flashy, tricky, and disconcerting in the kaleidoscopic illumination."

The chorus earned mostly favorable critical comment. Six young women, decorously dressed in classic style, "shrink, cower, quiver, shimmer and by other gestures intensify the emotions of the play," according to Alexander Woollcott (*New York Times*, 23 March 1920), who continues a bit later on, "At all events, the disporting Corinthian ladies of Mr. Browne's production do prettify the piece distressingly." The *New York Evening Sun*'s critic, on the other hand, complained that the chorus was too static, that he would not have been surprised to learn that these serious women were all "doctors of philosophy." For this reviewer, their movements of "statuesque grace and studied gesture" in forming beautiful stage pictures were all part of the production's failure: a performance that "was all Art with a capital 'A' and drama with a small 'd.' "

To close critical comment of the 1920 production the words of Alexander Woollcott are appropriate. We have seen how Gilbert Murray's translation, which now seems so dated, appeared in 1918 as contemporary and somewhat attuned to feminism. This held true two years later. Thus could Woollcott proclaim: "It is interesting to watch a twentieth century audience at this great feminist play . . . [from which have stemmed] all plays about forsaken women since the world was young and men have been faithless. After all, Medea was just a Madame Butterfly who showed a little proper spirit."

The version of *Medea* most frequently staged is not Euripides' "original" but the free adaptation Robinson Jeffers wrote for Judith Anderson. The 1947 program note describes the play as "a tragedy in two acts about the vengeance of a woman scorned by her ambitious husband." *Medea* opened with Jason played by John Gielgud, who also directed the show; he was eventually replaced by Dennis King. The show was revived for a limited run (sixteen performances) at the New York City Center in May 1949, at which time Henry Brandon played Jason to Anderson's Medea.

"If Medea does not entirely understand every aspect of her whirling character, she would do well to consult Judith Anderson. For Miss Anderson understands the character more thoroughly than Medea, Euripides, or the scholars, and it would be useless now for anyone else to attempt the part." So does Brooks Atkinson begin his review (*New York Times*, 21 October 1947) of the Jeffers/Anderson show. His praise extended to the entire performance: John Gielgud's Jason is described as "lucid [and] solemn"; Albert Hecht, he claims, "has the commanding voice and the imperiousness of a working monarch." The chorus, comprised of just three women, was well directed by Gielgud; indeed, all of the acting, according to Atkinson, was "innocent of the stuffiness peculiar to most classical productions." He closes his review with further praise of Judith Anderson: "She has freed Medea from all the old traditions as if the character had just been created. Perhaps that is exactly what has happened. Perhaps Medea was never fully created until Miss Anderson breathed immortal fire into it last evening."

Atkinson was so struck with Anderson's performance in Jeffers' *Medea* that a few days later (26 October 1947) he wrote a two-column piece on the play. Here he had the opportunity not only to praise Anderson's acting abundantly, but also to write about Greek culture. A few lines will serve to illustrate the further superlatives Atkinson found to describe Judith Anderson's interpretation of the role:

We are used to more temperate theatre. . . . But Miss Anderson's outpouring of barbaric feelings is so intelligently designed and controlled and so flaming in expression that it convinces and consumes the audience. . . . The details supply the logic, which in turn gives the character a solid foundation. But the quality that makes your scalp tingle in the theatre is the vehemence of the passion.

The drama critic then turns to Greek culture. Atkinson dares to break away from the common assumption that the civilization of ancient Athens was innocent of any wrongs. It is to Euripides' credit, he asserts, that he did not "conform to the accepted patterns." Thus in *Medea* he portrayed the marriage of a Greek to a foreigner—"still an abomination in cultures that are pure and intolerant" and "faced honestly the injustice that a Greek man had done a foreign woman." Such attitudes would eventually earn the playwright exile to Macedonia, since the Creons of ancient Athens "felt safer when he was out of the way."

In the final sections of his article Atkinson deals with Jeffers' sensible and dramatic updating of Euripides' text and Gielgud's directing. The only cavil he made was against the decision to tame Medea's murder of her two sons. Such a drama as *Medea*, he states, "needs that climax of inhuman horror to complete the design," and such a great actress as Anderson does "not boggle at violence." Gifted with such praise, Judith Anderson in the title role of Jeffers' *Medea* went on her extensive tour of the United States and Europe.[17]

Andrei Serban's interpretation of theater as mystery and ritual, a nonverbal experience of tragedy, attracted attention when he staged *Medea* at La Mama in New York City during the 1970s. His 1974 *Fragments of a Trilogy*, a vision of the Trojan War formed from *Medea*, *Trojan Women*, and *Electra*, and, somewhat later, the innovative production of *Agamemnon*, earned him special acclaim. But his first venture into Greek tragedy was with *Medea* in 1972. Here his texts were those of both Euripides and Seneca; Medea speaks the former's Greek, Jason the latter's Latin. The effect of the play in no way depends on the viewer's command of either: the intent is to be foreign and to base understanding on sound alone, or, more properly, on emotion alone.

To hear Serban's *Medea*, the audience was conducted to La Mama's candlelit basement, where its members sat on benches along the wall to watch what Clive Barnes termed a fascinating and remarkable *Medea*. Writing in the *New York Times* of 25 January 1972, Barnes assured his readers that although he lacked any understanding of the ancient languages, the impact of Serban's theater was powerful. He described the experience at some length:

A production such as this *Medea* seeks to shake the ordinary into the realm of the extraordinary. It tries to review by ritual what has been lost by acceptance. . . . Verbal comments are meaningless compared with the physical realization, the simple spectacle of [Medea's] despair. . . . Ambiguity and mist are both qualities that can enhance life into art. . . . This was a theatrical occasion of great interest.

Priscilla Smith played an intense Medea in this production, while Jamil Zakkai offered an outstanding Jason. The unique combination of language as sound, of set as a mere open space in a dark basement, and a belief in theater as ritual produced an experience both "pristine" and "persuasive." As Barnes concluded, Serban's *Medea* "opens doors to the possible theaters of the future."

The following year Clive Barnes saw another production of Euripides' play. Here he understood the words but found them wanting. In his review (*New York Times*, 18 January 1973) of *Medea* as adapted and staged by Minos Volanakis at the Circle in the Square's new uptown location (linked to the Joseph E. Levine Theater), Barnes voiced reservations about Volanakis' conversational language; he found it at times successful but at other times too idiosyncratic and "unnecessarily jazzy." He also questioned the elabo-rate staging and the inconsistent use of masks; in an interpretation attempt-ing to be naturalistic, the purpose of the masks, especially since they were put on and off, was unclear.

Walter Kerr, who saw the play ten days later, was equally displeased with Volanakis' language and interpretation. With the lines she had been given, he asserted, the powerful Irene Pappas had been reduced to a put-upon hausfrau. In his review (*New York Times*, 28 January 1973) he used harsh words to condemn the inconsistencies evident in this production. "The evening is constantly inverting itself, both visually and verbally," he com-plained. The masks and costumes apparently tried to be both archetypal and contemporary at the same time: "The mask says one thing; the deport-ment defies it or simply throws it away." The random gathering of effects, some good, others clearly askew, indicated to Kerr that Volanakis had not thought through all the effects he intended to use, especially when he used them all together.

However, despite their criticism of Volanakis' artistic decisions, both Barnes and Kerr had nothing but praise for Irene Pappas' Medea. Even though Volanakis desired her to be portrayed with more sympathy than is usually accorded the barbarian princess, Pappas still brought to the role the dramatic intensity for which she is justly famous. Here, while she kept her fires subterranean, she portrayed the character with "her unrelenting de-termination and unwavering desire for justice," to use Barnes' words. For this critic she stood out in fiery contrast to John P. Ryan's male chauvinist pig Jason, a creature who won no sympathy from the audience, even at the end when he stood ruined before his now-empty palace. Far from being a play of ritual and emotion, Volanakis' *Medea* of 1973 was based on a very real belief in a contemporary woman's firm resolve to ruin the man who broke his oath to her. Thus could T. E. Kalem (*Time*, 29 January 1973) assert that this version was a social tragedy, and that to humanize Medea's part was "to make it somewhat less than awesome in its sweeping horror." In so doing, Kalem believed, Volanakis' altered Euripides' probable intent to show the tragedy that results when passion overcomes reason.

Albert Bermel, writing in the *New Leader* (5 March 1973), heralded Volanakis interpretation. In a thoughtful article titled "Medea in Negative," Bermel praises the modern Greek director's understanding of Euripides, how he understands the ancient playwright's heroine as "driven by her private, uncompromising code," who can be a tragic figure despite her horrible deed. In Volanakis' version, according to Bermel, Jason is the villain who wronged Medea, and the creation of a sympathetic woman is the triumph of Irene Pappas' fine acting. The "negative" of Bermel's title lies in the inversion of the setting (described below), in the costumes—the contrast of Medea's black *peplos* with the brilliant red of Jason's cloak and the blazing white, offset with blue, of Aegeus' outfit—and in the masks used to separate Medea from those who surround her, either as supporting friends (the chorus) or as hostile foes (the three leading males). Although Bermel did not stand alone in his thoughtful acclaim of this production, his enthusiasm and generous understanding were not generally shared by other critics, who, while enjoying Irene Pappas' acting, had doubts about other aspects of this *Medea*.

Leonard Harris of CBS proclaimed the show a success, praising Irene Pappas' acting and the play itself as one that speaks to central problems of the modern world in a voice loud and clear. ABC's Kevin Sanders received the exact opposite impression. For him the production was "redeemed" by Irene Pappas' presence, and the staging was stunning, but *Medea*, he proclaimed, is a play "rapidly becoming obsolete through irrelevance."

Walter Kerr comments at some length on the staging and theatrical effects of the production; these were sufficiently unusual that it is surprising that Barnes (and others) make no note of them. At center stage "a vast wound opens up, a red-tinged crater ringed with steps descending into the netherworld of womb or tomb." This replacement for the traditional palace, created by Volanakis and Robert Mitchell, would seem to infect any figure coming from it with savage purpose. As it developed, however, Medea's entrance, according to Kerr, rather implied she had come from the kitchen. The ending of the play also tried for a special effect that apparently fell flat. The giant lid of this cauldron was lifted on high against the back wall, thus to be transformed into the chariot of the sun. But Volanakis could not place Medea onto this golden disk, so a mere symbol glowed in her place, while her final lines were piped in. The intent was a failure—and Kerr accurately sums up why: "At the moment of Jason's humiliation we want to see Medea in her power; the more human he, the more divine she. And we are cheated."

He has been humanized to deal with no more than a sound-track, an absence. The conclusion is impersonal after all, and flat."[18]

The opening years of the 1970s, then, saw two productions of *Medea*, the one introducing new possibilities for theater—although preserving the form of drama's earliest history—and the other trying to be contemporary—while including remnants of ancient ways. Serban's staging, which looked to the future via the past, was more effective than Volanakis' production, which looked to the past while clinging to the immediate present.

In the spring of 1982, Judith Anderson returned to the American stage in *Medea*, but this time as the Nurse, playing the servant to Zoe Caldwell's Medea. Some critics thought that even in the lesser role she still dominated the performance; they found Caldwell's acting much weaker than Anderson's had been in the lead role. Douglas Watt (*Daily News*, 3 May 1982) proclaimed, "Judith Anderson [as the Nurse] is the one moving thing about the revival [of Jeffers' *Medea*]. . . . Even in repose Anderson, whose electrifying Medea is still vivid in the memory, commands our attention."

But Watt was in the minority. Most critics had only praise for the interpretation given the role by Zoe Caldwell. Continuities abounded: Ben Edwards, who designed the 1947 production, also staged that of 1982, and he maintained the classic concepts that had worked forty years earlier. Thus the young actress had to re-create Medea in the setting her elder supporting actress had made famous. To the majority of New York critics her attempt was eminently successful.

Frank Rich, writing in the *New York Times* (3 May 1982), asserts that Zoe Caldwell "brought her special flame" to the revival. Her "intense psychological realism" brought her audience into "the thunderclap of Euripides' tragedy," leading them to believe in her warped logic. Her physical appearance set her off from those around her: she looked the part, states Rich, as well as interpreting it. He praises her wit, her sexuality, and her speech. While Rich cannot acclaim the entire production, he finally hails the play as powerful and exciting. He is echoed by John Beaufort of the *Christian Science Monitor* (6 May 1982), who, in a review titled "Zoe Caldwell's *Medea*, a Theatrical Mountaintop," accords accolades to the entire show. Caldwell, he states, "scales the histrionic heights" in the title role. She portrayed guile, cunning, deep hurt, and sorrow as she commanded "the spectator's understanding of this jealousy-maddened creature." While his approval of Judith Anderson's performance as the Nurse was expected, Beaufort even liked Michael Ryan's Jason: "the middle-aged power-conscious Jason is a plausible climber, the one-time varsity hero now angling for a place in the executive suite." Setting, direction, music—all moved this member of the audience: "Count *Medea* a theatrical event in the grand tradition. In other words, a summit." The critic takes time to discuss Greek drama as well.

Although one of the most popular plays from the alien world of Greek tragedy, *Medea* presents special problems for a latter-day audience. Oedipus, after all, didn't realize that he was committing patricide and, ultimately, incest. However, given her extreme emotional disarray, Medea knows what she is doing at every step. . . . Was Medea ignoble and base or was she rather a primitive (a "barbarian" as she scornfully proclaims), a woman totally ruled by extremes of passion? . . . The bottom line of Medea's motivation is reached in her explanation to [the] distraught father: "I have done it: because I loathed you more than I loved them."

Other critics equally praised the performance. Clive Barnes, now writing in the *New York Post* (3 May 1982), proclaimed in a review bursting with superlatives that "in Miss Caldwell's mighty and supremely variegated performance you have the inestimable joy of seeing a magnificent actress . . . a sight to be watched, a memory to be savored."[19]

The Caldwell-Anderson *Medea* had come to New York from its opening at the Kennedy Center in Washington, DC. There, too, the theater critics found superlatives in order. Joseph McLellan of the *Washington Post* (12 March 1982), who gives high praise to the leading actresses, chose an unusual way to describe Euripides' play. Beginning by suggesting that "Greek tragedy is not everybody's cup of retsina, but *Medea* is one of the few exceptions to the rule that this art is box-office poison" and quoting a lengthy passage from Schlegel, McLellan continues:

Euripides is the Puccini of Greek tragedy . . . *Medea* is both his *Madame Butterfly* and his *Tosca*. It is, in fact, a *Butterfly* with a *Tosca* clone as a heroine, the story of an Eastern woman wooed and married by a seafaring man from the West who ultimately abandons her for a more socially advantageous marriage. But this *Butterfly* does not quietly commit suicide; she exacts a revenge enormously more devastating than Tosca's and coldly premeditated.

The Washington critics focused particularly on the dramatic tradition that the two actresses were creating in this new production, a passing on of the torch of a great role from one leading lady to another. There was an additional unusual aspect to this *Medea*. The 1982 production was directed by Robert Whitehead, Zoe Caldwell's husband, who had produced the 1947 version. During that run, however, Whitehead and Anderson had had a falling out, and the two had not communicated for nearly thirty years.

Then in 1979 Anderson, seeking funding for the restoration of Jeffers' home, Tor House, in Carmel, California, considered the possibility of staging his most famous play again. She knew Caldwell's ability and thought she would be right for the part. Anderson indirectly contacted Whitehead about the script, then invited him and Caldwell to meet with her, and finally persuaded them to mount the show. Thus it was through Judith Anderson's vision that, once again, Jeffers' *Medea* was brought to critical acclaim.[20] While Anderson's portrayal of the Nurse was praised, she herself willingly accorded the top laurels to Caldwell, whose acting "completed the circle." Responding in an interview about the production, Judith Anderson said, "It's a great role, all right, and it was written for me. Once it was mine. Now it belongs to Zoe."21

As I noted above in the discussion of *Trojan Women*, an interest in Japanese-style Greek tragedy became popular both in the United States and Europe during the mid-1980s. Two productions caught critical attention, one of which earned international acclaim. Chronologically first was the Kabuki *Medea* of Wisdom Bridge's Chicago-based theater troupe. This show, conceived and directed by Shozo Sato, was brought from its Midwestern home to the Kennedy Center as part of the AT&T Performing Arts Festival in the summer of 1985.22

"Brilliant" was the word used by Louise Sweeney (*Washington Post*, 15 August 1985) to describe the Kabuki *Medea*. Sato retained the basic story line, but the legend took place far from Corinth. Medea, played by Barbara Robertson, was an Okinawan princess and Jason, portrayed by Dean Fortunato, a prince of the Japanese imperial court who captured a golden dragon; the two went into exile in Korea, where Euripides' tragedy in Japanese style took place. Critic Sweeney hailed the "dramatic tension between the stylized beauty of the Kabuki tradition and the visceral action of Euripides' tragedy." Strong emotion marked the acting of all cast members, none of whom were Asian; this production, unlike other Kabuki shows playing at the Kennedy Center during that summer, was performed in English. The blending of music, dance, and acting ability, the traditional triad that forms Kabuki, was eminently successful in the Wisdom Bridges performance.

The following summer the Delacorte Theater in Central Park was the setting for the Toho Company's version of Euripides' tragedy. In this production Yukio Ninagawa directed an all-male, Japanese-speaking cast who enhanced the Greek text with traditional Noh costumes and gestures. These, according to reviewer Glenda Frank (*Theatre Journal*, May 1987), "trigger retrospective plot-memory and arouse an emotional nexus keyed by visual coding." Searchlights, for example, indicated the "mythical world beyond Corinth, Medea's arrival and departure, and the superhuman forces of destiny." The lower world of mortals was lighted, in contrast, by torches and braziers.

Ninagawa's production brought audience sympathy to the side of Medea by presenting Jason and Creon as swaggering samurai: against such men the woman's anger is justly vented; she is, in Frank's words, "no monster [but] a powerful woman driven half-mad by her impotence in the face of abuse." Medea may have groveled, but the character still dominated the stage. Frank described the actor's appearance and presentation:

Resplendent in a glittering multicolored, forty-four pound costume, a fuchsia wig capping his six feet and false breasts bared, Mikijiro Hira as Medea . . . relinquished power through a slackening of posture during the confrontation scenes and then stripped to an ankle length red dress and headwrap that made his six-foot-plus [*sic*] frame both serpentine and sculptural in his postures of dejection, defiance and rage.

According to Ninagawa, the company was trying to create a new under-standing of the text by blending Japanese tradition and European realism, a universal theater spanning the different cultural styles. Although he took his direction very seriously, he ended his interview with the *New York Times'* Jennifer Dunning (31 August 1986) with a joke: "If *Medea* succeeds in New York, it will be because the Japanese imported American culture in a very good way. If *Medea* fails, it will be because we imported it the wrong way. Either way, it's the Americans' fault."

Any play that "has bonfires, a star dressed in a glittering headdress and a multicolored 44-pound robe . . . and ends with that star flying with a howl up into the sky" was bound to succeed.[23] In addition to the engagement as a part of Joseph Papp's New York Shakespeare Festival, Ninagawa's *Medea* toured to festivals in Greece, Italy, France, Great Britain, and Canada.

In the winter of 1991, the Guthrie Theater mounted a performance of Euripides' *Medea*. The text was that of the Athenian playwright in a trans-lation by Philip Vellacott. This was the first Greek show directed by Garland Wright, an undertaking he claimed to approach with fear, but his venture was defined by Mike Steele (*Minneapolis Star and Tribune*, 14 January 1991) as a "first-rate merging of archaic grandeur and contemporary sensibili-ties." Its grandeur and power lay in the acting of Brenda Wehle as Medea, and in that of the three women of the chorus, Isabell Monk, Jacqueline Kim, and Sally Wingert.

At first Wehle felt some trepidation about playing the title role in this play. Wright thought it important that Medea be played by a mother, but Wehle had to come to terms with a woman who would slay her own children. In an interview with Mike Steele in the *Minneapolis Star and Tribune* (11 January 1991) Wehle spoke about her relationship with the play's main character. To experience Medea's passion, she stated, "was scary, no fun at all." But as she developed the character, she came to understand drama itself as a cleansing ritual, one that allowed people to admit their darkest fears and not carry them out.[24] At last she achieved a balance between her anger and her sadness, all the while amazed at Euripides' understanding of Medea.

The critics acclaimed Brenda Wehle's rendition of the barbarian princess. They described her performance as powerful, full of energy, one that brought to life the grief and rage that would ultimately compel her terrible deed of revenge. Those upon whom she vented that anger, however, the men of the play, were uniformly described as weak actors, cold, flat, lacking in both vitality and intensity. The Guthrie *Medea* was ranked a success through the vibrant interpretation given by the women of the cast.

Zoe Caldwell won a Tony Award in 1982 for her portrayal of the title role in the Euripides/Jeffers play, as had Judith Anderson in 1947. The award was granted to an actress in the ancient play once again in 1994. Diana Rigg, who first created the role in London,[25] brought life to Euripides' text (in a new translation by Alistair Elliot) on the New York stage, and most printed reviews pointed out her talent. Edwin Wilson, theater critic of the *Wall Street Journal*, hailed Rigg's "incredible vocal range," "her presence and bearing." In his 13 April 1994 review he continues: "Ms. Rigg moves like quicksilver from one emotion to another but always with an unmistakable resolve. Her Medea is not a mindless barbarian but rather someone who knows exactly what she is doing . . . [she] moves relentlessly toward her goal. This makes the outcome that much more awesome and appalling."

Even the critics who were less fulsome in their praise termed the performance a "theatrical event" and Rigg's interpretation regal, if overly civilized; Vincent Canby (*New York Times*, 17 April 1994) complained that by her costume this Medea looked less like a barbarian than "the fashion plate of Corinth."[26] William A. Henry III, writing for *Time* (25 April 1994), had some reservations about Diana Rigg's acting, finding she did not equal Caldwell's power, but he hailed the final tableau as making the competent production unforgettable. In the surprising last scene, the bronze wall toppled

to reveal Diana Rigg apparently already at sea. Hunched during her period of rage and oppression, she stands proud as a ship's figurehead, clouds streaming past, golden light burnishing her. Then she turns and looks back, toward the scene of her unrepented misdeeds and, surely, toward an audience agape at the beauty and power of this finale.

Rigg's Medea was not at sea, but airborne, for as the legend tells us, her grandfather Helios, the sun god, had sent his chariot to carry her to Athens. The vision of her triumphant flight persists and offers a fitting closure to this show's production history, a show which in each revival has rested upon the power of an exceptional actress.

EURIPIDES: *HIPPOLYTUS*

During the 1950s, Greek tragedy received scant attention. A few single performances were offered, but even plays that had previously appealed no longer earned applause—*Trojan Women*, as we have seen, garnered poor reviews. Only Euripides' *Electra* was at last granted a chorus during the 1950s; if the time frame is extended back to 1948, the same playwright's *Hippolytus* can be considered here. Thus in the final pages of this chapter I have included the production histories of these two psychologically interesting dramas.

Greek drama generally languished in the American commercial theater during the period 1945 to 1960; tragedy and its issues were not a concern in this nation during the 1950s. In addition to the star-dominated productions of *Medea*, however, a second Euripidean play, *Hippolytus*, was brought to the boards at this time. The misogynist hunter first appeared on a New York stage in 1948.[27] Son of Theseus, king of Athens, Hippolytus devotes his life to the virgin huntress Artemis and completely ignores Aphrodite, goddess of sexual love. One does not spurn a Greek deity with impunity: Aphrodite, angry at his neglect and vaunted piety, takes her revenge upon him. She imbues Phaedra, his stepmother and wife of Theseus, with hopeless love for the hunter-acolyte. Events unroll to their inevitable and tragic conclusion when Theseus, believing his wife's false suicide note, activates a deadly curse against his innocent son. Three mortals, caught up in the petty disputes of Olympian deities, are ruined despite their attempts to live moral lives with good reputations.

In November 1948, the Experimental Theatre of ANTA (American National Theatre and Academy) resumed its invitational series by offering four performances of *Hippolytus* at the Lenox Hill Playhouse in Leighton Rollins' adaptation. A program note is worth mentioning: The action in this production was to suggest the time of the story, 1250 B.C., rather than the time it was first presented in Athens, 428 B.C. Just how this temporal distinction was indicated was not reported; the costumes in an accompanying press photo appear similar to those used for fifth-century B.C. productions.[28]

Brooks Atkinson (*New York Times*, 22 November 1948) judged the Experimental Theatre's performance to be "stimulating, simple, and impassioned." Although the play "reveals gods and their earthly victims in a series of sadistic relationships requiring the services of a licensed psychiatrist," the direction, acting, and setting were successful. Donald Buka, offering an Hippolytus "vigorously intolerant in its smugness and virtue" was the best actor, but Muriel Smith's Phaedra was forceful, portrayed in a "poignant tragic style." Osceola Archer, as the Nurse who always believes that "second thoughts are best" (*Hipp.* 211), struck a good balance between the "dignity and unction" the role requires. Only Horace Braham as Theseus, in Atkinson's opinion, seemed to miss the majesty of classical acting.

Atkinson concluded his review with praise: "Altogether it is a refreshing evening of pure theatre. . . . Thanks, and let's have some more, if you don't mind." His request was not granted, however, for ANTA's Experimental Theatre did not continue to stage Greek tragedy.

There were, in fact, no other productions of this Greek play on the New York stage for twenty years.[29] Then in 1968 the Piraikon Theatron under the direction of Dimitrios Rondiris brought Euripides' tragedy to the Felt Forum of Madison Square Garden. While earlier performances by the

Piraikon Theatron had garnered good reviews, this production was not judged successful.

Dan Sullivan, writing in the *New York Times* (20 November 1968), found the group's approach to Greek tragedy to be "fatally misguided and, worse than that, fatally boring." A play that seethes with emotion—"sex and death, lust and hatred, fire and ice"—failed to reveal these passions. The company's modern Greek seemed to Sullivan to be concerned more with rhythm than emotion, their listless movements more interested in tableaux than in expression. The reviewer knew what he had come to see: a play featuring a jealous goddess, a queen with an illicit passion for her stepson, this youth caught up in pious virginity, and a father who by his oath and prayer causes his son's death. He found instead a production that confused classical poise with static prettiness. The interpretation of the Piraikon Theatron, he summed up, would lead anyone who did not know the play "to conclude that Greek tragedy is by nature dull. That would really be a tragedy."

After another hiatus of nearly twenty years, *Hippolytus* was staged in Chicago by Painted City Productions in November–December 1987 at the Belfield Theatre on the campus of the University of Chicago. The story of "revenge, deception, madness, suicide, betrayal and family strife" was presented in a fast-paced, hundred-minute production that thoroughly charmed reviewer Chris Scott. Writing in *Crain's Chicago Business* (9 November 1987), he praised the stark set, flashy costumes, and "the often riveting performances" of the eighteen-member cast under the direction of Liucijia Ambrosini. All in all, Scott could proclaim this production a triumph.

Although the reviewers have found power in the various productions of *Hippolytus*, the play lacks a prominent position in the repertoire of oft-produced Greek tragedies. Perhaps its theme of incestuous and illicit passion, effectively taken over by Eugene O'Neill in *Desire under the Elms*, and which surfaces with regularity in the daily soap operas, has become too common to be interesting in its original form.[30] Or perhaps Euripides' text fails to attract directors because it lacks the more traditional grand and heroic characters. In this play no one figure is worthy of admiration or emulation: the gods are cruel, Phaedra vindictive in her jealously guarded reputation, and Hippolytus too smug in his overtly proclaimed piety.

EURIPIDES: *ELECTRA*

As noted above, Euripides' *Electra* had been absent from the American commercial stage since the production by the Coburn Players in 1910. In 1951 a fringe group known as the Laughing Stock Company offered the play, but it was not until 1958 that Euripides' *Electra* was performed again in a commercial theater when Milton Miltiades staged the play at the Jan Hus Theatre during the month of May. Lewis Funke, writing in the *New York*

Times (10 May 1958) determined that despite some limitations in the acting Miltiades' production was "sufficiently endowed to convey some idea of the tragic power of the most tragic of the Greek playwrights." Tresa Hughes headed the cast in the title role and gave an intelligent portrayal of the woman "whose royalty has been denied by her mother." The critic found somewhat less to like in Lee Henry's Orestes, who relied "mainly upon panting chest, tense brow and roaring" to indicate his purpose, although the play's headlong action served to hold audience attention.

Reviewer Funke noted that at the play's close Electra has attained her vengeance but cannot revel; she can only suffer remorse and guilt. His description of Euripides' character shows he understands the playwright's drama; the critic does not seek the classical simplicity associated with Sophocles, but rather recognizes the psychological depth Euripides gave to this woman. Finally Miltiades had brought the power of Euripides' *Electra* to the stage.

In the spring of 1962 this play was staged at the Players' Theatre by Shakespearewrights, using (surprisingly) Gilbert Murray's very dated translation. Arthur Gelb (*New York Times*, 22 March 1962) found little to like about the production, although some things to praise about the individual performances: Laura Stuart in the title role was "emotional," Byrne Piven's Orestes "intense and guilt-ridden," and Lorraine Serabian's Clytemnestra "impassioned." But, proclaimed Gelb, self-styled expert on Euripidean drama, "Euripides' *Electra* cries out for a production of space, grandeur and stylistic brilliance," but on the Players' Theatre's cramped stage "it seemed a stuffy and academic, if earnest, exercise." Perhaps, he opines, "this classic precursor of contemporary Freudian theatre" had been given a treatment too literal: the director has substituted reverence for inspiration. We note that Gelb has recognized the psychological underpinnings of Euripides' text, a further step forward in contemporary appreciation of the third Athenian playwright. Nevertheless, the remaining preference is to give "Euripidean realism" to Sophocles' character, leaving the real Euripidean drama on the shelf. The American commercial theater still awaits a major independent production of Euripides' *Electra*.

During the period 1935 through the 1950s, the Greek plays that were most popular deal with the emotions of those caught in individual passions. The themes do not look to the larger issues of the polis; the city-state holds no interest for Medea, Phaedra, Hippolytus, or Electra. The woman from Colchis takes vengeance upon the man who betrayed her; the fact that she was brought to Greece, a detail pointed out to her with pride by Jason, offers no consolation when she is set aside for her husband's political career. Phaedra, tracing the stain of her illicit passion to her Cretan ancestors, cares for her reputation and her husband's thoughts of her, but little for the land he rules.[31] Even Hippolytus, aloof within his piety, prefers the inviolate meadow to the political arena. Electra, meanwhile, is consumed with jealousy and her personal desire for vengeance.

Political plays, *Antigone* or *Trojan Women*, for example, so popular in other eras, received negative reviews if staged during this period. The American audience, now enamored of dramas focusing upon individual passions, preferred those Greek plays that treated the same themes. Overall, however, Greek drama held little appeal in the 1950s. Within the next two decades this would change.

NOTES

1. Even at that moment the reviewer of *Time* (3 June 1946) foresaw the lasting power of Olivier's exclamation; he writes: "Twisting and turning between confidence and fear, [Olivier] became both less and larger, a tragic figure of an early world, uttering at the climax two primitive animal howls that no one who heard them will ever forget."

2. So wrote Edgar Price in the *Brooklyn Citizen*, 21 May 1946. He commented that many of the women in the audience turned away from the bloody Oedipus, for "it was not a pretty picture, but then, tragedy is never pretty."

3. See Chapter 1. Only one complete satyr play exists, Euripides' *Cyclops*; a large portion of another, Sophocles' *Ichneutae* (*The Trackers*) completes current extant examples of the genre. We know the names of several other satyr plays; we have, also, the most tantalizing "fourth place substitution": Euripides' *Alcestis* was offered in lieu of the comic tag. While this aspect of the ancient festival is difficult for a modern audience to understand fully, one explanation is that given by William Arrowsmith in the introduction to his translation of *Cyclops*: the tragedies and final satyr play reflect the death and rebirth of Dionysus. (See William Arrowsmith, "Introduction to *Cyclops*," *The Complete Greek Tragedies*, ed. Richmond Lattimore and David Grene (Chicago: 1959)3: 224–226. For a full discussion of the satyr play in English, see Dana Ferrin Sutton, *The Greek Satyr Play* (Meisenham am Glan: 1980).

4. Such as Levi Strauss, René Girard, Marcel Detienne, and Jean-Paul Vernant; see also Mircea Eliade, *The Sacred and the Profane* (New York: 1959).

5. The idea of the primitive ritual and sacrifice was that of Michael Langham. In a letter to Burgess of 19 April 1972, he tells of his plan, drawing from an assortment of primitive cultural sources, and writes: "All male chorus, elders and lesser elders, with an assortment of symbolic headdresses, hand props, and instruments, opening the work by performing varied acts of sacrifice, possibly human— all of which fail to produce results." The exchange of letters between translator and director are published with the text of the play (Minneapolis: 1972) and in the program for the play.

The music, composed by Stanley Silverman, underscored the primitive and timeless qualities desired, being performed on a blend of both Eastern and Western instruments (from piano and cello to Buddhist bowls and bamboo chimes). Burgess created a libretto of chants that he termed Indo-European—which he insisted not be printed in any text (they are not).

6. Anthony Burgess, in his introduction both to the printed text of his translation/adaptation, "To the Reader," and in the program notes, "An Introduction," writes:

I have committed at least one unforgivable sin in this version: I have made Oedipus blind himself in full view of the audience. The Attic aesthetic forbade the presentation of violent action, but it is not easy for ourselves to forget Seneca and the Elizabethan Senecans. To a present-day audience the demand to see what happens, however bloody, has been so long sanctioned by Kyd, Marlowe, Shakespeare, Webster, and Ford that it seems to be a perversion of the aesthetic of the stage merely to recount what happens.

7. Of this passage Burgess wrote:

Oedipus, seeing himself as a creature of unknown parentage, exults in being a sort of creature of nature, an animal-human member of a family which is itself the cycle of the seasons. But he ends as a kind of mutilated god who helps keep the cycle alive. In both images he is not unlike the Sphinx. . . . The riddle may stand for the intriguingly easy but inexplicably forbidden . . . or for the knot which holds natural or social order together, untied at our peril though so tempting to untie. . . . Oedipus is the cause of the state's disease and disruption but also, through his discovery of and expiation for sin, the cause of its recovered health. He is a criminal but also a saint. In other words, he is a tragic hero.

8. Robert Sonkowsky discusses the function of this chorus in his article "Classical Theater and the Burgess-Langham Production of *Oedipus the King* at the Guthrie," *Miscellaneous Papers of the Bell Museum of Pathobiology* (1973): 27–33; he points out that the entire production was based on the idea of the "cleansing year-spirit," by which interpretation Oedipus is both the year-spirit and the Christ figure, and the riddle is part of the communion service.

9. By popular demand the Guthrie revived *Oedipus* for its 1973 season; the lead roles were played by Kenneth Welsh and Pauline Flanagan. Set and costumes remained virtually the same.

10. Carrie Nye played Cassandra; Jane White, Helen. Other roles were played by Joyce Ebert, Robert Mandan, and Alan Mixon.

11. I saw this performance as an undergraduate and have always remembered it; others who saw it, with whom I have talked, also have vivid recollections of the Cacoyannis production.

12. For a full discussion of Suzuki's Little Theater and this performance of *Trojan Women*, see Marianne McDonald, *Ancient Sun, Modern Light. Greek Drama on the Modern Stage* (New York: 1992): 21–44.

13. This quotation and other information about the Olympic Arts Festival cited from Paul Hertelendy, "Arts Festival Takes Chances," *San Jose Mercury*, 25 March 1984, and Welton Jones, "The Theatrical Cup Will Runneth Over," *San Diego Union*, 11 March 1984. Olympic Rule 34 requires a cultural component to any summer games; Fitzpatrick took this rule to heart.

14. *Sic*; just why Hornblow so termed Medea is unclear, for, while accurate, she is usually identified as daughter of the barbarian *king*, more usually as granddaughter of the sun. Review is in "Mr. Hornblow Goes to the Play," *Theatre Magazine* 27 (18 April 1918): 217; I have emended the odd grammar (or printing error) found in the magazine.

15. So deemed the reviewers from the *World* (23 March 1920): "The difficulty was that intention and method were not always skillfully carried out"; the *New York Evening Sun* (23 March 1920): "*Medea* is highly artistic. But it has one fatal

defect. It does not live"; and the *New York Times* (23 March 1920): "[It was] artfully and painstakingly managed. . . . Yet it becomes cloying."

16. Indeed, when Anglin returned to New York City for a brief ten-day run at the Gallo Theater in December 1927, her skill in bringing ancient Greek drama alive for the modern audience was again acclaimed. The writer in the theater's *Program Magazine* praised her ability to make the ancient dramas touch the modern audience, to make them "robust reality." Her performances of classic Greek plays were always greeted by large and enthusiastic audiences: "Such [was] the miracle of Margaret Anglin."

17. It is not to my purpose here to catalogue Anderson's European tour, but a brief quotation from a review in the *New York Times* (14 September 1951) is relevant:

[The Allied audience] found *Medea* by Robinson Jeffers out of Euripides somewhat harder to take than last night's American offering to the Berlin festival, *Oklahoma!*, but many were thrilled and chilled by Judith Anderson's bravura performance in the title role. . . . The theme of the monstrous forms that revenge can take is of interest in Berlin.

18. Despite these negative reactions, Volanakis' staging was repeated at the Theatro Athenaion production at the Herod Atticus in Athens in 1985. There again characters emerged from and descended into a fiery oval opening center stage. All characters, with the exception of Medea, were half-masked. In Athens as in New York, Medea (Tzene Karezi) sat cross-legged in front of this would-be palace to tell her story. And at the end, most amazing and most ineffective, a huge crane lifted up a golden disk on high—very high to surmount the back wall of the Herod Atticus theater—on whose center was pinned a Medea doll while her voice was piped in. If this was to be the ancient equivalent of the deus ex machina, the modern forklift was less believable than the crane that lifted in the gods in the ancient Greek plays. How the Greeks staged the sun-chariot, which carries away Medea at the end of this play, however, remains an unsolved problem in classical staging scholarship.

19. Equal praise is to be found in Jack Kroll's review in *Newsweek* (17 May 1982), in Howard Kissel's in *Women's Wear Daily* (4 May 1982), and in Edwin Wilson's in the *Wall Street Journal* (7 May 1982); the latter also talks in terms of height, terming the show "a lofty experience of another kind."

20. Much of this information is available in James Lardner, *"Medea's* Winding Road to Washington," *Washington Post* (28 February 1982). Lardner's subtitles are *"Medea*: 3 Lives & a Play" and *"Medea*: Strange Encounter."

21. Quoted by Robert Berkvist (*New York Times*, 2 May 1982).

22. The American National Theater hosted four productions from Chicago as part of this festival, shows that were "so violent and angry in tone" that officials of the Kennedy Center were pleasantly amazed at AT&T's sponsorship, to quote the *Washington Post* (24 April 1985). The plays: Steppenwolf Theatre Company's *Coyote Ugly* and *Streamers* and Wisdom Bridge's *In the Belly of the Beast*, in addition to *Medea*.

23. Jennifer Dunning begins her review with this description of the Kabuki and Noh *Medea* (*New York Times*, 31 August 1986).

24. Wehle said further that as she worked on the role it seemed that every news article she read concerned "the murder of children out of anger and pain." For a scholarly study of this seemingly unthinkable act, see P. E. Easterling, "The Infanticide in Euripides' *Medea,*" *Yale Classical Studies* 25 (1977): 177–191.

25. Rigg was also acclaimed there, where she won the *Times'* readers Accolade for best West End actor and an *Evening Standard* drama award. Information from the *Times* (14 June 1994).

26. Canby tries to be cute in his text, starting off with, "Let's face it: Medea . . . is not your prototypical battered wife"; he continues, "Friendless in a foreign city, what is a witch to do?" He fusses, too, about Peter Davison's set, claiming that its harsh design seems to indicate that Rigg's elegant Medea is to civilize the barbarian world of Corinth.

27. *Hippolytus* had been performed before this period only at Yale for the commencement season of 1935. Broadway actress Selena Royle was engaged to play the role of Phaedra, and her presence brought this academic production to the attention of the New York theater critics. But while the reviewer of the *New York Times* (15 June 1935) noted that there was a fairly good audience, he did not mention the quality of the production.

28. Program note and photo are from Daniel Blum, ed., *Theatre World*, 1948–1949 (New York: 1949): 128.

29. In 1954, Robinson Jeffers' version of this story, titled *The Cretan Woman*, was performed at the Provincetown Playhouse. It was so successful that its run was extended although, to quote Brooks Atkinson (*New York Times*, 1 September 1954),"the summer is not supposed to be the time when people like to be purged by pity and terror." Atkinson praises Jeffers' style as austere and relentless; his themes, the critic continues, did not win him a wide audience. His revisions to the Hippolytus story were extensive: first in making Phaedra the dominant figure, second in having Theseus slay his openly homosexual son onstage. Despite the extended run, however, Atkinson found the acting in this staging less than grand.

30. The theme has reappeared on the American stage in foreign dress. In June 1990, the American Repertory Theater sponsored the Taganka Theater of Moscow's production of Marinaa Tsvetaeva's *Phaedra*. Played in Russian at the Loeb Drama Center in Boston, the performance was to reviewer Kevin Kelly (*Boston Globe*, 18 June 1990) interesting in form but too complex in theme to be effective. The intermingling of ancient myth and Tsvetaeva's own life, one of suffering under Soviet brutality, was difficult to follow; he found it effective in mood and interesting in staging, but overall too complex to be a success. (In May 1990, the play had received its British premier and garnered more favorable reviews.)

La Mama E.T.C. offered a production of *Hippolytus* in November 1992, done by the State Theatre of South India. The summation of this interpretation, given in the flyers announcing the show, indicates that Hippolytus changed when appearing in Eastern guise: "Hippolytos . . . breaks the apparent world of *maya* (illusion) and follows his 'bliss' on the pathway to the Sun, the eternal *Light*, the ultimate aim of human existence. Hippolytos reaches 'dharma.' "

31. For a discussion of the relationship between Phaedra and Crete, where her mother had been afflicted with an unnatural passion for a bull, see Kenneth Reckford, "Phaedra and Pasiphaë: The Pull Backwards," *TAPA* 104 (1974): 307–328.

6

Greek Tragedy Responds to War, Drugs, and Flower Children: 1960–1970

During the decade of the 1960s, America became involved in the Vietnam War. Protests against this conflict and against all authority figures became the order of the day, while freedom of expression was carried to the realm of sex as well as speech. The use of drugs marked the culmination of these protests, as American youth—and those who wished to be so—sought ecstasy and escape via various narcotic substances. It was a time of self-expression, combined with a sense of community; free love blended with a subconscious narcissism. Violent demonstrations were led by those who put flowers into guns, while others led peaceful protests and civil rights marches: brotherhood was the operative idea, a brotherhood with clearly marked boundaries. A Dionysian "union of opposites" marked the culture of the day.[1]

Several "new" plays appeared in the repertory of Greek tragedy production in America during this period. While, as we have seen, *Trojan Women* was still staged as a protest against the Vietnam War, a second tragedy also gained appeal as an antiwar play, Euripides' *Iphigeneia at Aulis*. This heartrending drama of delusion and self-deception had played but once in a commercial theater until the 1960s (in 1921), but the play moved from the college campus to the professional theater for at least three productions in 1967 and 1968. Also new were initial stagings of Euripides' last Athenian play, *Orestes*. The drama was first performed in any venue that might be considered commercial in 1968. This *Orestes* was very much in tune with its time, as we shall see, for it was a "hippy" version of the ancient text.[2] Two further newcomers to the repertory were Aeschylus' *Oresteia* and Euripides' *The Bacchae*; the former marked a significant moment in American theater history, the latter was considered to be an accurate measure for the temper of the times.

Until the 1960s there had been little interest in Aeschylus in the commercial theaters of America; perhaps the grand sweep of his themes and the major role played by his chorus were thought too foreign for a modern audience. At any event, the first full-length production of *Oresteia* took place in Ypsilanti, Michigan, in the summer of 1966. Following upon this venture was the innovative and provocative staging of the tragedy, now titled *The House of Atreus*, with script and direction by Douglas Campbell and Sir Tyrone Guthrie in the winter of the same year. *The House of Atreus* played during the 1966–1967 season at the Guthrie Theater in Minneapolis, then toured to New York and Los Angeles during 1968.

With the dawn of the 1960s, with its emphasis on communion with nature, free love, and self-awareness, Euripides' *The Bacchae* suddenly became a popular text. The fact that the play does not, in fact, celebrate the sexual license Pentheus believed the women were observing in the bushes made no difference; it was a text far more meaningful for the generation of flower children than was the intellectual search of *Oedipus Tyrannus* or *Electra*'s exhausting quest for justice. For the directors of the 1960s *The Bacchae* extolled the pleasures of freedom achieved by breaking social standards. The culmination of this understanding of the play came in what would become the notorious version, *Dionysus in 69*. Because they are so closely tied to this decade, the production histories of these texts, *Oresteia*, *The Bacchae*, and *Iphigeneia at Aulis* form the focus of this chapter.

AESCHYLUS: *ORESTEIA*

The Greeks stand first in the production history of Aeschylus' great trilogy. In 1961, the Greek Tragedy Theatre/Piraikon Theatron, whose production of Sophocles' *Electra* was well received during the same tour (see Chapter 4), included in its repertoire *Choephoroi* [*Libation Bearers*] and *Eumenides*, the last two plays of the *Oresteia* trilogy. The choice to skip *Agamemnon* was unusual, for the Greek company ran a risk of playing to an audience unfamiliar with the king's story. In following years the initial play was favored and the later ones avoided, so the Greek Tragedy Theatre's choice to offer these dramas of revenge and propitiation was particularly interesting. The decision to stage *Eumenides* is especially odd, for it portrays the inauguration of jury-court justice, a theme not as exciting for a modern audience as watching *Agamemnon*'s story of the vengeance taken by a wife against her husband.

Nevertheless, although these performances at the City Center were done in Greek, they received favorable notice. Milton Esterow proclaimed (*New York Times*, 27 September 1961) that in these productions "the imagery is magnificent. The style is lofty and dignified. There is majesty and power."

He urged his audience to attend the plays and listen to their language, whether or not it was obscure. For, he asserted, "masterpieces from Greece 2,000 years old are rarely presented in town by such professionals. . . . The visitors offer a rewarding night in the theatre." Jim O'Connor stated (*New York Journal American*, 27 September 1961) that the troupe "cast a spell over the audience that verged on fascination." After praising in particular the acting of D. Veakis as Orestes, portraying clearly a man possessed, and the glowing performance of Aspassia Papathanassiou as Clytemnestra, O'Connor wound up his review by lauding the staging and direction of Dimitrios Rondiris, acclaiming it as "startling in its theatrical effect."

Even "Georg" of *Variety* (4 October 1961) gave this Greek performance high marks. The distinguished company, he asserted, invited its audience to the realms of nobility. He commended several members of the cast, but waxed eloquent in his praise of Papathanassiou. Switch off the simultaneous translations during her tenure onstage, he suggested, for the majesty of her performance "transcends the barrier of language." Despite its success, this production was in Greek. America still waited for an *Oresteia* in English. Five years later the performances began.

"Majesty is our theme, majesty in Michigan." So begins Stanley Kaufmann's review in the *New York Times* (30 June 1966) of the Ypsilanti Greek Theatre production of *Oresteia* in June 1966. This performance, which inaugurated the Ypsilanti company,[3] was the first *Oresteia* to be staged outside and played in its full three-part form. Alexis Solomos as artistic director staged the show, for which Iannis Xenakis did the music; the text was a condensed version of Lattimore's translation.[4] The performance preserved an illusion of tradition while modernized sufficiently to appeal to a contemporary audience. Certainly the casting emphasized the importance attached to the venture: Judith Anderson (now Dame Judith) played Clytemnestra, Donald David did Agamemnon and Apollo, John Michael King offered an adequate Orestes, and Ruby Dee performed Cassandra with "extraordinary physical intensity." Kaufmann concluded his review of this seminal performance benignly: "The Olympian gods smile and smile on Ypsilanti."

Tom Prideaux, writing in *Life* (29 July 1966) also had high praise for this initial production of the Greek drama outdoors. In a review titled "Two Great Greeks in a Ball Park,"[5] Prideaux proclaimed that the power of the play "emerges in its staging," for Solomos incorporated techniques from Epidaurus for the Michigan stadium: "When the procession of elders lift their fiery torches against the darkening sky, or the writhing Furies toss their snakelike tresses, this is heroic theater at its best." Prideaux was so entranced with the setting that he could not resist further comment on the show's unusual site; thusly does he open and close his review:

Apollo stood in the infield like a Big League umpire. Mercury in his winged helmet seemed to sneak across the field as if he were stealing second. For one astonishing instant it appeared that the gods were playing baseball. . . . [Festival founders want to build a theater.] I like it better in the ball park which has an easy-going and friendly feeling that accommodates even high tragedy. The sports-loving Greeks, I imagine, would like it better there, too.

That fall Douglas Campbell and Sir Tyrone Guthrie opened their version of Aeschylus' play. The poster for the Guthrie's production of *Oresteia* displayed a broken stone fragment with the name ATREUS in block capital letters. The design was significant, indicating that the current play was neither the traditional *Oresteia* nor even *Agamemnon* alone, but a new conception of the House of Atreus legend. The script of the trilogy, titled, indeed, *The House of Atreus*, was John Lewin's version, adapted from a number of English texts, but the artistic conception and direction which made the show famous lay in the hands of Campbell and Guthrie.

The entire production was *big*. Although the boast (given in the program) that it was "the first professional production of the complete trilogy in America" was false, as we have seen, it certainly was the first such massive conception. Walter Kerr (*New York Times*, 10 September 1967)[6] commented in particular on the size of the performance: "The images, swollen close to the proportions of nightmare, become more real than reality." These, he continued, filled the stage with "massive mobile bronzes" for the "sheer dramatic *effect*; Clytemnestra is not temptable flesh but naked human will." This critic felt a mythic power in the play, especially in the third act, where the supernatural solution, featuring a "sunburst Apollo" and Athena as "an inhabited sculpture," dominated. A final statement on the effect of the play's physical size is that given by Robert Sonkowsky, writing in *Arion* (Spring 1968):

The giant gods do not merely represent removed grandeur compounded by gothic alchemy, but they are great, live, witty carnival figures, protecting mankind, realistic, intelligent Mardi Gras miracles, to whom the great problems of justice are presented. They move with uncannily naturalistic coordination of their immense limbs. . . . The device is pushed only a little too far. Athena, the largest of the three, is a seated cult statue, but even she, after Apollo and Hermes, moves, at first, one arm; then, after we are thoroughly titillated with wondering whether the rest of her will also come to life, she moves her head, and then later, both of her arms and her head. Meanwhile, her dialogue is so witty and her movements so bemusing that the Furies go unnoticed and do not get their due.

While the Guthrie *Atreus* impressed with its magnitude, many aspects of the production did not please everyone. Nevertheless it commanded vast critical attention, both during its run in Minneapolis in 1966 and 1967 and its revival in New York City the following year, the first time the Minneapolis-based company had gone to the Eastern theater center.

The performance at the Billy Rose Theater in December 1968 stirred as much controversy as had the original production two years earlier. Walter Kerr was among the minority who praised the play, for other critics took issue with text, acting, or interpretation.[7] The play and its characters were accused of lacking any of the ancient themes and of "replacing" classic stature with "entertainment and spectacle," of being "ludicrously anachronistic," while its directors were charged with making the "deathless legend lifeless and sexless."[8]

The excesses of the Guthrie production are surprising in view of Guthrie's own views of Greek theater in general and classic drama performances in particular. He had been enamored with the simplicity of several productions he had seen at Epidauros, believing strongly that the classics are truly more important than "showbiz" and that theater should not be based on commercialism.[9] Guthrie also believed in the basically religious and ritualistic nature of theater, and this might partially explain his conception of the House of Atreus story.

John Lewin's adaptation (he himself eschews the word "translation," and hence titled his work *The House of Atreus*) is in no way excessive. The verses flow smoothly in direct English; some passages echo closely the Greek text and share the power of Aeschylus' script, others are freer and lose some of their original intensity. The text does not demand the staging created by Guthrie and Campbell. Only one passage of Guthrie's introduction to Lewin's published text offers a slight clue to their creation:

In brief, our performance will make an endeavor to suggest the removed grandeur of the archetypal events and persons presented. In doing so, we shall make use of some of the devices which the Greek theater is known to have used—not only choral speech but impersonal masks and so on. But we shall not use these devices in order to try to reconstruct the sort of impressions which an Athenian audience may have felt twenty-five hundred years ago.

The classical scholars in our audience will be asked to forget, if they can, their preconceptions.... Rather let them consider whether the archetypal situations have been re-created in a manner which makes them an interesting and vivid theatrical event.[10]

The Guthrie-Campbell-Lewin production was certainly that. In spite of the critics and their reviews, this *House of Atreus* remains a significant moment in the history of Greek tragedy in the United States, one of the key performances of this century, important, if for nothing else, for its daring and disregard of classical restraint.

The Guthrie version dominated the late 1960s and seemed to satisfy interest in Aeschylus' trilogy; his text was not a popular choice for the stages of the 1970s. With the exception of a few scattered performances, mainly in regional theaters or on college campuses, *Oresteia* did not enjoy a major staging for another ten years. Then, in 1977, New York audiences were offered the unusual, if not bizarre, production of *Agamemnon* (only) staged by Andrei Serban and Elizabeth Swados at the Vivian Beaumont Theater. Here, as he had done in his earlier *Fragments of a Trilogy* (see Chapter 5, under *Trojan Women*), Serban put his emphasis on the sounds of language as a self-contained medium, and added to this interpretation both ritualistic spectacle and unusual character doubling.

Violence seems to have been the subtext of his conception. On a dark, harsh, chain-mesh set, the cast enacted the various murders of the myth in a preshow mime. Thus the audience got to "see" both the sacrifice of Iphigeneia and the slaying of Agamemnon and Cassandra. The linguistic mixture emphasized harsh sounds; Serban's Argos was a dangerous place.

He attempted to do the show with only two actors; Jamil Zakkai was effective in the male roles, and Priscilla Smith had some fine scenes as Clytemnestra and Cassandra. But while the doubling of killer and victim in the same character is an interesting idea, it cannot work out logistically in this play. Agamemnon can be Aegisthus, and may well have been the same actor in Aeschylus' three-actor version, but Clytemnestra cannot simultaneously be Cassandra. Disturbing to the critics, in addition to the doubled characters, was the twenty-six-member polyglot chorus.

Whereas *Fragments* worked because the theme was largely that of *Trojan Women*—grief, lamentation, and despair, emotions that can be fairly effectively transmitted by sound and gesture—*Agamemnon* has an intellectual depth that cannot be presented merely by voice and mimed violence. The heart of *Agamemnon* (or of most Greek tragedy) is not ritual and spectacle; these add to its effect, but it is the power of persuasion, *Peitho*, "daughter of designing Ruin," used in well-crafted speech, and the delusion of the efficacy of deeds done apparently in the name of justice that render Aeschylus' play a great tragedy. While some part of these ideas is carried in Clytemnestra's words, the majority lie in the magnificent verses of the chorus. By having the chorus chant in indefinable and largely unintelligible sounds, the Serban-Swados interpretation stripped the text of its strength and its meaning.[11]

The critics, for the most part, realized this. The most harsh reviewers were perhaps T. E. Kalem (*Time*, 30 May 1977) with his headline "Vandal Sacks Atreus," and Martin Gottfried (*New York Post*, 19 May 1977), who found the show "cultish and silly," "an excuse for artistic masturbation." Edwin Wilson (*Wall Street Journal*, 19 May 1977) commented that Serban was guilty of "directing by whim, not design," that he had found a chorus but not the idea of the play. Walter Kerr (*New York Times*, 29 May 1977), who was put off by the forty-minute "delay" of the preshow mime, claimed that Serban's play lacked any value because Aeschylean values were gone. Kerr, indeed, discovered the greatest flaws in the Serban-Swados conception: the polyglot chorus and the (amazing) cancellation of the carpet scene. Without the enactment before the eyes of cast and audience of Agamemnon's trampling of tapestries, his visible deed of hybris, the first play of Aeschylus' trilogy lacks its powerful message of the personal responsibility for significant choice. A rendition of Greek drama such as Serban presented strips the classical texts of their power. Fortunately, in the 1980s, the search for an updating gimmick has usually been laid aside in favor of productions that look to the text for the meaning of the play and offer an artistic style based on the simplicity of the ancient performances.

Several critics were rather more favorably impressed with the Serban production. Clive Barnes (*New York Times*, 19 May 1977) found the show fresh and vibrant; Serban, he claimed, "succeeds in involving us in a life experience that happens to be theatrical." Jack Kroll, in a review titled "Greek Fury" (*Newsweek*, 30 May 1977), praised Serban's approach to the foreign nature of Greek tragedy production. Serban created, he decided, "an atmosphere of psychic crisis in which the play becomes a kind of inspired dream reaching back through time—a vibrating three-dimensional image of an entire people driving their way from barbarism to civilization."

The most extensive and balanced view was offered by Bernard Knox in the *New York Review of Books* (14 July 1977). The classics scholar found much to criticize in the performance; like the other critics he found the steel net only partially effective, the use of but two actors unwieldy, and the nonlanguage of the choral songs largely impenetrable. Nor was he impressed with the pantomime illustrating Cassandra's visions:

[A chart of the family crimes in the lobby is intended to help the audience, but it is not enough.] Serban does put most of Cassandra's visions on stage, but without the sureness of touch which made the sacrifice of Iphigeneia so electrifying. The Fury dancing with her blazing torch is impressive enough, but the children carrying their own cooked entrails are merely grotesque, especially since the objects they have in their hands look more like dried out lobster shells than liver and lights.

But unlike the other reviewers, Knox found the preshow mime extremely original and effective, an "attempt to deal with the poetic and intellectual content of the lyric portion of the play." The enactment of Iphigeneia's sacrifice, he wrote, "is a theatrical *tour de force*, an irresistible assault on the emotions of the audience." He also found the music compelling and dramatic, a blend of Byzantine church music and the lyrics of Mikis Theodorakis. And although scene transpositions were troubling, Knox concluded that, while it is possible to cry "Alas," at last the good prevails. Thus he closed his review on a strong, positive note:

The richness of its music, the care that has been taken with the training of the chorus, the insistence on clear delivery in the spoken dialogue, the restraint of the actors, whose passionate intensity is somehow raised rather than lowered by the solemnity of their gestures, above all the imaginative attack on the problem posed by choral lyric—all this means that Serban has set standards against which future productions of Greek tragedy will be measured.

Future performances did not follow immediately; several years passed before the House of Atreus legend returned to the American stage. Then in 1981 began a series of productions of a new and fuller version of the story titled *The Greeks*. This script binds together in chronological order the various plays that tell the legend. As created by John Barton and Kenneth Cavander for the Royal Shakespeare Company, the shows ran for nine hours over three evenings. For the American stage, Cavander and Nikos Psacharopoulos, producing the show at the Williamstown (MA) Theatre Festival, cut the playing time to a mere six hours over two evenings, and the trilogy became a two-part script, *The Cursed* and *The Blest*. Several familiar figures of Greek tragedy production in the American theater appeared in the cast: Jane White played Clytemnestra, Carrie Nye portrayed Helen. Christopher Reeves offered a petulant Achilles, and, according to Charles Michener (*Newsweek*, 27 July 1981), Donald Moffat's Agamemnon was exceptional as "this ungodly father figure in each of his five plays." The total cast list numbered sixty: there was no doubling and no principals played in the chorus.[12]

This first American performance of the Barton/Cavander text attracted wide critical attention: the staging of a Greek tragedy is always a theatrical event; to mount seven plays as one is a special occasion. Robert King (*New York Times*, 12 July 1981) found much to say about the Psacharopoulos production. He quotes the author's desire "to dramatize a progressive degeneration in society . . . as it became more materialistic, more violence prone, like our own." The show opened with the question, "Who is to blame?" Thence the audience was led through the twisted turns of the family's violent story, wherein could be seen (to quote Michener) "their brilliant, deluded, irrepressible quarrels about what it means to be human." Glenne Currie (UPI's Lively Arts Editor)[13] declared the sweeping canvas to be both exhausting and rewarding. Since the story told in these plays lies at the heart of Western civilization, she urged her readers to see the show, for it offered "something rare to see and think about."

The Greeks was later presented by the American Conservatory Theater in Seattle and in 1986 opened at the Back Alley Theater in Hollywood. Sylvie Drake, theater writer for the *Los Angeles Times*, found some aspects to praise about the performance, but had many reservations about Allan Miller's adaptation of the Barton/Cavander text. Titling her review "Mixed Bag of Greeks," Drake declared (29 April 1986) that in this production the theater was in over its head and out of control. The reduced script was played more for laughs than for philosophy, thus turning the show into an experience: "The Greeks Go to Hollywood." The opening scene of the sequence taken from Euripides' *Helen*, for instance, is written to be amusing, but to make it "a Judy Holliday version of Liz Taylor running amok with ad-libs" did no justice to the Barton/Cavander theater epic.

In 1985, the City Stage Company presented a version of *Oresteia* (*Agamemnon* and *Electra/Orestes*) under the direction of Christopher Martin, using Robert Fagles' translation and starring Karen Sunde as Clytemnestra and Tom Spiller as Agamemnon. Rush Rehm, writing for *Theatre Journal* (December 1985), had nothing good to say about the performance: set, direction, actors, and chorus fell before his condemnation. Rehm took time to point out the relevance of Aeschylus' trilogy for the modern audience, a play "of sexual politics, of the idea of progress through defeat, of the relationship between vengeance and justice."[14] The City Stage production, in his opinion, took no account of these ideas. Mel Gussow (*New York Times*, 17 January 1985) shared Rehm's disappointment; but although he pointed out the oddities, he found some details to praise, e.g., Ginger Grace's feline ferocity as Electra and the shafts of light that served as the temple at Delphi. But as to why Apollo appeared in sunglasses and white fatigues, followed by an actress on roller skates, or why the dirge-like chorus took its masks on and off were left unexplained. Gussow's summation was that "the production itself could be considered intriguing in its unevenness."

John Beaufort (*Christian Science Monitor*, 24 January 1985) noted some further peculiarities in Martin's interpretation, but gave a more positive final verdict. At the City Stage, Agamemnon returned from Troy in an actor-powered chariot that whirled around the stage, "illuminated by a battery of hysterical spotlights that would do credit to a Hollywood premiere," while Cassandra hung on for dear life. Beaufort liked Charles Patterson as the handsome black Apollo and found Amy Warner's homecoming queen Athena persuasive. He concluded that the workout this performance gave actors and spectators was worth the challenge and that the City Stage deserved credit for its venture: "The production marks a further step in the career of a producing group that occupies a unique position in New York's institutional theater, founded on a devotion to major classic works and a dedication to repertory."

Touring the United States in 1986–1987 was the Suzuki Company of Toga. As we have seen (Chapter 5), the troupe had made their American debut in Milwaukee in 1979 with *Trojan Women*, then won national acclaim when they performed the play at the 1984 Olympic Arts Festival in Los Angeles. They opened *Clytemnestra* in La Jolla, California, in the spring of 1986 and at the Guthrie Theater in Minneapolis the following year.

Tadashi Suzuki calls his interpretation of the Greek classics "requotations," to indicate that they have been rearranged to give new meanings. In the words of Sylvie Drake (*Los Angeles Times*, 12 May 1986), his works are "theater that just is." She continued that "the director capitalizes on the way in which the intransigence and inexorability of Greek tragedy marries well into the intransigent formality of ancient Japanese custom." Kent Neely, reviewing the performance for *Theatre Journal* (December 1987), noted that the significance of Suzuki's work lies "in the attempt to reconcile the balance of nature . . . with the imbalance of an over-commercialized and indulgent postmodern western world."[15]

These philosophical themes underlay but did not overpower the beauty and imagination of the production. The action took place within Orestes' mind: he envisioned the action, the actors then performed it. Thomas Hewitt, playing the troubled prince, was the only actor to speak English; through his words the American audience understood the play. Suzuki mixed contradictory symbols and styles to give the special effects he desired: dual languages, costumes varying from kimonos to sweatshirts, and music both Japanese and Western punk rock. These disjointed symbols, according to Neely, "served to emphasize the conflict which is central to the tragedy." Drake's review concludes with strong affirmation: "The sounds and visions in this hour and 10 minutes are potent, its special effects much stronger than any attempt at realism could have been and the carefully structured, ritual aspect of its staging pure tonic. When theater can do that, it has done everything."

In the summer of 1992, the Guthrie Theater turned to the other side of the House of Atreus story and presented a trilogy focusing on Clytemnestra. The idea for this production arose when the Guthrie wanted a vehicle for Isabell Monk, who especially wanted to play Clytemnestra in Sophocles' *Electra*. Not wanting to do the single play in isolation, Garland Wright, with Michael Lupu, Jim Lewis, and Thomas Kohn as dramaturges, decided to do the three plays that outline Clytemnestra's story: the outrage, the revenge, and the punishment, plays that feature the child-killer, the husband-killer, and the mother-killer. The idea was to have the story line of the House of Atreus carry through and override the fact that the three plays were written in different time periods by different authors; indeed the possibility of having the three authors' interpretations of the myth was one of the deciding factors in the final selection (not, for instance, using Euripides' *Electra* or including *Eumenides*). To further the differences the director chose to use translations by three different writers: *Iphigeneia at Aulis* by W. S. Merwin and G. Dimock, *Agamemnon* by Robert Lowell, and *Electra* by Kenneth McLeish.[16]

The concept worked surprisingly well, given the differences inherent in the idea. The production of these three plays, originally composed over a fifty-year time period by the three playwrights, offered an encapsulated study of drama history: the differences among the three were immediately evident (even allowing for the translators' varied style) in language, in staging, in the chorus' role, in character portrayal. Euripides' *Iphigeneia at Aulis* really is a modern domestic tragedy set in an archaic legend; Aeschylus' formality of language and sweeping thematic structure come through even in a cut text and a less-than-perfect translation; Sophocles' primary interest in character-in-circumstance is amply proved.

Since the trilogy began with a ninety-minute *Iphigeneia at Aulis*, followed by a two-hour break, then *Agamemnon* and *Electra*, broken by a ten-minute intermission, the total immersion time was around seven hours. For the audience, however, there were other problems and unanswered questions, for they did not come for a demonstration of drama history but for plays that both posed and answered questions. As must inevitably happen, when the House of Atreus story is told without the resolution given with such grandeur by Aeschylus, or with such scorn by Euripides, the audience is left wondering if there is any end to the cycle of violent killings. When the three shows were done on a single day, the Guthrie version added a voice-over ghost of Clytemnestra taken (in part) from *Eumenides*. Since this did not show that Orestes was the last of the killers, that the legend ended with him, the extra ending was no ending at all.[17]

On the other hand, as a study of how violence begets violence, how the miasma of murder can stain into the next generation, and how it can destroy the *arete* (inner virtue) of an individual, this grouping of the plays worked exceptionally well. At the Guthrie as in the ancient Athens, Clytemnestra was a good mother interested only in her daughter's happiness in *Iphigeneia at Aulis*; she became a spirit of evil vengeance in *Agamemnon*; and was a cruel and frightened *ameter* (no-mother) who earned her fate in *Electra*. Overall, the 1992 Greek show at the Guthrie was an extremely successful venture. While it was not true that the story can fully transcend the discrepancies of time and authorship, as a dramatic production the Guthrie "Clytemnestra project" deserved acclaim.

However, in spite of the fact that the trilogy was advertised as the "Clytemnestra project," that symposia were held on the role of women in antiquity and Greek tragedy, that extensive program notes and a hundred-page study guide addressed the issue of women in classical Athens, and that Isabell Monk did an excellent job in portraying the queen in her three guises, the emphases of the original playwrights still came through. Thus in the first play we wept not with Clytemnestra but with the doll-like Iphigeneia and her tormented father. The greatest moment of terror in *Agamemnon* was not the king's death cry as his wife wielded her ax (offstage) but when he set his feet on the crimson tapestries, his fateful treading on the forbidden cloth. In Sophocles' text, the exceptional interpretation given to the lead character by Jacqueline Kim dominated the stage; her joyous reunion with Orestes drew shared tears from the audience, and her silent contemplation of the dead queen, enacting if not speaking the line of Euripides' heroine, "The mother I loved and could not love," remained the final vision from the trilogy.[18]

For some reviewers, however, the emphasis on the female was successful. Mike Steele (*Minneapolis Star Tribune*, 24 June 1992) declared that despite some weaknesses the productions had great stature. For him the "feminine power . . . and the cruel results of patriarchal dominance" were fully evident, perhaps because the male actors, with the exception of Stephen Pelinski's Agamemnon, were weak, while Isabell Monk, and in particular Jacqueline Kim as Electra, offered a gripping emotional truth. David Richards (*New York Times*, 9 August 1992) titled his review "A Trilogy for Clytemnestra, the Feminist," with the subtitle "Ancient Greek Tragedies Tell a Modern Tale of Women Facing the Messy Consequence of Male Ego."

The set for the "Clytemnestra project" was minimal but extremely effective, evoking both the ancient Greek theater and the Mycenaean age. Gray transparent curtains hung in a semicircle upstage, with a deep red panel to indicate Mycenae. A dark reflecting metal circle defined the stage, suggesting both the ancient orchestra and the great Mycenaean hearth; it thus replaced, in a way, the ancient *eccyclema* by bringing the inside out. To take the king within, however, the red carpet is always a brilliant and disturbing prop, and on the Guthrie's stark stage it was especially dramatic. Richards described the action well: "A covey of handmaidens lay down a path of blood-red silk squares to the palace door. They flutter to the ground, making a carpet of deceptive delicacy. . . . Agamemnon has no qualms about crushing it under foot. Overhead, drums and cymbals erupt in mad tumult."

Richards pointed out further how Wright's interpretation showed that not only did the gods come off poorly—as was to be expected—but so did the men. He seconded Steele's verdict when he defined the males of the story as "patronizing, arrogant, cowardly, headstrong and, for all their ringing appeals to might and right, amazingly ineffective."

The directors chose, in each play, to stage a silent and significant action intended to offer an effective answer to an ambiguous situation. Thus, in *Aulis*, they included the disputed final Messenger's speech, then directed Clytemnestra to show that she did not believe his words. But since she was given no words to speak, some members of the audience felt the vengeance was unnecessary since she knew (apparently) that her daughter was not dead. At the close of *Agamemnon*, where Aeschylus left a silent chorus to file offstage, Wright borrowed from Cacoyannis' *Electra* and directed the young daughter to run quietly to her slain father and weep silently over him before dashing off; the revenge, we were to think, would come from her. Again, the decision to enact (but not speak) the line of Euripides' heroine, "The mother I loved and could not love," served to enhance further her tragedy and her greatness. The silent scenes cast doubt upon the action, but since these doubts were without verbal expression, ambiguity remained. Wright's decision was a daring, but risky, way to give his production a final meaning.

But the message of the plays for the modern world was not ambiguous. As reviewer Richards summed it up, the plays are representative of our times because the characters "are not the playthings of the gods; they're one another's playthings. They evoke the gods simply to justify the havoc of their lives." Warming to his theme he continued: "Our leaders, too, refer endlessly to a national mythology, which is supposed to inform our collective destiny. In its name, ideals are advanced and sacrifices exacted. And yet that mythology may be no more than a smokescreen masking errantly self-interested deeds."

In the early years of the 1990s, Aeschylus' trilogy appeared to be an apt description of the American political and social situation. The show, and the shorter version of the story, Euripides' *Orestes*, became two of the defining dramas of the times.

Also playing in the United States during 1992 was a very different interpretation of the Atreus legend. Ariane Mnouchkine's Théâtre du Soleil's *Les Atrides* arrived from Europe and swept into American theater headlines. Certainly this show was the most ambitious version of the story, surpassing both Aeschylus' original offering and the Guthrie's *House of Atreus* of 1966, not to mention the concurrent "Clytemnestra project." The four-play, ten-hour cycle, featuring a cast of sixty, took New York by storm when it opened in October at the Park Slope Armory, under the auspices of the Brooklyn Academy of Music.

Mnouchkine's *Les Atrides* also played *Iphigeneia at Aulis* first, but then continued with all three plays of Aeschylus' trilogy. Frank Rich, writing in the *New York Times* (6 October 1992), found *The Libation Bearers* (although altered from the Greek script) to be particularly powerful. Rich waxed eloquent, if somewhat ambiguous:

In the Théâtre du Soleil rendition, the storytelling is neither modern nor archaic . . . but timeless. Ms. Mnouchkine fulfills her idea of a cosmopolitan, ritualistic theater that is beyond language, plot or any kind of realism and that instead digs deep into the primordial passions, many of them ugly, that seem the eternal, inescapable legacy of the human race. . . . The most extraordinary coup de théâtre in *The Libation Bearers*—and, for that matter, in *Les Atrides*—arrives after the blood is spilled: as the lights dim to black and the barking of approaching dogs rises to a terrifying pitch, individual attempts to remove the bloodied mattress bearing the mutilated corpses of Clytemnestra and her lover, Aegisthus, come to nothing. Finally the entire chorus must advance to do the macabre deed, and the apocalyptic spectacle leaves the anxious audience in dread of an unchanging world in which blood inexorably begets blood and evil forces are never tamed.

This was the moment in the performance, declared Linda Winer, writing in *Newsday* (6 October 1992), when Aristotle's requisite pity and fear were fully realized.

Rich praised the appearance of the chorus of Furies, "snarling, mutated hellhounds, part canine, part simian." Winer described the several choruses more fully:

[Mnouchkine] turns the Greek chorus into both a ritualized unisex folk-dancing ensemble and a full-throated complicated character, which changes from play to play. Sometimes the chorus shares the sorrow on stage like a kindred soul, sometimes it checks out the action like a nosy neighbor on the fence, sometimes it does flying somersaults over the walls like violent splats of color.

Overall, however, the multicultural casting and controlling aesthetic sense were compelling. The cultural blending was dominated by Kathakali choreography, but ceremonial costumes suggested other Asian or African origins, while stagehands revealed a Kabuki influence. All of this rendered *Les Atrides* an important moment in the performance history of Aeschylus' trilogy.

One final production of *Oresteia* illustrates further the fascination the trilogy holds in recent years. In the spring of 1994, Tim Robbins directed the Actors' Gang Theatre of Los Angeles in a performance of the story. This version comprised Charles Mee's adaptations of Aeschylus' *Agamemnon* and Euripides' *Orestes*, a script performed as a single drama two years before (see Chapter 8); Ellen McLaughlin's adaptation of Sophocles' *Electra* replaced Aeschylus' *Libation Bearers* and rounded out the trilogy.

Dan Cox (*Daily Variety*, 23 March 1994) applauded the Actors' Gang for "adroitly blending the lyrical tragedy of the classic cycle with the apocalyptic punch of two postmodern scribes." The production, he continued, was typical nuclear-age: the soldiers wore World War I fatigues, the Greek chorus wore black. The game-show staging of the third show saved the evening "from another postmodern depiction of historical figures with black sunglasses." While the pop culture references played for laughs, Robbins did not lose important ideas in a maze of disparate symbols. The aim of director, translators, and actors was to offer a contemporary tale of a dysfunctional family. Certainly no one could dispute that the House of Atreus fits that description, but the tragedy of the traditional story can get lost when the larger themes are disregarded.

Inventive staging marked each play of the Actors' Gang production. For *Agamemnon* the stage was covered with open-faced hardcover books which Dan Cox described thusly: "Nimble Thesps [*sic*] dance lightly over the pages. While the image might be an ironic, unintended metaphor for Mee's free use of Aeschylus, it still provides a gripping visual in the small warehouse of a theatre." *Electra* was played on a stage full of dirt (why is not stated), while *Orestes* was set within a mental institution marked by hospital beds and plastic curtains. The latter setting had been widely acclaimed, when *Orestes* played alone, as an appropriate metaphor for the late years of this century. The trilogy was intended to give full expression to this interpretation.

During the nearly thirty years following the initial production of Aeschylus' *Oresteia* in America (1966), staging style, directorial interpretation, and critical reception gradually but strikingly changed. The star-studded cast of the Ypsilanti open-air performance and the masked grandeur of the

Guthrie-Campbell staging emphasized the fateful power of the story. This was theater writ large, and we were to see in its magnificent sweep the power of emotions and the dangers of justice taken into mortal hands. Even the Serban version, which narrowed the focus to the single play, concentrated on violence and used the terror it inspired to teach its errors.

The Barton/Cavander script continued to show the story in epic style. In this version, however, humor amid the tragedy was recognized when Euripides' *Helen* was added to the cycle—although the serious message of the ancient text, the illusions for which men go to war, remained the overriding theme. The idea that the tale has validity but needs to be updated in performance began in the commercial theater with the City Stage Company's production in 1985. That the message can transcend language barriers and comprehension, a belief initiated by Andrei Serban's *Agamemnon* in 1977, continued with the Suzuki performances in 1986–1987 and culminated in the widely acclaimed tour by the Théâtre du Soleil with Ariane Mnouchkine's *Les Atrides*. The latter production can only be termed epic: its length and its return to atavistic rituals rendered Aeschylus' play lengthier and more primitive than the Athenian original.

The Guthrie's cycle focused on Clytemnestra and developed more fully an idea suggested by Mnouchkine's version. The Atreid myth in the 1990s emphasized male brutality versus female suffering, even though no one could deny Clytemnestra's power when she took vengeance into her own hands. The grand sweep of the Greek trilogy had become a feminist text as well as a domestic tragedy. It took but a few steps further, at almost the same time, to make the story illustrative of the dysfunctional family, a unit that had come to symbolize the degeneration of contemporary society. By the 1990s, the gods and the inevitability of Fate left the House of Atreus; mortals' ruin lay in their own hands. Aeschylus probably would not have denied this view, but the theme gained greater power when the actions of men and women were seen within the context of a larger universe.

EURIPIDES: *THE BACCHAE*

Not once during the first sixty years of the twentieth century did the conflict between Dionysus, the god unrecognized, and Pentheus, the tyrant who refused to honor him, appear on the American commercial stage. Euripides' penultimate play[19] portrays the doomed attempt of Pentheus, young ruler of Thebes, to block Dionysus from bringing his new cult into the city. But the deity is determined to be recognized in the city where his mother, Semele, conceived him and died, and thus he returns, disguised as a mortal, to his native Thebes. In *The Bacchae*, a chorus of bacchantes, or *maenads*, women of Asia who follow the god by choice, tell the deeds of the women of Thebes, who maddened by Dionysus left their looms and rushed to the mountains to become members of his *thiasos* (holy band) by force.

There they live at one with nature, happily performing the god's rites when left in peace; but when threatened with capture, their staffs turn to weapons and their violence knows no bounds. In the play's central scene, Dionysus takes control of Pentheus' mind and body, dressing him in women's garb and leading him to spy on the Theban women. The tyrant who wanted to control his city and its people becomes the helpless victim of the god's power and the hunted prey of the Theban bacchantes. In the spell of the god's punishing madness Queen Agave rends apart her own son's body. Returning to Thebes in exultation, she is guided by her father, Cadmus, to the bitter truth. Dionysus appears to the wretched Cadmus and Agave and affirms that now, indeed, Thebes and its citizens recognize his power. Political decisions and military force cannot stand against religious beliefs; the latter are too powerful.

Such is the plot of Euripides' *The Bacchae*, such its message. But neither appealed to directors in American theaters in the earlier years of this century. The play was known, but the violence it described was too strong, its theme too disturbing to allow it a place on the commercial stage. Then, suddenly, in the 1960s, the events of this strange drama began to appear relevant. To live at one with nature, to celebrate the god who gave mortals the gift of wine, to follow new cults, and to overpower those advocating staid and traditional values were ideas that spoke to the generation of the 1960s. Never mind that Euripides' play also cautions against excess, be it in acceptance or rejection of a new religion; never mind that Pentheus is wrong in his assumption that the Theban women are engaged in drunken debauchery and lascivious unions, never mind that to accept Dionysus fully is dangerous. The god must be recognized and revered, although his rites are repulsive as well as exhilarating. The producers who now turned to *The Bacchae* found in this script a celebration of the natural life and free love, a play that extolled freedom won by breaking social standards, thus a text meaningful for the generation of flower children. This celebration of *The Bacchae* finally reached its orgiastic culmination in *Dionysus in 69*.

In the early years of the 1960s, however, Euripides' play held more appeal for the academic audience than for the general public. On the campus the play was selected not as an academic exercise but as reflective of the social scene; at least one of the many versions staged during this decade is worth discussion.

While the initial staging of *The Bacchae* in the eastern United States was as the commencement play at Smith College in June 1934, a production remounted the next year at Bryn Mawr College,[20] for thirty years thereafter *The Bacchae* remained absent from the American commercial stage. Then it was a Greek who directed one of the first productions of the 1960s. In the spring of 1963, Minos Volanakis was invited to Pittsburgh by the Carnegie Institute of Technology to produce *The Bacchae* "in an attempt," as a press release states, "to remedy the tendency toward academic and uninteresting productions of classic Greek plays in America." The translation used was that of Volanakis himself, and the choreography was designed by Zoozoo Nicoloudi, also specially invited by Carnegie Tech.

The program notes reveal that the ideas behind Volanakis' interpretation are singularly reflective of the times. Dionysus was envisioned as being a combination of Mick Jagger and John Lennon, and, overall, the attempt was to infuse the production

> with a feeling of ecstasy and, in some parts, a sense of hallucination. The ecstasy of Dionysus and the ecstasy of LSD seem to have a similar dual nature: transcendent beauty on the one hand, and violent disorientation on the other. . . . We have tried to create a theatrical experience that transcends the melodrama of the bare plot line of *The Bacchae.*

Whatever the errors behind this venture, the critics claimed the play was worth seeing because the acting was sufficient to overcome the flaws of its conception.[21]

The Bacchae was first staged in New York in the winter of 1967 by the Group of Ancient Drama at the Library and Museum of Performing Arts at Lincoln Center. Dan Sullivan (*New York Times*, 24 February 1967) allowed that to see it "was not an overwhelming experience," but that the production had its points. He found its strengths to be Thomas Pasatieri's music, Bruce Harrow's neo-primitive costumes, and the chorus, who moved and spoke as a single group. Despite the "emotional opportunities" of the script, however, the cast did not, in Sullivan's opinion, live up to them. In his view Aliki Nord as Agave, Ken Kliban as Pentheus, and Alex Cort as the god made good attempts to bring the play to life, but fell short of their goal. Thus with little fanfare the first New York staging of Euripides' great play opened and closed after a brief run.

Within the next two years, however, *The Bacchae* became the play of the year. In the spring of 1969, the Repertory Theatre of the Yale School of Drama mounted a production using the Kenneth Cavander translation, directed by André Gregory. The drama critic of the *New York Times* (23 March 1969) opened his review thusly:

> Every age, I suppose, searches among the classics for those works which seem most particularly to mirror its own nature; and our age has found *The Bacchae*. This late tragedy of Euripides has never been so widely ignored as, say, the *Ion* or the *Helen* . . . but until recently it had not been widely read, and it had almost never been produced.

Then he continued:

> *The Bacchae* is important to us because Dionysus, especially as Euripides here depicts him, is for better or worse the god of our times: the god of intoxication, of frenzy, of release-your-inhibitions and blow-your-mind . . . the god who makes you

dance "until the mind splits open, and the world falls in, and Dionysus is glad." Dionysus is glad a lot these days. We had better learn as much about him as we can; our survival may depend upon it.

His review of the actual performance focused much upon the technical aspects of the production: the set, the lights, the movement, and direction that seemed to offer theatricality for its own sake, not for that of the play. The set he found to be a metallic limbo, despite its poles and steps for the active chorus, a chorus skilled in acrobatics but lacking in joy or any connection to the service of Dionysus. Perhaps the disjointed nature of the chorus arose from the fact that it had been trained by the associate director, Stanley Rosenberg. Clive Barnes, also writing for the *New York Times* (15 March 1969), allowed that to conceive of the chorus as contemporary hippies was a "relevant insight, and the most meaningful part of the production," but the conception led to no coherent interpretation; he too found the athletic figures lacking in passion.

The actors, according to the *Times* (23 March 1969) drama critic, gave competent to powerful performances. David Spielberg as a black-booted dictator was plausible, Mildred Dunnock exulted as Agave, but "[made] it touchingly clear that this is a gentle nature wrought up by the god to a totally uncharacteristic savagery." The dominant figure, as he should be, was Alvin Epstein as the god, a Dionysus sensual and strange, full of mystery and power. Once again we can turn to the drama critic of the *New York Times* for a description of the final scene:

He stands on a platform high above the unfortunate mortals whose lives he has ravaged, rolling his knees and hips with cold, ironic sexuality, while his voice gives grim judgments over the loudspeaker system, and a live snake twists in his hands. There are not many actors who could upstage a live snake, but Mr. Epstein does it; the snake becomes only a part of the horrible triumph of Dionysus.

The production revealed the power of Euripides' play, this critic asserted, and justified the revival. At Yale *The Bacchae* was fully successful.

Meanwhile in New York the Performance Group's staging of its version of *The Bacchae, Dionysus in 69,* was still running. Richard Schechner's extreme conception of Euripides' text had opened, despite its title, in the summer of 1968, and at once drew attention. Few of New York's drama critics found the show appealing, and few gave it a full measure of praise. They did, however, devote many words to the show, both because it was so strange and new and to advise its audience of what an evening at the theater might mean should they choose to attend this interpretation of Euripides' classic play.

The script, such as it is, mingled lines primarily from *The Bacchae*, but also from *Antigone* and *Hippolytus*,[22] but consisted of many improvisations that changed each evening. The form of the show also regularly changed, as the actors responded to their own whims and involved the audience variously; those who paid to see the show were not allowed merely to sit and watch. The end result was, in the words of Clive Barnes—more generous than others—a performance that was "probably the strangest hit even off Off Broadway has achieved."[23] Schechner's intent was to make the theater "an environment and an experience" which were intended to alter the way people think about drama and theater. But Barnes had some words of sage advice to those who would change the familiar concepts. The development of the new style created by Schechner need not crowd out the prosperity of traditional theater; while difference does not rule an interpretation out of court, difference does not, on its own, make a play great.

Walter Kerr did not enjoy his evening at the theater. Writing in the *New York Times* (16 June 1968), he complained, "My problem is that I am not divine." Were he divine he could do what he wanted, but during the performance of *Dionysus in 69* he was permitted no freedom at all. He could not sit quietly and watch, but was constrained to dance, was not allowed a place or time to smoke, nor, most annoying of all, he was not allowed to think. He wished to think about Euripides and his very fine play, a play that "will still be there when we're all through roughing it up." But it was not only the swarming, squirming melee that kept Kerr from his thoughts, but "Mr. Schechner's careful determination that I get no hard information to work with . . . probably half the evening is unintelligible by design."

Kerr did not miss the successful moments of the show. He picked up on the suggestion—or made it in spite of the company's attempts otherwise—that excesses such as those going on in the dramatic space[24] could only end in violence. He felt the terror of Pentheus' vain attempt to silence the ecstatic whispers of Dionysus' ever-expanding *thiasos*. Finally Pentheus' frantic flight, jumping from platform to platform over the audience's heads, provoked sympathy as well as fear. Nevertheless, Kerr closed his review with an important question: is physical contact more conducive to empathy than Euripides' "awful penetration of words?" He concluded it is not.

From this strange version the momentum of *The Bacchae* productions continued through the 1970s—the play apparently appealed at some level to the "me generation." In 1972 the Roundabout Theatre in New York City staged a version that blended a straightforward style and strong acting with several bizarre touches; the direction and adaptation by Leslie Ann Ray offered a poetic narrative and a vision of the chorus, daubed in fluorescent paint, wildly racing in the dark. A production in 1977 at the National Arts Theatre, playing with a script titled *Socrates on Trial*, added as subtitle on the program "Wine, Women and the Gods." The Pacific Repertory Company came to Pittsburgh in 1979 with a version directed by Dennis Aubrey. Howard Clack's press release (21 February 1979) outlined the philosophy of this interpretation:

Why do *The Bacchae*? The theatrical violence of *The Bacchae* directly reflects 20th century violence. After two world wars and the development of scientific warfare, we have perfected a sophisticated system of genocide and daily witness mass murder, suicide and terrorism in a more callous but no less barbaric world than the world of *The Bacchae*. Dennis Aubrey's production investigates this barbarity and the results of its repression in a modern approach to the work.

In the 1980s the play finally was dared as a straight text in the commercial theater. Here I include several of the productions of *The Bacchae* and one modern adaptation. While the drama critics did not find these shows particularly effective theater, they used the opportunity to present their views of Greek drama and its significance for the modern world.

Most notable in New York City was the Cacoyannis version at Circle in the Square in 1980. While his 1963 *Trojan Women* had been hailed as extremely effective, many drama critics were disappointed with his *Bacchae*. Most noted, first of all, that in this performance the cast did not sustain the power of Euripides' play. Brendan Gill (*New Yorker*, 3 October 1980) found that Dionysus and Pentheus were "light-foot lads, closer to Houseman than to Euripides," while Frank Rich, in the *New York Times* (3 October 1980), said that Pentheus in disguise was "closer to the farce of Charlie's Aunt," and Robert Brunstein (*New Republic*, 1 November 1980) asserted that the chorus were not "earthy primitive peasants" but "actors who work close to the ground and clutch themselves." John Simon's typically cynical comments (*New York*, 20 October 1980) are most memorable (and least generous): "[The girls] are an ethnically mixed group in sluttish costumes whose movements are rather like the floorshow in a medium-priced third-world bordello."

In contrast, Clive Barnes found Cacoyannis' staging sufficiently magnificent. He asserted (*New York Post*, 3 October 1980), "Cacoyannis has directed with his customarily sure sense of ritual . . . and stressed the grandeur of the play." And while he accorded success to all the actors, he had special praise for Philip Bosco as Cadmus and Irene Pappas as Agave.[25] Indeed, these two artists won acclaim from most of the critics; these two characters, however, are not the key roles in Euripides' *Bacchae*.

Thus the reviewers chose to devote much of their time to discussing the playwright's ideas. *The Bacchae*, wrote Frank Rich, is "about men's souls, not murder, about choice, not fate," while of the same production T. E. Kalem (*Time*, 13 October 1980) proclaimed: "[*The Bacchae*] shows man in a precarious magnetic field between what is aspiring, rational, noble, and demigod-like in his nature and raw, timeless instinctive drives that would shame the beasts." The playwright, trumpeted Clive Barnes, "anticipated certain Judaeo-Christian views of God, Man and Nature, [and thus] seems closer to us in time"; Dionysus is furious with the Thebans because "they reject his divinity and his virgin birth." Jack Kroll in *Newsweek* (13 October 1980) claimed that *The Bacchae* ought to be closer to us, as it is "a conflict of repressive moral law vs. sensual excess." This critic left the theater disappointed but thinking Greek thoughts, for he closed his review by noting that Greek tragedy was more alive at that evening's boxing match.[26]

Among additional New York productions of Euripides' late play was the version staged by the Meat and Potatoes Company at the Alvina Krause Theatre in 1985, where the emphasis was on latent sexuality. In the press release Andrew Sackin credited the play's "profound erotic undertone and orgiastic spirit" with keeping it off the boards for centuries. It was the 1960s, he claimed:

with its hippies, yippies, flower children, and drug culture, all in conflict with a rigid, patriarchal power structure, [that] provided a new and first-hand sense of the Dionysiac spirit—and once again the play became a living organism with a voice that can bridge the gap of twenty-four centuries and speak directly to our time.

The critics, however, while noting the sexuality of the production and that the topic seemed "ripped from yesterday's headlines" (Sy Syna, *New York City Tribune*, 18 July 1985) or as "pertinent as tomorrow's" (Ron Mullen, *Backstage*, 2 August 1985), found the performance lacking in power. Pentheus was "tricked out" in a black *chiton* and Dionysus was "a mocking macho man," according to reviewer Syna, while Steven Steinberg (*Stages*, September 1985) complained that, in the Meat and Potatoes Company production, "the play depicts the boy next door in a fit of pique at the star of the local little league."

In 1987 an adaptation of Euripides' play was staged at the American Music Theatre Festival in Philadelphia. With a script titled *Revelation in the Courthouse Park*, Harry Partch created a play whose events alternate between those of *The Bacchae* and those taking place in a courthouse of a Midwestern American city. Here Dionysus is Dion, a pop idol, followed by bands of ecstatic females, while Pentheus is Sonny, who questions Dion's power and is destroyed, lynched to death by the rock star's groupies. The critics praised the acting, the music, and even the possibility of transforming Dionysus to rock star. But they questioned Partch's adaptation. Leighton Kerner (*Village Voice*, 3 November 1987) complained that the playwright had reduced the tragedy of Agave and Pentheus to a "maudlin soap opera of Mom and Sonny."

We return to middle America and to the Guthrie Theater for the final *The Bacchae* of the decade, where in the 1987 production the director's emphasis at last left the sexuality of the last twenty years and focused upon a philosophical idea. Here it was the necessity of balance, a conflict not between sexuality and repression but between "absolute control and absolute freedom." Dennis Behl proclaimed the intent in his press release (3 August 1987) for the show: "In this regard the task of our production has been to unearth the undying shades of Greek mythology and find out how the ancient myths and the stunning poetical power of Euripides mirror our deep emotions and universal human truth." The artistic conception of the production, however, rested on a different premise. As clearly articulated in a post-performance discussion by director Livui Ciulei and the chorus leader, the central message of Euripides' play is the primacy of balance. "Balance is all," sing the chorus, and these words are offered as a translation of the difficult and often (mis)quoted *o ti kalon philon aei* (*Bacch.* 881, 901).[27] It is true that excess is to be avoided in interaction with the divinities, but this is not exactly what the verse teaches, for taken in context the lines refer to exulting victory, not careful moderation. Further, while balance is proper for mortals, neither balance nor restraint is part of Dionysus' actions nor of those under the spell of his rites.

The staging of the Guthrie's *Bacchae* blended the traditional and the modern. The set featured two huge boulders forming, as a corbeled vault, the palace entrance, above which was suspended a massive gold ball. Downstage center the pit-grave of Semele flamed at key moments in the play. In familiar Guthrie fashion the palace miracle scene was given full measure of action: the ball fell, the flame flared in the darkness, smoke billowed out, and a carpet of ashes fell upon the stage which buckled as the bacchantes shrieked in terror. This climactic scene closed Act I; the palace remained shattered for the rest of the performance.

The use of masks marked a further blending of traditional and modern. All major characters—Dionysus, Pentheus, Cadmus, and Agave—as well as some chorus members had masks of smooth, shining metal lacking any particularizing characteristics. These were slipped off and on as a crown might be, donned and removed to mark changes in emphasis, mood, or meaning. Pentheus in transformation, of course, gained a female mask which he wore for his final moments onstage. The production thus utilized the tradition of the mask, but modernized the interpretation by allowing the characters to speak in front of the metal disguise as well as from behind it. The polished and undistinguished form universalized the mythic characters but did not deny them either individualization or the expression of emotion.

While Ciulei successfully individualized members of the chorus by dividing the lines so as to give each a consistent point of view, he failed to give them any unified dance. This prevented the audience from seeing a choreographic echo of bacchant revels familiar from vase paintings, an action necessary so Pentheus' imitation in the travesty scene may be recognized. Furthermore, as Thomas Disch commented in his review of the play in the *Nation* (12 September 1987):

The ladies of the chorus did not appear to pose any discernible danger to the civil order of Thebes. They swirled their heavy gypsy skirts and shook their bangled arms at the balcony and declaimed their fortune cookies, but the effect was rather of a feminist rally than of women mad for Bacchus.

The transformation (or transvestite) scene should be terrifying, but in the Guthrie version the farcical almost outweighed the fearful. As Disch noted, here "the audience just had a safe giggle at a silly drag queen." But in Agave's recognition scene a full sense of terror came through: Trazana Beverly, as she understood her deed, gave a chilling silent scream. Her moment of quiet recognition spoke as loudly as any cry of pain.

The final moments of the Guthrie *Bacchae* marked a severe departure from the text as we know it, even in its mutilated form. In the Guthrie/Cavander version, man and god did not meet: mortals did not learn from the deity who worked their ruin and demanded their exile. The final speech of Euripides' Dionysus-in-epiphany, ex machina, defines his nature and asserts the power of the Olympian gods. Cavander's deity gave some cheerful tag lines showing his pleasure in the outcome, but he did not inspire awe. To accept this deity seemed a good idea, but it did not seem necessary. The 1987 Guthrie *Bacchae*, with its emphasis on balance, seemed rather to be a prescription for man to hold his temper than for a mortal to recognize a god. As Disch suggested, the Guthrie *Bacchae* finally lacked excitement in its attempt to be safe.

Interpretations of *The Bacchae* altered during the twenty years of its production history. During the 1960s the text was played as a celebration of free love united with a back-to-nature life-style. Within the next decade, directors realized that the rites practiced by the Theban women had a more dangerous side: the law of the wild cannot endure the eyes of civilization. But in its attempt to counter the misunderstanding of the earlier generation, to announce the importance of balance in human life (against which no Greek would argue), the Guthrie version went too far; the performance staged in Minneapolis tamed both man and god too much. Balance kept the audience from the brink of terror and skirted the power of Euripides' daring play. The interpretations of the 1980s, however, are closer to the Greek original than the excesses of the 1960s; directors of *The Bacchae* have come to recognize the union of opposites that the deity exemplifies and expects mortals to accept. But the commercial stage in America still awaits a performance that will celebrate both the nature and the power of the Greeks' most unusual god, and acknowledge the tension between military and religious power that Euripides' text portrays.

EURIPIDES: *IPHIGENEIA AT AULIS*

Euripides' last extant drama returns to the story of the Trojan War, to the very beginning of that conflict, when the possibility existed that it would not take place. He removes the tale of the great battle to the straits of Aulis, where the anger of Artemis kept the ships beached, and focuses attention on Agamemnon as the king makes the choice for war. The playwright asks the audience to consider what forces can compel a man to sacrifice his first-born daughter, and what can compel her to go unbound to the altar. The issue is both martial and domestic, as Euripides brings to the military camp a familial crisis, personalizing a political decision and turning the sympathy of his audience from the man who would lead the troops to the girl whose sacrifice is needed for those troops to sail, and to the mother whose daughter has been tricked to camp and altar. To answer Artemis' request for Iphigeneia's sacrifice—or, at least, as the prophet Calchas claimed the deity so requested—Agamemnon has lured his daughter to Aulis with the promise of marriage to Achilles. In Euripides' play, the king agonizes over his choice but finally believes he can do nothing but obey the gods. Rightfully angered over the slaughter of her daughter to restore Helen, her own wanton sister, Clytemnestra challenges his decision. In the end, Iphigeneia accepts her father's reasoning; her final exit is brave, but the play's action has cast such doubt upon the validity of Agamemnon's choice that the audience questions its necessity and pities the young girl's delusion.

Iphigeneia at Aulis raises strong emotions. In one reading it can be understood as an antiwar play, in another as the pain caused by fate's implacable force. Agamemnon's decision at Aulis has become a paradigm for a choice where neither option is without suffering, where each side is both right and wrong. In Euripides' version of the story, the audience is compelled to consider the personal over the political, to vote for family over army, even while knowing that the military decision is the only viable one. The play also raises male-versus-female issues: is the choice for army, the male decision, the only valid one, or is the female preference for family correct? Such disparate ideas garnered different interpretations over time; the production history of *Iphigeneia at Aulis* reflects the changing attitudes of the American audience.

It is strange, perhaps, that the play has not been staged more frequently, for both military and feminist concerns have been at the forefront of thought in the United States during the past century. But the play's antiwar theme was overshadowed by that of *Trojan Women* in the early 1900s. Again, those wishing to play a strong female found Electra or Medea more exciting options, for in *Iphigeneia at Aulis*, the title character ultimately accepts her father's logic, a choice difficult for the contemporary audience to approve. Meanwhile Clytemnestra, whose role allows the actress a greater range of emotions, remains the wife scorned, who does not—during the course of this script—take any definitive or successful action. She is, finally, a figure more appropriate to modern domestic tragedy than to traditional concepts of Greek drama, a character who gained stature only when the play was made a prologue to the *Oresteia* trilogy.

In the spring of 1921 Margaret Anglin appeared before the New York audience as Clytemnestra in this play under the direction of Maurice Browne. Ludwig Lewisohn, writing in the *Nation* (8 April 1921), praised her boldness in doing such dramas: "To dare to be heroic is to dare greatly." He found her acting not superlative, but nevertheless passionate; she was better suited, he opined, to soaring energy than to rage and reason. All in all, however, he proclaimed the performance interesting and beautiful. The play, on the other hand, Lewisohn termed "curious . . . full of conscious or unconscious but unmistakable world-historic irony." He continued with a strong and sarcastic indictment of the cause for war, recognizing that Iphigeneia's death was not for Greece, but for "the shabby interests of an individual and a class." To this critic, Clytemnestra's logic is correct, and Agamemnon is a pitiable figure. And Lewisohn made no apology for being "ultra-modern and irreverent."

Alexander Woollcott was displeased with the overall interpretation of the play, especially Maurice Browne's direction of the chorus, both its dances and its costumes. "Mr. Browne's way of bedizening and prettifying these austere Greek tragedies is nothing short of an abomination," he thundered (*New York Times*, 9 April 1921); he "has tied up the *Iphigeneia* as one might a box of bonbons."[28] Nevertheless, he continued, through the power of Anglin's acting, the power of Euripides' play came crashing through. With the addition of Walter Damrosch's lovely music, the production provided its large audience a memorable experience.

Woollcott had little to say about Euripides' play itself; he apparently did not find its theme worthy of comment. His description of the final scene, however, gives us some taste of the style and interpretation that appealed to the audience of the 1920s. Having told us that the play closed not with Iphigeneia's exalted march to the altar but with the messenger's report of Artemis' last-minute rescue, and the soldiers then "whooping off to Troy," Woollcott continued: "Clytemnestra is left leaning against the pillar, weary, relieved, smouldering, resentful, with her husband marching off to war in gay oblivion of her thoughts of him and with only Achilles to bend and kiss her hand in homage and understanding."

Mr. Hornblow (*Theatre Magazine*, June 1921) considered the production, especially the acting of Margaret Anglin, an overwhelming success. Although he praised her interpretation of Clytemnestra at some length, he was enamored of the whole performance; he especially singled out Maurice Browne's direction as deserving highest acclaim. Anglin, he asserted, showed "regal dignity, splendid depth of feeling, defiance, anguish and relief; [she] demonstrated herself the genuine leader of the heroic stage."

Hornblow also noted the popularity of good drama in New York City. The reception accorded this performance demonstrated, he stated, "in no uncertain fashion that there is a public here for the very best." After scornfully acknowledging that some might find the "undraped girly-girly shows" enjoyable, he suggested that to others Greek drama would have appeal: "We have also an intellectual, cultured public today, actually starving for, and deeply appreciative of, the best, [as] no one can doubt who witnessed the extraordinary and enthusiastic audience that gathered to see the Greek tragedy acted by Miss Margaret Anglin and her associates." At least a portion of the American audience of the 1920s had become more sophisticated; many were ready to accept and even enjoy ancient Athenian drama.

But other Greek dramas were staged for the next forty years; *Iphigeneia at Aulis* did not reappear on the boards until the 1960s. Then the play was considered to be an appropriate antiwar play, especially as a protest against a war many believed should not be waged. The message of a military conflict for the wrong reasons was not appropriate for the war to stop Hitler, but it hit on target for that in Vietnam. While the play remained most popular on college campuses, although less so than *Trojan Women* or *Lysistrata*, Euripides' text had a long run in New York in 1967–1968 at the Circle in the Square, followed immediately by a version staged by the Piraikon Theatron again on tour in the United States.

Michael Cacoyannis' production of *Iphigeneia at Aulis* opened at Circle in the Square in November 1967. The translation was that of Minos Volanakis; Irene Pappas played Clytemnestra, Jenny Leigh was in the title role. Director, cast, and theater as well as the inevitable pull of Greek tragedy drew critics to the performance. Their evaluations were mixed, as we shall see, but they were united in their belief that Euripides' play was both powerful and significant for the time.

Clive Barnes accorded the show very high marks. The play was, he declared (*New York Times*, 22 November 1967), "great theater and an adornment to the New York stage." He waxed eloquent as he awarded laurels to Irene Pappas:

That fine Greek actress Irene Pappas is a Clytemnestra of the most noble passion, with a wine-dark voice that rolls like distant thunder and a cry of anguish that echoes in the soul. . . . She plays Clytemnestra as a wife and mother more than a tragedy queen, and not once could one forget that here was a woman giving up her child.

Jenny Leigh as Iphigeneia also earned Barnes' praise for her superb interpretation of the young girl's changing nature; he considered Mitchell Ryan's Agamemnon a "subtly judged performance" of this man who "lacks the moral equipment to know what the right thing is."

Barnes included in his review a summary of the plot and of Euripides' interpretation of it. He concluded that the theme and very human motivation of the play gave it a contemporary significance: "For one of the things *Iphigeneia in Aulis* is about—or, rather, now seems to be about—is a person's duty toward a nation pursuing a war he feels to be worthless."

Walter Kerr's review of the play (*New York Times*, 1 December 1967) ran to five columns, and only a portion of his text treated the performance. He liked the production, praising Pappas' impressive "leonine silences" as she watched men "plot to barter her daughter for the deceptive triumphs of war." He admired also the acting of Alan Mixon as Menelaus and Mitchell Ryan as Agamemnon, and found Jenny Leigh's Iphigeneia well acted, although wrongly directed. Much of his review, indeed, was devoted to Cacoyannis' misdirection of the title character: her innocence evoked pity too soon and thus too much. Thus, Kerr asserted, "Sheer pity . . . tends to close in on itself, to stand still, to tread the same ground without digging a much deeper trench." At the last, however, Kerr declared, when Iphigeneia put aside her innocence and accepted her fate, "she binds us back to her."

Kerr spent much of his review proclaiming that Euripides' play is rife with melodramatic devices current playwrights would hesitate to use, such as the Intercepted Letter, followed by Innocence Deceived and Mistaken Identity, culminating in the Begging for Clemency scene. While he was dissatisfied with the overplaying of the Innocence Deceived trope, he found special power in the Intercepted Letter scene and in the bitter argument between Menelaus, the betrayed husband, and Agamemnon, his politically ambitious (and more capable) brother. Kerr described better than anyone their confrontation:

Whether one wishes to think of them as trapped by the playwright or by fate, they are trapped beyond retreat. They must expose themselves to each other utterly, standing on ultimate thresholds of pain, each demanding of the other what it is impossible to give, impossible even to ask for. . . . Before the battle is done, Menelaus wishes no more of Helen, no more of Troy, not at this cost; and Agamemnon understands that he must go on.

Clive Barnes reviewed the play again when Jane White replaced Irene Pappas in the role of Clytemnestra. He advised those who saw the earlier portrayal to return to see the play again, for White's interpretation offered a rewarding contrast. Jane White, Barnes declared (*New York Times*, 6 April 1968), "is more Greek than the Greek" when she concentrated not on the humanity of the play but on the "massive tragic power of a mighty queen betrayed by destiny." He closed this review by affirming that he had called the play great theater when it opened and "great theater it remains."

Amid these garlands of praise for Cacoyannis' *Iphigeneia at Aulis*, one voice raised a dissenting note. Robert Sonkowsky, writing in *Arion* (Summer 1968), said the production wasted the talents of Irene Pappas, Cacoyannis, and Euripides. The entire venture was "a tame theatricality" which could be admired but which did not reach any true emotional level. The power that lies in the Greek text was missing from the Circle in the Square performance, according to Sonkowsky. There was a vague antiwar message, but that did not outweigh the loss of a "full representation of Iphigeneia's discovery of her freedom from the ugly constraints into which *tyche*, character, human adulthood, have locked the others." But he stood alone, for the show was emotionally satisfying to most who saw it.

In November 1968, the Piraikon Theatron returned to New York to play *Iphigeneia at Aulis* at the Felt Forum of Madison Square Garden. Although Dimitrios Rondiris' work had been admired during earlier visits to this country, Clive Barnes found little to like in this performance. He was annoyed by a show done in modern Greek with no simultaneous translations available and by the archaic approach Rondiris favored, a static and declamatory acting style. Writing in the *New York Times* (13 November 1968), Barnes noted that he thought there was more movement in the auditorium as people departed than there was onstage. He did admit, however, that he was judging the performance against that of Cacoyannis earlier in the year, and in this comparison, the Greek theater's version failed. For Barnes, it was an evening "of almost unmitigated boredom." Within the space of a few months one reviewer found such pleasure in one interpretation, such dissatisfaction in another. In this instance, however, it was the quality of the two performances of *Iphigeneia at Aulis* that made the difference, not the events of the times.

Euripides' tragedy remained virtually unseen for the next two decades. It did from time to time appear as an introduction to a retelling of the House of Atreus story, e.g., in the Barton/Cavander epic cycle *The Greeks*, the Guthrie's "Clytemnestra project," and Mnouchkine's *Les Atrides*. Then in 1992, *Iphigeneia at Aulis* was staged as a double bill with *Iphigeneia at Tauris* by the Huntington Theater Company in Boston. Tazewell Thompson decided the two plays would work well together to give a more complete picture of this key figure of Greek legend. The critics hailed the dual scripts, but not the full performance; while critical reception of the play was mixed, the negative prevailed.

Thompson cast the plays color-blindly and did not maintain the actors in consistent roles. Thus Iphigeneia was white at Aulis, black among the Taurians, her brother was white, her father Asian. The multicultural casting was, in the words of Arthur Friedman (*Boston Herald*, 8 March 1991), "gilding the lily. Euripides . . . is already universal, whatever the color or gender or ethnic origin of his performers."

Friedman determined that although the performance was visually appealing, the quality of the acting left much to be desired. This critic understood the power of Euripides' script, but in this production, he stated, the audience was led to laughter at the wrong moments, while the actions of the chorus were of the sort that gives Greek drama a bad name. Kevin Kelly (*Boston Globe*, 7 March 1991) declared the drama both insistent and slack. He, too, was put off by the chorus, "artfully arranged as a taverna poster" but a difficult distraction to bear. He praised the powerful acting of Karen Evans-Kandel in the lead role at Tauris; in his opinion the other roles were less successfully portrayed.[29] The recognition scene, one of the most celebrated in all drama and most admired by Aristotle in his day, was well done, all critics agreed, so that the final verdict was that the production was worth seeing. Once again, Euripides' texts offered good theater even if the interpretation did not merit a first-place crown.

As an individual play, *Iphigeneia at Aulis* was not performed in the commercial theater again until 1994, when the Jean Cocteau Repertory Company staged the play at its East Village theater in New York.[30] The translation used was the excellent version by W. S. Merwin and George E. Dimock, Jr. Eve Adamson directed the show in the style Julius Novick (*Newsday*, 1 April 1994) claimed characteristic of the Jean Cocteau Repertory: "energetic, unpretentious, straightforward."

Novick, however, did not find this direct style sufficient for the ironies of Euripides' text. While he was willing to read the play as a celebration of Clytemnestra, heroic feminist avenger, in this production he judged that actor Craig Smith gave the strongest performance as the tormented King Agamemnon, while the sentiments of the women lacked conviction. Jonathan Slaff, writing in the *New York Times* (30 March 1994), also considered the male characters better acted than the female, thus undermining the otherwise well-interpreted staging. This critic liked the presentation of these ancient figures as "real people struggling for life and reason in a world they abhor but cannot escape." Although the casting of Clytemnestra and Iphigeneia was not first-rate, Slaff declared the Jean Cocteau Repertory show to be "a wonderfully satisfying production of a great drama that usually frustrates the efforts of modern companies . . . [one] that holds the audience in its grip from the first word to the last."

Euripides' play has remained on the edges of commercial theater productions in America, for although it has served as an introduction for the Trojan War cycle, it has had limited popularity as an individual text. The rejection of the play from the standard repertoire probably does not rest upon the uncertainty of Euripides' ending, for this script eschews the difficulty of ancient gods; despite the king's protestations, it is quite clear that the responsibility for action lies in mortal hands. But the very absence of the traditional divinities renders this play less grand in theme; in Euripides' telling, the House of Atreus is very close to modern domestic drama, not Greek tragedy. Thus the play defeats itself: by being too accessible to the contemporary world, it languishes on the threshold. When it is staged, however, even if the particular production falls short of critical expectation, its painful message touches the audience: how easy it is to cast away blame onto invisible deities and deny one's own responsibility. *Iphigeneia at Aulis* deserves a chorus for the modern stage.

NOTES

1. In *The Bacchae*, his play telling of the introduction of the cult of Dionysus into Greece, Euripides presents the god as a "union of opposites." Dionysus is both citizen and stranger, man and god, god and beast; his rites blend the holy and the

horrible. For an excellent study of this play, see E. R. Dodds' introduction to his text edition (Oxford: 1944); for further analysis, see his *The Greeks and the Irrational* (Berkeley, CA: 1951) or R. P. Winnington-Ingram, *Euripides and Dionysus. An Interpretation of the Bacchae* (Cambridge: 1948).

2. Although *Orestes* first appeared in the 1960s, both singly and as part of an *Oresteia* trilogy, its performance history peaks somewhat later; hence the full discussion of this play appears in Chapter 8.

3. The citizens of Ypsilanti who began the Greek festival with this star-studded production hoped to make it an annual event, and the initial response, with great attendance, nationwide reviews, and funding from Henry Ford II, encouraged the dream. But the dream died young; Greek shows were not regularly done there after all.

4. Kaufmann approved the condensation as "essential if it is to take less than a full day." Although this belief is common, *Oresteia* can be done in just over three hours, as proved by the Herod Atticus production in Athens in 1983, a version of all three plays played without interruption. For further comment on the length of Greek tragedy production, see Peter Walcot, *Greek Drama in Its Theatrical and Social Context* (Cardiff: 1976): 11–21.

5. In addition to *Oresteia*, Aristophanes' *Birds* was performed at the festival; Bert Lahr and Jack Fletcher played the lead roles.

6. Kerr's words quoted here are actually of the revival of the following summer.

7. A few reviewers were at least impressed with the magnitude of the performance. Richard Watts (*New York Post*, 18 December 1968) found that he liked it in spite of himself, and Richard Cooke (*Wall Street Journal*, 19 December 1968) claimed the spirit of Aeschylus was not offended.

8. Such accusations were leveled by, among others, Douglas Young, writing in *Theater Research/Recherches Theatrales* 9 (1968): 122–124, and Richard Schechner in *Educational Theater Journal* 21 (1969): 101. The cover photo of this issue of *ETJ* is of Douglas Campbell as Clytemnestra and Robert Pastene as Aegisthus. Schechner roundly pans the production: "[The show] is campy, corny, ill-conceived (and whatever else truly philistine art is)." Men playing female roles is interesting, but not in this "falsetto, pseudo-singing, limp-wristed" way.

Clive Barnes (*New York Times*, 18 December 1968) also vented his hostility at some length. Claiming that the show was but a "bundle of stage tricks," Barnes found the masks grotesque, the dancing poor, and the male impersonations of females a failure: "[There is] a Clytemnestra who appears to be giving a drag impersonation of Hermione Gingold and an Electra who seems to be wondering just what Miss Gingold is like."

9. His sentiments are expressed in his book *In Various Directions: A View of the Theater* (New York: 1965): 50–54, 191–192. He also affirms that a director should not override the author, that the dramatist should not be a "victim of dominant interference" (175).

10. Quoted from "A Version for the Stage," in *The House of Atreus* (Minneapolis: 1966): 10.

11. As Bernard Knox points out in his review of the performance (*New York Review of Books*, 14 July 1977, reprinted in *Word and Action. Essays on the Ancient Theatre* [Baltimore: 1979]: 70–78), Serban's use of classical Greek was a mere pre-

tense. While Jack Kroll (*Newsweek*, 30 May 1977), who did not know Greek, considered the blending of languages to be "a linguistic rite of spring," Knox points out that two of the "words" are not words but exclamations, one of which does not occur in Aeschylus' text, and to accompany the violent stabbing with cries of *kai! kai!* [and! and!] was hardly appropriate.

12. The actors, who had only three weeks to rehearse this massive show, all worked for minimum Equity wages just to be a part of this extraordinary performance and to work with Psacharopoulos, whose directing ability they all praised. Unlike John Barton preparing the Royal Shakespeare Company's version in London, Psacharopoulos withheld full scripts from his cast so that they would be surprised by the final performance.

13. The text of her review ran in the several papers published under the aegis of UPI.

14. Rush Rehm (later) directed the single performance of Euripides' *Suppliants* performed in this country; see Chapter 9.

15. For a full discussion of Suzuki's *Clytemnestra*, see Marianne McDonald, *Ancient Sun, Modern Light. Greek Drama on the Modern Stage* (New York: 1992): 45–58.

16. Isabell Monk played Clytemnestra throughout; Stephen Pelinski played Agamemnon in his two plays. Jacqueline Kim gave a spectacular performance as Electra in the Sophocles drama. Other cast members included Kristin Flanders as Iphigeneia and Paul Eckstein as Orestes. Chorus members also reappeared in two or three plays, and a few played character parts in the individual pieces.

17. Questions such as these arose when I was leading a post-show discussion at the Guthrie on 27 June 1992; I believe these were typical issues of concern for any audience.

18. The decision to cut her damning line "Strike, if you can, again!" also helped to keep sympathy on the side of the princess; this Electra escaped any guilt Sophocles placed upon her.

19. Often regarded as his last play, since it was produced posthumously at the City Dionysia in 406 B.C., it was probably completed before *Iphigeneia at Aulis*, since the latter seems to have been left unfinished. Whatever the truth, *The Bacchae* is one of Euripides' last works.

20. Both were of sufficient merit to earn comment in the New York papers, especially the effective costuming and music, designed and composed under the direction of Eva Sikelianos. While the play had been done at University College London in 1921 and at Cambridge in 1930, apparently the first American production of *The Bacchae* was at Occidental College in 1924, followed by performances at Rockford College in 1926, the Experimental College of the University of Wisconsin in 1931, and the University of California at Berkeley in 1932; this listing from Domis E. Plugge, *The History of Greek Play Production in American Colleges and Universities 1881–1936* (New York: 1938): 14–30. Only the productions at Smith and Bryn Mawr attracted critics from the major newspapers, whose interest probably rested in the participation of Eva Sikelianos.

21. Volanakis' script was staged again at the Kennedy Laboratory Theatre in Honolulu in 1967. The program notes were repeated for that performance.

22. According to Marianthe Colakis, the adaptation "used nearly 600 lines of William Arrowsmith's translation of *The Bacchae*, and some lines from Elizabeth

Wycoff's translation of *Antigone* and David Grene's translation of *Hippolytus*." This information cited from *The Classics in the American Theater of the 1960s and Early 1970s* (Lanham, MD: 1993): 44. Readers are encouraged to see her full discussion of this performance.

23. Clive Barnes (*New York Times*, 19 November 1968) closes his review with a gentle admonition to his readers: "Meanwhile, go and see *Dionysus in 69* with a pure heart and an open mind. Thank me if you love it, forgive me if you hate it, and go in peace."

24. Critics tended to eschew the word "theater" for the converted garage on Wooster Street in Greenwich Village where *Dionysus in 69* was performed. Neither exterior nor interior conformed to the traditional understanding of a theater.

25. Barnes writes further of the chorus that other critics found so poor: "[The chorus is composed] of nine beautiful women . . . who move sinuously around the stage with the timelessness of women as creatures of fate and the timeliness of women of circumstance."

26. Kroll ends his review thusly:

> But an hour later the closed circuit telecast of the Mohammed Ali–Larry Holmes fight became true contemporary Greek tragedy, with Ali like Oedipus reeling to disaster from the tragic sin of hybris, overweening pride, while the chorus of spectators howled vainly against fate. You could almost see Euripides taking notes in his seat.

27. The most literal translation of this phrase is, "Whatever is beautiful is always beloved"; thus it is tempting to render the line as, "A thing of beauty is a joy forever." Since, however, the verse concludes by defining this "thing" as "to hold your hand triumphant over a crushed enemy," the Keats' quotation seems inappropriate. Nor does the phrase seem to mean "balance is best."

28. Woollcott generally scorned Maurice Browne's Greek tragedy productions. This show, he stated, reminded him of Browne's *Medea* at the Garrick in 1920, a show he roundly panned. He described the *Iphigeneia* chorus thusly:

> [Browne] fills his stage with a weaving and writhing Delsartian chorus that is like festooning a severe Greek temple with pink cheesecloth. . . . [T]hese twenty love-sick maidens chanted platitudes in stained-glass attitudes [and] could do nothing but yearn helplessly for another Gilbert and Sullivan to come out of space and deride them.

In a review the following day, Woollcott continued his derision, proclaiming, "It is Mr. Browne's way to drench the Greek plays with roseate light and wreathe them with choric damsels, who look as though they had stepped down from a lot of 1895 art calendars." Oddly enough, Lewisohn proclaimed that these dances "had a wild and natural grace." One wonders what the critical expectation for a Greek chorus was.

29. Francis Ruivivar as Agamemnon and Jonathan Peck as Menelaus played their parts well, and Matthew Loney offered both a good Achilles and Pylades. Shari Simpson as Iphigeneia at Aulis was only fair in the role, but for this critic Lizen Mitchell as Clytemnestra and Athena only played at the emotion, not in it.

30. At the Telluride Drama Festival during the summer of 1994, an adaptation of this text was performed. Debbie Falb created a version titled *Impossible Things before Breakfast*, wherein moral choices are still possible when faced with political atrocities. In this version, Agamemnon makes the proper choice and is joined by

his daughter. According to the review and summary by Marianne McDonald (*Hellenic Chronicle*, 30 June 1994), Falb's version was an enjoyable play that became a modern parable.

Paul Shenar as Oedipus and Carol Mayo Jenkins as Jocasta in A.C.T.'s 1970 production of *Oedipus Rex*. A.C.T. Photo.

Ken Ruta as Teiresias in A.C.T.'s 1970 production of *Oedipus Rex*. A.C.T. Photo.

Kenneth Welsh as Oedipus, Oliver Cliff as the Shepherd, Wilberto Rosario and Douglas Hamilton as Guards in the Guthrie Theater's 1973 production of *Oedipus the King*.

Judith Anderson as Medea in the National Theatre's 1947 production of *Medea*. Photograph courtesy of the Billy Rose Theatre Collection, the New York Public Library for the Performing Arts, Astor, Lenox and Tilden Foundations.

Brenda Wehle as Medea and Stephen Yoakam as Jason in the Guthrie Theater's 1991 production of *Medea*. Photo Credit: Michael Daniel.

Isabell Monk as Clytemnestra in the Guthrie Theater's 1992 production of *Iphigeneia at Aulis*. Photo Credit: Michael Daniel.

Katharine Cornell as Antigone and Cedric Hartwicke as Creon in the Cort Theatre's 1946 production of *Antigone*. Photograph courtesy of the Billy Rose Theatre Collection, the New York Library for the Performing Arts, Astor, Lenox and Tilden Foundations.

Elizabeth Peña and Vilma Silva in A.C.T.'s 1993 production of *Antigone*. A.C.T. Photo.

Ken Ruta as Creon surrounded by Chorus (Gerald Hiken, Ken Grantham and Joy Carlin) and Mo-Fracaswell Hyman as Messenger in A.C.T.'s 1993 production of *Antigone*. A.C.T. Photo.

7

Greek Tragedy Echoes a Period of Self-Reflection: 1970–1980

The youth of the 1970s were often characterized as members of the "me generation," as a certain narcissism seemed to mark the period. It was also a time of reevaluation and self-reflection, as Americans tried to come to terms with the events of the past decade. Ambivalence prevailed as well. While the anti-intellectualism that has run consistently through American culture retrenched and the old continued to be rejected, at the same time an interest in anthropological and psychological archetypes gained both credence and popularity. The performance histories of several Greek tragedies have already indicated these interests, i.e., the Serban productions at various times throughout the decade, the Guthrie *Oedipus* in 1972–1973, and Volanakis' *Medea* at Circle in the Square.

The texts of Greek tragedy selected for production on the commercial stages of America during the 1970–1980 decade do not appear to follow any obvious pattern: the antiwar plays no longer dominated, and misconceptions of Dionysus seem to have faded. The echoes of war were not forgotten, however, for the 1970s saw Aeschylus' *Persians* performed, not once but twice; this play would not gain an audience again until the 1990s, when it became almost the play of choice. Another "new" text selected for production during this decade was the last play of Sophocles' "Theban trilogy," *Oedipus at Colonus*. The final salvation of society's scapegoat attracted attention for the first time, perhaps because of the new found interest in ritual origins and individual redemption. Thus in this chapter I have chosen to review these two plays which in some ways frame extant Greek tragedy: Aeschylus' early *Persians* and Sophocles' final text.

AESCHYLUS: *PERSIANS*

"The particularity [of Aeschylus' *Persians*] would seem to date the work. As it turns out, the opposite is true. The nature of the aggression . . . is timeless." So Clive Barnes begins his review of the 1970 production of *Persians* in an adaptation by John Lewin at St. George's Church, 207 East 16th Street, New York City (*New York Times*, 16 April 1970). A performance of this play had not been mounted earlier on the American commercial stage—if, indeed, we can call that of St. George's Church commercial; the fact that the Phoenix Theatre presented it permits me to include the staging here. It is seldom played because the virtual absence of any action, which characterizes several of Aeschylus' extant plays, is especially marked in this drama written for performance at the City Dionysia in 472 B.C. Then it was both unusual in theme, being based on an actual historical event, the defeat of Xerxes and the Persian forces at Salamis eight years earlier, and in perspective, since it portrayed the defeated rather than the victors. This latter aspect of the play has attracted modern directors, who have found the work a powerful indictment of those who seek to earn a certain glory by conquering other lands. *Persians*, previously absent from American theaters, has enjoyed several productions during the last twenty years, and each time the play's relevance, loudly announced by its directors and producers, has been noted by the critics as well.

John Lewin's "free adaptation" staged in the spring of 1970 maintained the essentials of Aeschylus' text; its innovations rested upon more current language and references—perhaps overly stated—to all recent wars. The performance was a mixture of old and new: there was a good deal of ritualized action by the chorus, while the actors and actresses had to climb scaffolding so raked that reviewer Barnes wondered if they were wailing with grief or vertigo; even Darius returned to earth by *ascending* the "majestic stairway covered with crumpled threads of gold," according to Walter Kerr (*New York Times*, 26 April 1970). A single lighted eye hovering above the set stood for Persia. Lewin frequently added to the text and took as his closing injunction the phrase "Remember Persia," a directive Barnes found effective as "an agonizing admonition to the future."

Furthermore, whatever the limitations of Gordon Duffy's direction, the actors played their parts well. Jacqueline Brookes offered a powerful interpretation of Queen Atossa waiting to hear the name she desires—and dreads—to hear. "Xerxes" is then "hallooed in such a way that its reverberations come back from all corners of the auditorium, waves of power," to use the words of Walter Kerr. David Spielberg as the resurrected King Darius and Stephen McHattie as the vainglorious and hence defeated Xerxes were equally compelling.

Reviewers thought that seeing *Persians* had a historical as well as a philosophical value. It is not often, they noted, that a modern audience has the opportunity to see a well-staged version of drama's very beginnings.

Kerr enthusiastically proclaimed that in this production we were able "to touch the source of drama, feel the first impulse that made theater stir." He closed his review by encouraging his readers to see the production, since "it is extremely unlikely that you are going to get another opportunity to make the acquaintance of *The Persians* in your lifetime." Kerr, guided by the past, could not know the future. Four years later a second production was staged again in New York City.

In May 1974 the Circle Repertory Theatre Company closed its season with Aeschylus' *Persians*. The reviewers found little to like in this staging by Rob Thirkield. Joseph Mancini, writing in the *New York Post* (20 May 1974), claimed the play to be "lively . . . in its way, with a ghost, echoes of epic battles, an heroic queen and an ambitious prince guilty of godless insolence." But he had no praise for the production. He complained that the play's numerous prototypes required "imaginative direction and superior acting," but that neither was present in the Circle's presentation.

Although the static nature of the text (for all its exciting theme and being "a play of firsts") makes *Persians* difficult to bring to life, critical comments indicate a weak interpretation and unimaginative setting marked this production. One line of Mancini's review, however, reveals why the drama offered little enjoyment: "It's an anti-war play (last revived four years ago when the U.S. troops were still in Vietnam)." As we have seen, plays speaking against war fail to please when our country is not involved in any open military conflict: *Trojan Women* was seldom staged during the 1950s, but was almost the Greek play of choice during the following decade. Timing played a role in the critical dissatisfaction with this mid-1970s offering of Aeschylus' *Persians*. The play did not ring true in 1974 for the same reason that *Trojan Women* was found hollow in the 1950s.

Arthur Sainer, writing in the *Village Voice* (30 May 1974), deemed the setting, an imaginative construction of webbed cords and wooden planks suggesting the "worn stones of an ancient era," the most effective aspect of the performance. He also found a kind word to say about Ron Seka as the Ghost of Darius, but for the other actors and the chorus Sainer had no praise.[1] Debbie Wasserman (*Show Business*, 23 May 1974) was equally disenchanted with the performance. Onstage chaos was increased by the incomprehensible mutterings of the chorus, she asserted, and she closed her review by substantiating its title, "Circle Company Uncomfortable with Classics": "Director Rob Thirkield's attempt to cover up a vague concept of *The Persians* with emotional gymnastics and group mumbling only results in pointing up his actors' lack of classical training, and consequently making them look uncomfortable." In 1974, *Persians* was unsuccessful in both text and production.

The brief Gulf War prompted several productions of *Persians*. Those who chose to stage the play, however, did not realize that its antiwar sentiment might not earn popular appeal: President George Bush's attack against

Saddam Hussein was favored by many. Furthermore, the war itself was so brief the show's opening could not be completed before the troops were home. Thus a director's intent to use the script to speak against the Gulf War became instead a statement against any military conflict, a warning of the danger any war involved.

Peter Sellars took up the attack with his production of *Persians* in Los Angeles at the Mark Taper in the fall of 1993. Using an adaptation by Robert Auletta, who had written the text for his *Ajax* in 1986 (see Chapter 8), and recalling actor Howie Seago to play the Ghost of Darius, Sellars recast Aeschylus' play as an indictment of American foreign policy against Iran. Sylvie Drake of the *Los Angeles Times* was not impressed. Under the headline "Muddled East vs. West: Gulf War Is the Focus in This Adaptation of a Greek Classic, but It's a Misfired Exercise in Misplaced Activism," Drake (2 October 1993) accused Sellars and Auletta of offering a version not innovative, just blatant. The actors did a good job in carrying out Sellars' directives, she admitted, but the conception was too flawed to merit approval; the flagellation of America was too heavy-handed, the borrowing and blending of Kabuki, Kathakali, and rock too disparate. The murky staging illuminated by low-level spotlights and the hand-held microphones added to audience discomfort and disappointment.

While the message of Aeschylus' early play is clear, it is an uncomfortable, if not meaningless, message to a contemporary audience. Americans do not want to see a drama that celebrates the victims of war; United States citizens of recent years are more interested in victims of domestic, not military, violence. Only the most powerful performance of *Persians* could overcome both its static nature and its unpleasant message; to date that performance in English has not played on the American commercial stage.[2]

SOPHOCLES: *OEDIPUS AT COLONUS*

Oedipus at Colonus has been brought to the commercial stage less often than *Antigone* or the play that records the king's downfall, *Oedipus Tyrannus*. The earliest performance of Sophocles' last play that I have been able to identify was at St. Joseph's University in Philadelphia in 1905.[3] This was the only staging of the play, at academic or professional theaters, for the first half of the twentieth century, a performance notable also because it was done in classical Greek. But since college drama departments might well shy away from a text in which the main character is so aged, it is not unreasonable that the play has remained in the hands of the professional theater producer.[4]

Oedipus at Colonus is a play marked by confrontation, anger, a display of strong leadership, grief without long passages of lamentation, and an ending that is both mystical and uplifting, but it did not appear on the American commercial stage until midpoint in the twentieth century.[5] Since that time, however, audiences in this country have had the opportunity to see this powerful script performed at least once in each of the last four decades. Two times *Oedipus at Colonus* stood alone, twice the production was part of a "Theban trilogy," an "Oedipus cycle." This choice to do "cycles" or "projects" is in itself an innovation of the past twenty years. As we have come to expect with the opening of Greek tragedies at commercial theaters, all performances of *Oedipus at Colonus* received a considerable amount of critical attention: classical drama arouses the philosophical mood and cultural awareness of the drama critics.

Sophocles' last play, however, was not attempted by an American producer. It was the Greeks who brought *Oedipus at Colonus* to the United States. The earliest production was offered by Milton Miltiades at the John Hall Memorial Theatre in New York City in 1955. From 17 to 29 October, audiences were able to see the play in which, as the press release announced, the long suffering Oedipus "was made into the patron saint of Athens."

In the Miltiades production Lee Henry played Oedipus and Virginia Royce, Antigone; Lionel Kingsley and Harold van Geldern rounded out the cast as Creon and Tiresias respectively. The success of this production encouraged Miltiades to stage the three Theban plays as a cycle. For two weeks in the late spring of 1956, New York audiences had the chance to see the three most familiar plays of Sophocles performed as a group, albeit a different one each evening.[6]

A fully American professional staging of *Oedipus at Colonus* was finally done in 1972 by the Equity Library Theatre at the Masters Theatre in New York City. In a translation by Theodore Bank, under the direction of David Bamberger, James Harkey played Oedipus; Hillary Wyler, Antigone; Benjamin Flack, Creon; and Gregory Abels, Theseus. For the most part the production earned praise from the critics. Howard Thompson (*New York Times*, 14 February 1972) stated the Equity Library Theatre had mounted the play "with intelligence," so that it was a "sharp and thoughtful show anchored to a rich lucid language." Under Bamberger's direction, the play "is a tribute to Old Athens," wrote Thompson, "a study in compassion for a symbolic martyr." One might wonder about Thompson's understanding of the play; to describe the ending he wrote, "The old king marches off stage for a quick act of heavenly evaporation," while he decried Harkey's failure to play Oedipus "as a wounded dying lion." Jennie Schulman of *Backstage* (19 May 1972), however, claimed Harkey played Oedipus "with searing power" and gave the entire production a strong review. Thus finally, in 1972, *Oedipus at Colonus* joined the ranks of American commercial productions of Greek tragedy.

During the 1960s and into the 1970s, one actor's interpretation of the aged Oedipus dominated the stages of the United States, Canada, and England, as well as his native Greece. Alexis Minotis, acclaimed for many roles for many years with the National Theatre of Greece, toured extensively as the long suffering Theban king. As a gift from the government of Greece to the United States in celebration of the American Bicentennial, the National Theatre sent Minotis and his *Oedipus at Colonus* to New York and neighboring cities.[7] The actor told Nicholas Gage, in an interview in the *New York Times* of 12 November 1976, that he regarded *Oedipus at Colonus* as his mission. "I am not only playing Oedipus," he said, "I am playing Sophocles. I have spent 70 years preparing to play *Oedipus at Colonus*. . . . [The play] has a happy ending because Oedipus accepts death on his own terms." Mel Gussow (*New York Times*, 11 November 1976) admired the "stately, almost monumental quality" of the production and commented further that "Oedipus is leonine and chalky white, weighted by his beard, his trials, and his woes." Photographs from the performance show that Minotis' Oedipus was a massive character, powerful in appearance despite his age and suffering.

Critical acclaim, however, was mixed. The 1976 show was again done in the Greek text of Gryparis, and despite Minotis' fine acting, several critics found the foreign language limited the show's appeal.[8] Gussow complained that since words are the action in this play it was difficult to appreciate this performance without an adequate translation. Roderick Faber of the *Village Voice* (29 November 1976) found the performance overall a bit stiff, but thought the chorus was magnificent, a view shared by both Gussow and Sylviane Gold of the *New York Post* (11 November 1976). She stated further that although the performance was a "mitigated" delight, it still should be seen, especially since the play was so seldom staged. The reviewer of the *Daily News*, one Harry Stathos (perhaps as might be expected), praised the production overall.[9]

The year 1980 marked a key moment in the history of Greek drama in the United States,[10] when the Classic Stage Company of New York City mounted a production of the full Theban cycle. Titling the performance *The Oedipus Cycle* and using a new translation by Paul Roche, director Christopher Martin dared to do all three plays as a continuous piece.[11] The venture was, according to the critics, one of the most significant events of the 1980–1981 season.[12] While the whole cycle was praised, it was *Oedipus at Colonus* that the reviewers found most compelling.

The cast was headed by Robert Stattel as Oedipus throughout; Karen Sunde portrayed Jocasta and then Antigone, while Eric Tavaris played Creon. All the actors had many credits to their names and all performed the ancient "trilogy" very well. Stattel, wrote Mel Gussow (*New York Times*, 14 December 1980), was heroic; "he stalks fate with the unswervable intensity of an attorney prosecuting a puzzling crime." Holly Hill of the *Soho Weekly Review* (12 November 1980) found Karen Sunde as Antigone "intense and inwardly focused." Eric Tavaris developed, according to Glenn Loney of *Other Stages* (18 December 1980), from modest helpfulness to tyrannical rage in a frightening manner. The six-man chorus was effective both severally and in unison; according to Clive Barnes of the *New York Post* (3 December 1980), both the translation and direction humanized this key element of a Greek tragedy.

The cycle's production evoked from the critics some of their more philosophical and imaginative prose. Loney wrote a lengthy piece on *The Oedipus Cycle* in *Other Stages*. He encouraged his readers to see the whole trilogy, but if they could not, then they should see at least one play. His suggestions echo the song of Nankipoo in *The Mikado*: "Are you in a mood for a powerful clash of wills? See the *Antigone*. Do you wish to watch man challenge fate? See *Oedipus the King*. Or do you yearn to learn the meaning of suffering: See the *Oedipus at Colonus*."

While all of the critics hastened to point out that the three plays were not, in fact, written as a trilogy, they also found that the "Sophoclon," as David Sterritt of the *Christian Science Monitor* (8 December 1980) termed it, brought a new understanding to the dramas. Loney noted that the decision to perform *Oedipus at Colonus* between *Tyrannus* and *Antigone* was "a stroke of genius" (one wonders where else it might be placed!), and Sterritt remarked that the three plays work well together on the stage, "for this allows us to follow Oedipus from ignorance to exultation, Antigone from anonymous girlhood to courageous maturity, Creon from amiable courtier to troubled statesman." When the three plays are seen together, asserted Clive Barnes in the *New York Post* (3 December 1980), one is able "to comprehend the Greek view of the tragic step,"[13] or, again, as Sterritt put it, "one sees the philosophical overview of the Theban legend, with its rising and falling curve of fate, resignation, and redemption."

As noted above, of the three plays, *Oedipus at Colonus* garnered the most praise, perhaps, again, because it was the least familiar. Loney, like nearly all the other critics, found *Colonus* especially moving, describing it as a "curious ambiguous play." In it, trumpeted Howard Kissel of *Woman's Wear Daily* (16 March 1981), "psychology, morality, religion and politics all hang directly on one another." Sterritt waxed even more eloquent when describing *Oedipus at Colonus* alone: "[It offers] metaphorical variety as Creon and Theseus contend for the power to harm or help Oedipus. . . . It is the most mysterious and transcendent play of the series." Finally, Thomas Ryan writing in the *Villager* (23 October 1980), said of *Oedipus at Colonus*: "[It is] about supplication and betrayal, care and ingratitude; it is also about redemption and 'the numinous feel' of reality. Its ideas are so great that a performance demands magnitude."[14]

Apparently the Classic Stage Company's performance of *The Oedipus Cycle* achieved sufficient magnitude in all its aspects: acting, language, set, costumes, and lighting. All reviewers ended by encouraging their readers to run to see this performance, one that was, in the words of Howard Kissel a "powerful reminder of what theatre should—and can—be."

In spite of such resounding success, however, neither the "cycle" nor *Colonus* has been staged in this country since 1980–1981. While the other plays of the trilogy remain at the top of the Greek theater production repertoire, the end of Oedipus' tragic story has had little appeal. Perhaps the mysterious manner of his death discourages contemporary directors: how can they make the inexplicable event meaningful to a modern audience which demands the verification of action, especially when that action is not seen but is told in the words of a messenger? Perhaps theater companies fear we cannot understand the power emanating from the possession of a religious relic, how there can be political benefit from a religious event. But when well done, the power and majesty of the play are recognized.[15] For *Oedipus at Colonus* offers not just the final outcome to the story of the king of Thebes cursed with the worst destiny a man could have. Sophocles' last play presents at least one answer to the question of suffering: how it should be endured and what resolution it might have. Furthermore, the mysterious death of Oedipus at Colonus is an assertion of Sophocles' belief in both man and god, and the blessings possible when both are acknowledged.

NOTES

1. Throughout his review Sainer compared Aeschylus' play with an improvisational play *Stone*, staged at the same time by the Keystone Company; in this play an alchemist living in New Mexico in 1945 has found the "philosopher's stone," and various Greek gods battle to regain the object from mortal hands. Sainer preferred the modern production, with its very present deities.

2. There were at least two other productions of *Persians* in the 1993–1994 season. In the summer of 1993, in Utah, the Classical Greek Theatre Festival staged the play in Salt Lake City and environs as its annual production (see Chapter 9). In June 1994, at Chicago's fifth International Theatre Festival, the Attis Theatre, an experimental group from Athens, offered the drama in "an intensely physical performance in which the essence of Aeschylus was preserved," according to Ann Scott Tyson (*Hellenic Chronicle*, 23 June 1994).

3. Although Plugge lists a performance at Bates College in 1912, the archivists at Bates have no record of a true performance. Apparently the drama coach had classroom readings of ancient drama from time to time, and *Oedipus at Colonus* may have been one of these. At St. Joseph's on 21–22 May 1905, at the college auditorium, a full cast (with extra attendants) and a chorus of fifteen achieved, in the words of a historian of the university, "the college's most notable scholastic and dramatic triumph." Playing to an "enraptured audience," Stephen McTague in the title role declaimed his part "with dignity and solemnity and genuine feeling," as the reviewer of the *Philadelphia Ledger* (23 May 1905) affirmed; the chorus of elders, indeed, was singled out for its excellence in both song and movement.

4. After the performance at St. Joseph's University in 1905, my research shows the next university staging of the play was at the University of Washington School of Drama in 1955—a hiatus of fifty years. The following year the Harvard Classical

club offered a performance of *Oedipus at Colonus*, and unlike the 1881 *Oedipus Tyrannus*, the show was not done in Greek; in 1960 the Carolina Playmakers also produced Sophocles' last play. The University of North Carolina version was a double bill, featuring both *Oedipus Tyrannus* and *Oedipus at Colonus*. The program adds an intriguing (and precise) detail about these two plays: *Oedipus Tyrannus* takes place before the palace of Thebes in 1300 B.C., *Oedipus Colonus* at the sacred grove of Colonus in 1275 B.C.(!) I have not been able to find record of any performance of this play on an academic campus since this 1960 production.

5. *Oedipus at Colonus* had been staged earlier in Europe, although also very rarely: the earliest production was in Berlin in 1929, followed by a performance in Paris and one at the Greek theater in Syracuse in the 1940s.

6. For some reason director Miltiades did not keep his characterization constant: Jack Aronson played Oedipus as king of Thebes, and Norman Roland portrayed the ancient ruler.

7. Minotis had earlier brought his interpretation of this play to the World Theatre Festival at the 1967 Montreal Expo, where he both directed and played the title role in a translation into modern Greek by Ioannis Gryparis. The theater festival at Montreal featured performances from around the world, offering bills as varied as an evening with Jack Benny to the Pop Stars of Prague, while the dramas enacted ranged from Shakespeare to Beckett. The National Theatre of Greece also offered performances of *Agamemnon* and *Plutus*; perhaps Minotis was interested in the late plays of each writer, but there are no program notes.

8. The narrative provided via headsets was more a description than a translation; the audience did not have a real opportunity to appreciate the lines of the play itself.

9. During the 1980s Minotis continued to play the aged king in Greece, where he always received attention and acclaim in both the Greek and international presses. Alexis Minotis died in November 1992, leaving a dramatic legacy enviable on any terms.

10. That same year there was an abortive attempt by the Classic Theatre in New York to stage the play. The performance was hindered by the company's tiny space but also, apparently, by the director's misunderstanding of Greek theater. These two factors led him to dismiss the physical presence of the chorus, whose songs, then, were taped and played while the actors waited for them to stop. This performance needs no further attention; it serves as an example of how not to do Greek drama.

11. Translator Paul Roche claimed, in his program notes, that he had tried "to render Sophocles' elusive Greek into natural speech, poetical and rhythmical . . . dramatically convincing and expressive to the human heart." He apparently succeeded.

12. The year 1980 was a banner one for interest in Greek tragedy production. In addition to *Oedipus at Colonus* by the Classic Theatre and *The Bacchae* at Circle in the Square, *Orestes* and *Electra* were mounted at Julliard, and *Oedipus Tyrannus* played at BAM (Brooklyn Academy of Music). However, only *The Oedipus Cycle* by the Classic Stage Company was considered fully successful.

13. Barnes offered other interesting comments, some dubious, others perceptive. *Antigone*, he claimed, "is the most complex because it deals with moral, not religious issues" (I do not follow his reasoning here). He felt that Creon, as seen

over the three plays, was similar to Oedipus, in that both were guilty of the "sin of unyielding pride," but Creon "had the gift of choice, Oedipus is a victim of fate."

14. Actually Ryan's statement was in response to the production by the Classic Theatre; but the ideas are valid despite their original context.

15. The resounding success of *Gospel at Colonus*, in which Lee Breuer and Bob Telson recast the play as a black Pentecostal gospel service, rich with music and emotion, fully demonstrates both the power of the text and its message.

8

Greek Tragedy and Reevaluation: 1980–1994

During the decade of the 1980s, Americans tried "to have it all," then realized that the basics were more important. The legacies of the 1960s began to be reevaluated: drugs and free love were recognized to bring consequences, not liberation. Social awareness vied with flaunted greed, while a series of natural disasters forced a sense of balance and an understanding of what was truly essential. In 1985 the Vietnam Memorial Wall was completed in Washington, DC.

The Greek tragedies chosen for production during this time reflect these varying trends. In the earlier years the grand sweep of Aeschylean drama held little appeal; the emphasis was on individual striving to find meaning in the traditional myths. But even as the times defied a single definition, so too the plays staged in this decade-plus: *Medea* with Zoe Caldwell and Judith Anderson in 1982, Diana Rigg in 1994; the Guthrie's balanced *Bacchae* (1987); and *Oedipus at Colonus* (offered as part of a cycle by the Classic Stage Company [1980]), three very disparate plays. The absence of Aeschylean dramas early in this era suggests the opening years of the 1980s did not favor thinking on the grand scale his texts demand; the emphasis was on character, on the individual, often in conflict with society. Thus in addition to *Medea*, *Bacchae*, and *Oedipus at Colonus*, the 1980s saw several stagings of Sophocles' *Antigone* and the sudden popularity of Euripides' *Orestes* as a single text, i.e., not part of a House of Atreus trilogy.

Two performances of unfamiliar texts, both also focused on an isolated figure, attracted widespread critical attention during this period. Indeed, in 1986 Greek plays lit up the drama reviews, as two directors chose to offer unusual, if not bizarre, productions of two tragedies. That year Robert Wilson opened his free interpretation of Euripides' *Alcestis*, and Peter

Sellars offered his bitter vision of society by staging Sophocles' *Ajax*, both productions marking a significant moment in the performance history of Greek tragedy in this country. In this chapter, then, I review these performance histories, with the familiar *Antigone* and *Orestes* framing the reception accorded Sellars' *Ajax* and Wilson's *Alcestis*.

SOPHOCLES: *ANTIGONE*

A favorite play on college campuses,[1] *Antigone* has seldom been brought to the commercial theater, although its theme appears readily accessible: moral beliefs coming into conflict with autocratic power. When producers have chosen to mount the play since World War II, they have preferred Anouilh's version to that of Sophocles. Thus as the performance history of *Medea* favored Robinson Jeffers' script, so that of *Antigone* includes Anouilh's retelling of the story.

While Californians were able to see Margaret Anglin in a performance of *Antigone* in the Greek theater at Berkeley in 1910, residents of New York had to wait until 1923, when the Bennett School opened the show at the Forty-eighth Street Theater. This was not really a commercial venture, but did feature two professional actors, for the student cast was led by Edith Wynne Matthison in the title role and Charles R. Kennedy as Creon. The performance received good reviews, and the limited run apparently played to full houses. But *Antigone* was not staged in a Broadway theater until 1946, 101 years after it had opened and failed at Palmo's Opera House.

When Katharine Cornell chose to play *Antigone* at the Cort in 1946, it was in Anouilh's script.[2] The fame of both the actress and the play drew the critics to the theater, where all praised her acting and that of Cedric Hardwicke as Creon. *Life* magazine (18 March 1946) ran a three-page illustrated spread of the performance, noting in its brief text that the play "offers to acute playgoers 99 minutes of absorbing and beautifully acted drama."

There was nearly unanimous critical agreement, however, that Anouilh's play was less than successful: each critic held the French text up to the Greek and found Sophocles' play more powerful. The reviewers were not disconcerted by the modern evening dress; they did not fail to recognize the conditions under which and with what intent Anouilh had penned his version of the ancient tale in Nazi-occupied Paris in 1944. The various critics and commentators missed the powerful force of inevitable fate they felt marked ancient tragedy. Thus does John Chapman write (*Daily News*, 19 February 1946), "As a tragedy in the pure Greek style it is something less than effective, for tragedy must be unswerving, inevitable, relentless—and the new *Antigone* makes frequent excursions into high comedy and a dip or two into low." Wolcott Gibbs of the *New Yorker* (2 March 1946), in an article titled "That Little Oedipus Girl," termed the play "a literary and political curiosity," and in words more accurate perhaps than he could know claimed "its interest . . . lies far more in its history than in its execution." *Time*'s theater critic was more harsh. "This *Antigone*," he proclaimed, "barring its one big clash between despot and defier, was flat, fumbly theater." He continued (4 March 1946):

This Antigone, shorn of her Résistance aura, was unmoving and unreal. And in a modernish setting, the burial issue on which the plot hinges seemed outlandishly bizarre. . . . In Sophocles' version the plot at least has the psychology of a superstitious age and a religious people behind it. . . . Creon is at once the least Sophoclean and the most successful person in the play. . . . If Antigone has ethics on her side, Creon has logic on his—which may explain why the Nazis raised no squawk.

Only Stark Young, writing in the *New Republic* (4 March 1946), praised both the acting and the play. Anouilh's drama needs no justification, he stated, for "we may use the legend to our own ends." This critic had good words to say about the natural and idiomatic style of the language, the spirit of the company, and the modern interpretation. Young's enthusiasm for the show led him to this hyperbole:

Sophocles, if he could have endured the play, the production, the audience or any of us at all, would have said here go ahead. (Euripides, of course, would have been a better bet. He would have applauded this slapping down of the traditional stuffed shirts. . . .) [Furthermore] if the whole company at the Cort is not filled with the height of tragic acting, I can only say that our audiences would not know the same if they encountered it.

Young closed his review with high praise of Katharine Cornell, who "might easily be making more money by being more Broadway, [is here] presenting an American version of a French version of something worth talking about, worth seeing, worthy of herself."

At the 1946 staging of this *Antigone*, most drama critics were reluctant to recognize the possibility that an ancient play could have modern political meaning.[3] While both brave and relevant to a French audience under Nazi occupation, Antigone's protest had no meaning to an American audience never held by a foreign power and free of military concerns. Katharine Cornell had toured the European theaters to play to the U.S. armed forces overseas, and perhaps her experience there (although playing *The Barretts of Wimpole Street*) influenced her decision to stage the play so popular in Paris upon her return to New York. But her choice was not acclaimed. *Antigone*, which was to become a viable statement for later decades, did not appeal in 1946, or, at least, did not appeal in Jean Anouilh's updated interpretation. We cannot know if the Sophoclean text the critics claimed they missed would have had any greater popularity, for the play was not staged again in the commercial theaters of the United States for some twenty years.

What remains intriguing is why Jeffers' *Medea* the following year should have had such appeal.[4] We can not assume that Judith Anderson was a more powerful actress than Katharine Cornell: both were leading ladies of the stage. Since this *Medea* garnered such praise, the updating of a classic was not the sole cause for critical disappointment with the contemporary *Antigone*. One might argue that Anouilh made a greater alteration to the ancient text than did Jeffers, but I think the dissatisfaction lay not in the text but in the understanding of it. The popularity of the one play over the other lay in the different situations of the two heroines. In *Medea*, a woman takes action against a man who has betrayed her, while in *Antigone* a young girl takes a stand against the new ruler; in short, *Medea* portrays a domestic issue, *Antigone* a political one. To Americans of the late 1940s, the former was understandable, the latter was not. Once again while the ancient legend remains constant, the modern interpretation changes.

It was not until the 1970s that Sophocles' script became a popular text for the commercial stage, but a 1969 production on the University of Southern California campus in Los Angeles by the Living Theatre might be noted in passing.[5] This *Antigone* was "Judith Malina's version of Brecht's version of Hölderlin's version of Sophocles' *Antigone*," to quote Dan Sullivan's review in the *Los Angeles Times* (1 March 1969), which, despite its "layers of authorship [was close] to the original." Sullivan continued, "[The play] may be the most effective weapon the company has in spreading its message of revolution." While the power of fate and "Sophocles' sympathy for King Creon"[6] had been removed from the Living Theatre version, the courage and pathos of Antigone, as played by Malina, remained unchanged and effective. Elements reflective of Japanese Noh drama were tamed by Brechtian echoes, so that although exaggerated gestures, bodies as props, and "grubbie hippie street clothes" costuming marked the production as typical of the Living Theatre, the actors' line delivery and sense of style made "the evening a calmer one than most offered by the Living Theatre, an evening more conducive to speculation and less to hysteria and impulsive acceptance of the company's message." Such praise from Sullivan was rare, for he usually had little patience for either the ancient or the avant-garde; his comments again indicate how a classical text can be used for a very contemporary message.

In May 1971 the Repertory Theater of Lincoln Center opened *Antigone* at the Vivian Beaumont as the final offering in their season, and the critics vied in their praise of the production. Douglas Watt (*Daily News*, 14 May 1971) led the acclaim by calling the play not only a "clean, spare, swift thing of beauty" but continued:

It is hard to believe but it is apparently true that last night's new production of *Antigone* at the Beaumont is the first professional mounting here in this century of the Sophocles masterpiece. . . . Oh, we've had the Anouilh version several times and the ones by Cocteau and Brecht, but aside from a few matinees in 1923 and a few off off Broadway showings in 1957, . . . this is New York's first encounter with the real thing since heaven knows when.

This is "a revival of Olympian stature" trumpeted T. E. Kalem (*Time*, 24 May 1971), "the finest work that has ever been done there"; he continued by describing Martha Henry's Antigone as "a female javelin." Philip Bosco's Creon also earned superlatives, as did, indeed, all aspects of the performance.

What nearly every critic found important to emphasize was the play's complete relevance to the modern world. Richard Watts (*New York Post*, 14 May 1971) claimed it was relevant and timely, while S. K. Overbeck (*Newsweek*, 24 May 1971) elaborated on the theme:

Antigone . . . resonates with so much contemporary relevance one feels batted back and forth between antiquity and today's headlines. . . . Thoughts come crowding in of Sisterhood, the Panthers, the Berrigans, Weathermen, etc. and you almost expect Creon to spread his palms and say, "Let me make one thing perfectly clear."

Equally assertive was Stewart Klein (WNEW, 13 May 1971), who announced: "*Antigone* burns with immediacy! Timeless in its wisdom, raw in its relevance. Its issues might have come out of today's newspapers. Should be seen by everyone, especially by every office holder in Washington!" "Even Leonard Harris, in a television review for WCBS (13 May 1971), although he alone found the performance less than compelling, had to assert, "Insofar as *Antigone* deals with social order and individual conscience, it has always been and will always be relevant."

Newsweek's Overbeck also praised the set, the music, and Bosco's Creon, "breathing volcanic fires of righteous indignation," although he was less impressed with Henry's Antigone. Overbeck closed his review by questioning the costuming of the chorus: "Why the Greek chorus girls wear heels is a mystery only the oracle can dispel."

Echoes of Anouilh's 1943 version have reappeared in more contemporary adaptations, e.g., Athol Fugard's *The Island* (1973), wherein prison inmates stage *Antigone* to point out their harsh guard's repression, or the version in Creole by Haiti's foremost poet, Felix Morisseau-Leroy.[7] An *Antigone Africanus* [sic], created by Joseph Walker and staged at Howard University, transferred the story to Africa, a concept that emphasizes its universality.[8] But the powers at which recent performances of Sophocles' play tilt might be somewhat less obvious. Thus in the 1980s, the appeal of Antigone lay less in her battle against Creon's autocracy and more in her assertion of personal belief: the young woman is willing to die for what she holds to be true. In a world that seems to have lost its moral center, Antigone's proud struggle offers a model not found in the heroines of more contemporary scripts.[9]

During the last twenty years, there have been the occasional single productions of *Antigone* and those included in the staging of a Theban trilogy.[10] The play's appeal seems to have been nationwide: Sophocles' drama was performed, for example, in New York, Washington, Chicago, Minneapolis, and San Francisco. In 1982 Joseph Chaikin staged in New York a version that emphatically underlined the play's political overtones, but his emphasis and John Chioles' translation strayed too far from the traditional to please the critics, whose warmest praise was a "half-successful *Antigone*" (David Sterritt, *Christian Science Monitor*, 12 May 1982) and whose strongest condemnation termed the play "a classic alright—a classic howler" (Frank Rich, *New York Times*, 28 April 1982). Rich, indeed, vented his anger at some length:

There is also Priscilla Smith—a female Teiresias who quite literally spits out her prophecies. She appears with a young boy who signs her lines—never mind that the prophet is blind, not deaf. . . . [Further miming includes the messenger, who] upon telling us that "Creon began to run," breaks into a paroxysm of jogging that, thanks to his heavy boots, reduces the rest of his speech to a Theban clog dance.

Attempts to be "political," according to Rich's review, were limited to Chaikin's insistence on relevant buzz words and Chioles' use of "person" for woman (but not for "man"). Of the productions of the 1980's, the Chaikin-Chioles' *Antigone* earned the lowest marks.

In 1984, the Round House Theatre of Washington, DC, usually a successful producer of Greek dramas, mounted an *Antigone* that the reviewers found more funereal than vital. Interesting to note, however, is director Mark Jasper's experiment with stage and actors: in an attempt to recall the ancient acting space, the stage was covered with a large bed of sand and, in classical convention, only three actors played all the roles. According to David Richards' review (*Washington Post*, 17 January 1984), the former impeded the actors' movements, while the latter experiment, since it was done without masks, rendered the different incarnations just short of amusing.

Two years later audiences in both Chicago and New York were treated to performances of *Antigone*, the former done in classic style complete with masks, the latter offered by a team known for treating theater as political protest.[11] Susan Padveen directed the Chicago Actors Project *Antigone* in a manner described by the drama critic of the *Chicago Tribune* (12 June 1986) as imaginative and intelligent. According to the critics, the version brought to New York City by the Living Theatre, under the direction of Julian Beck and Judith Malina, had lost the fire that made Sophocles' play great and Beck-Malina's productions controversial. Malina who had performed the title role some seventeen years earlier, described *Antigone* as "a synthesizing of the powerful, physical, visceral, emotional quality of the Artaudian actor and the cerebral, conscious, analytical, intelligent, intellectual quality of the Brechtian analysis."[12] John Beaufort (*Christian Science Monitor*, 31 January

1984) described the performance of the Living Theatre as "theatrically empty, tiresome and old hat." He continued: "The tragic tale threads its way through the Living Theatre['s] obstacle course—the howling and growling and chanting, the dispersals of actors into the auditorium, and assorted Malina-Beck directorial embellishments. The production spreads more fog than light."

In September 1992, the Northern Sign Theater opened in Minneapolis an *Antigone* with a simultaneous translation into American Sign Language. According to Mike Steele (*Star Tribune*, 22 September 1992), this version was "brimming with ideas and overflowing with contemporary complexities." Attempts by Peter Cook to modernize the ancient script led to such opening lines as "Why do you look so shook up?" while director Wendy Knox's intent to create "multiple perspectives" reduced the theme to a sexual-political game. An effective aspect of this performance, however, was the ritualistic forming of the cast into a chorus which repeated the play's story six or seven times. Thus, as Steele said:

Each account is more fragmented and cryptic than the previous one as the social order breaks down. With each ending, one candle is snuffed until the tragedy ends in darkness. Not only does this pattern rhythmically build tension, but in its repetitiveness it sets up something horrifying about the inevitability of the tragic dilemma.

Although this *Antigone* emphasized a feminist viewpoint probably unrecognizable to Sophocles, it offered some entirely satisfying moments of theater.[13]

Finally we turn to the production of *Antigone* by the American Conservatory Theater in San Francisco in February 1993. The scenic design for the ruins of war-torn Thebes was inspired by the extensive damage done to the Geary Theater by the Loma Prieta earthquake, ruins re-created for this performance at the Stage Door Theater as a frame for the dramatic action. The ruined theater, indeed, inspired the decision to stage a Greek tragedy, when director Carey Perloff sensed that the destruction of civil war, the play's central metaphor, echoes and "evokes the image of the random destruction . . . an earthquake can deliver."

In her program notes Perloff explains further her choice of the Greek play:

Productions of Greek tragedy are, in many ways, litmus tests of what a culture is experiencing at any particular time. . . . [Sophocles' Antigone is a defiant woman] who takes on the prevailing political establishment . . . to reassert the dignity of [her] own family and [her] own individuality. *Antigone* . . . is a play of chiseled logic and precise imagery, about rebellious youth and the rhetoric of democracy. Its immediacy beckoned to us instantly.[14]

The translation and adaptation was that of playwright Timberlake Wertenbaker. Her goal was to make the play both modern in its English and faithful to the Greek, and her "rhythmical prose" (as she described her translation) seems to have met both goals well. Perloff and Wertenbaker proved that Sophocles' play holds a message that speaks to our age and that his language can be made accessible to contemporary America.

Steven Winn (*San Francisco Chronicle*, 19 February 1993) gave the performance an overall three-star rating, although he found some aspects less than stellar. He thought a major problem of the A.C.T. *Antigone* was its creation of "a social order that's already in shambles," thus "reduc[ing] the stakes of the play's main conflict." Here his criticism is somewhat off target, for Perloff's intent to emphasize the social as well as the individual issues of Sophocles' script reveals her understanding of Greek drama. However, Winn's reservations about Perloff's chorus were on the mark, for the three-person group, dressed in matching gray suits, burgundy cummerbunds, and jaunty fedoras, "caper stiffly with walking sticks" and chanted some, sung others of their lines, and seemed to add little to a production that was intended to echo the ancient wisdom, albeit wisdom accessible to the modern world. Other innovative touches worked better, however, and although the *Chronicle*'s reviewer closed on a negative note, his rating of the show indicates, once again, the hold that ancient texts have over modern reviewers and, through them, modern audiences.

Sophocles' *Antigone*, then, has had relevance for the American theater when the national mood favored either political resistance or the expression of personal freedom. While Antigone is a young girl, she is able to speak for those who wish to highlight women's courage and integrity. The cause for which she dies in Sophocles' text, the right of burial, is no longer an issue, but her stand against political abuse of power remains a burning concern. Creon learns through suffering in this play, but it is pain that recoils upon him for his own actions, while Antigone's suicide stains the ruler's hands. Both mythic figures offer a message to any world where basic rights are trampled under political ambition.

SOPHOCLES: *AJAX*

A listing of the productions of Greek tragedy on the New York stage from 1845 until 1984 includes but one performance of *Ajax*. Sophocles' earliest play clearly was not a popular text. When this show was first "granted a chorus"—or at least a staging, it opened at a community hall in an "immigrant village" on the East Side of New York City. There, on 2 April 1904, the Greeks who made this part of the city their home put on a performance of *Ajax* that charmed the audience and was, in the words of the anonymous reviewer of the *New York Daily Mirror*, "lucid, direct and convincing."[15] The performance was apparently quite an event, an unexpected pleasure in all its aspects, a show that, under the able direction of Mabel Hay Barrows, was "more valuable than many of the exhibitions that have occupied the metropolitan stage this season."

The interest in any performance of Greek drama is shown by the very fact of its coverage in the *New York Daily Mirror*, which usually devoted its theater pages to reviews of major productions in Manhattan, Boston, and the "provinces" (as its editors termed New Jersey and Pennslyvania). The enthusiastic (if somewhat patronizing) words of this reviewer are worth quoting at more length:

Crowds of the picturesque inhabitants [of the Greek colony] gathered to see the uptown contingent arrive at Clinton Hall. . . . Nearly everybody attended because of curiosity and expected to be bored. . . . the pushcart industry is not regarded as a particularly promising school of preparation for a difficult style of dramatic art . . . and everyone knows the *Ajax* is especially boring. [But] every minute of the 1-1/2 hrs was interesting. . . . A tragedy written twenty-four hundred years ago, enacted by amateurs drawn from the humble ranks of a small foreign colony and wholly ignorant of stage technique . . . riveted the attention and won enthusiastic plaudits of an intelligent and exacting assemblage.

Ajax, however, was not to gain another staging for over eighty years. Then it opened not in New York at all, but was presented by the American National Theater in La Jolla, California; from the West Coast the show traveled east to play at the National Theater in Washington, DC, where it began its run, by accident or design, shortly before 4 July 1986. Flamboyant director Peter Sellars decided in 1986 that *Ajax* had a relevance for the modern world, a world apparently devoid of heroes but not of the need for them. He believed the message of Sophocles' text needed to be heard even though the United States was not at that time actively involved in a war, declared or not. However, he did not want merely to offer a traditional staging of the Greek play; he needed a version that would speak to his own understanding of the ancient text. Robert Auletta, a playwright himself, provided the updated "translation"—more an adaptation—of Sophocles' play. The result was billed as a new civic and military tragedy.

Much of the original was preserved: the cast remained the same, as did the suspect nature of the decision to award the armor to Odysseus, and so (naturally) did the hero's madness. The main emphasis of ancient text continued into the modern: that in the "new" world, be it fifth-century B.C. Athens or twentieth-century America, the political man who works to his own advantage is more in tune to current reality than the hero isolated in his individual and personal honor. Sellars and Auletta, however, used Sophocles' text as a springboard from which to develop a drama that virtually assaulted its audience with its political messages.

The Sellars/Auletta version took place in the "near future" after an American victory in a Latin American war; the setting was the Pentagon. The men of the cast were all American generals, the chorus Ajax' faithful troops, and Tecmessa, wife of Ajax, the daughter of a defeated South American dictator. Athena was Athena; as a modern equivalent for her role would have been difficult to devise, Auletta left her in her ancient realm but gave her a slinky silver evening gown. The issue of proper burial rites was equated with the honor of interment in Arlington National Cemetery. But the staging and casting earned this production its critical attention and acclaim.

Dead center behind the general's desk stood a large aquarium, in which was revealed the hero sitting amid ankle-deep, sloshing blood. While all of the actors who performed outside this tank did a masterful job, Howie Seago as Ajax, seated within his closed space, dominated the stage. The crazed hero, this "shaggy mountain of a man in stained fatigues,"[16] is deaf and had to sign his lines, first from within the tank, later from without, while any available actor onstage actually articulated his words.[17] In the words of critic Jack Kroll (*Newsweek*, 23 June 1986), "Seago creates a devastating, frightening, moving performance of a shattered spirit. Not since Olivier's Oedipus has an actor come so close to the primal power of a Greek tragedy." Seago's own interpretation of his role is equally noteworthy: "Basically I am a poet inside, and I just love getting involved with language that has double and triple meanings and a lot of imagery. I love the challenge of putting it out in the air for people to see."[18]

Dan Sullivan (*Los Angeles Times*, 2 September 1986) applauded Sellars' efforts "to dig out the myth under [the play] and to relate that myth to the national mind-set just now." He praises further the Sellars/Auletta attempt to make the modern text echo the ancient version by creating a "tough-minded, worldly wise play." Politics as practiced by the crafty shaped Sophocles' interpretation of the Homeric legend and certainly was the guiding principle of the Sellars/Auletta version. Here, as Marianne McDonald pointed out, "[it is] clear that politics are what succeed now, and the manipulation of information."[19] Thus Ajax, crazed warrior in disheveled attire, was an embarrassment to the neatly uniformed Menelaus. Sellars/Auletta made their point that war is waged by born-to-lose heroes in the trenches like Ajax, but managed by smiling men in well-tailored uniforms like Odysseus.

While in some ways Sellars' interpretation may have been overly graphic, overly audacious—he "outdares himself," claimed Kroll—the dramatic power brought to the role by Seago gave the audience a powerful and exciting evening of theater. Even when the lines are altered to suit the exigencies of the modern world, the ancient texts can maintain their vitality.[20]

EURIPIDES: *ALCESTIS*

The earliest production of Euripides' earliest extant drama, *Alcestis*, was by the Coburn Players in 1910, done in repertory with his *Electra*. Mrs.

Coburn played the title role, her husband played Heracles, and John Kellerd took the part of the man who accepts Apollo's offer.[21] The anonymous reviewer of the *New York Daily Mirror* (7 December 1910) offered but faint praise to the show:

The premier of Mrs. Wagstaff's poetic drama was not notable through the acting. No one imparted consistent strength to his role, although Mr. Kellerd and Mrs. Coburn at times injected considerable sincerity into their work. The stage pictures were attractive, except for an impossible chorus of men, for the costuming, lighting, and tableaux were intelligently supervised.

Of the poetry, it is hard to judge from a single presentation. Smooth and agreeable, it lapses sometimes into trite phrases that mark classic verse. The Greek play is considerably abridged, but sufficient remains to tell the narrative, if not to characterize the individuals firmly.

For the next forty years, the play remained the province of college and community theaters,[22] and was not performed again in a commercial venue until 1955, when for two days in October the Provincetown Playhouse of Greenwich Village mounted Euripides' drama. The press release for the show noted that it was the first production since 1910. Using the Dudley Fitts and Robert Fitzgerald translation, Denis Vaughn staged the play with classic costumes and in traditional style.

There were two commercial stagings of *Alcestis* in the 1970s: in 1973 by the Cubiculo Theater and the following year by the Roundabout Theatre. Neither won particular critical acclaim, for the play's message seemed irrelevant to a world where women were seeking an escape from male domination. Arthur Sainer, writing in the *Village Voice* (19 September 1974), panned the play as neither ancient nor modern, a naturalistic drama attempted but failed.

Then in 1986 Robert Wilson offered his interpretation of *Alcestis*. It was staged by the American Repertory Theater in Cambridge, Massachusetts, at Harvard's Loeb Theater in March 1986, and attracted instant critical attention. Heading the cast were Diane D'Aquila as Alcestis and Paul Rudd as her husband. Since Wilson's version would have been virtually unrecognizable to the play's Athenian author, it is necessary to set forth some of his innovations before turning to the show's critical reception.

Wilson was interested in the structure, movement, and lighting of the play. He began by discarding the text and running through the show in silence, then spent six days in designing the lighting effects; then and only then did he permit the actors' words to be heard. Even then Wilson was not satisfied: "I felt I was illustrating the text too much with the movements, that what I was doing with the actors was redundant. . . . I was working with a complete translation of Euripides' text then, but I felt I had to make it more my own. So that's what I did. Rewrote it myself."[23] The final production was only vaguely related to the drama Euripides offered in lieu of the expected satyr-play. Wilson's *Alcestis* was a series of scenes enacted before a set of primary images, marked by spectacular lighting, a set and lighting that played as much a part in the action as did the actors.

Downstage during the entire performance stood an eighteen-foot-high Cycladic figure. The main stage area was dominated by three primary images:

The first, a mountain range [inspired by Delphi's Mt. Parnassus] ran across the entire upstage width of the stage. . . . A river, the second main element, was sunk in the raked deck, and although the water was not visible, it could be heard as actors moved through it. And finally, between the river and the mountain stood three cypress trees. These trees appeared to burn at the end of scene two and were replaced by three Corinthian columns, which in turn were replaced by three industrial smokestacks.[24]

During the course of the performance, boulders broke off from the mountain and slowly rolled down its slopes and onto the stage. Boulders and actors moved while Jennifer Tipton's evocative lighting created a single day from sunrise to sunset, culminating in a green laser beam that finally cut a bright white, then red "eye of God" on the mountain. The main characters from Euripides' play were present, but an electronic chorus replaced any words from the ancient townspeople of Thessaly, while Death, wrapped in a shroud, appeared as a white bird.

Although the words of Wilson's chorus were proclaimed by an electronic voice, three women enacted various rituals onstage. Time sequences were illustrated by their costumes' changing from ancient to modern while they lamented for Alcestis with such ritual actions as hair-washing, planting, sacrificing, and forming a mournful procession. Finally, at the end, only the Cycladic fertility figure and the three women of the chorus survived.

Wilson added a prologue to the short play. Heiner Müller's *Description of a Picture*, which corresponded to the death and renewal theme of *Alcestis*, was staged first.[25] After *Alcestis*, Wilson offered a Japanese Kyogen, *The Birdcatcher in Hell*, as a short epilogue. Each story told of death and resurrection with the Bird of Death image uniting the three. Wilson's *Alcestis*, staged in the spring of 1986 by the American Repertory Theater in Cambridge, Massachusetts, became an event in theater history.

Critical acclaim was mixed. Each writer felt the power of Wilson's images, but each felt that too much had been lost, not enough gained: confusion mingled with admiration in their reviews. Elinor Fuchs, who assembled the "casebook" for *Performing Arts Journal*, tried to give a dispassionate statement of the play and Wilson's directorial decisions. She described what happened onstage during the 110-minute show, plus the intermission followed by the fifteen-minute epilogue, and identified what most marked Wilson's production as different:

The most important change that Wilson makes in Euripides' text is the elimination of the restorative ending. The Wilsonian world at the end of *Alcestis* is mysterious, frightening and uncertain. The lines of celebration have been omitted, and despite cues in the remaining text that Alcestis will be returned alive, Wilson regards the shrouded being who emerges from the underworld as a "fourth character" whose identity is a mystery.[26]

David Sterritt, writing in the *Christian Science Monitor* (21 March 1986), gave the most favorable review, proclaiming that all of *Alcestis* is "channeled into the best known Wilson trademark, a steady stream of dreamlike images that shift and merge at a glacial pace." Although Wilson's formality was less successful than might have been expected when applied to classical drama, nevertheless, Sterritt concluded, "even second-rate Wilson is exciting—e.g., white-winged Death, River Styx with glass coffin, and A.R.T. performers doing well."

Other critics were a little less generous. Kevin Kelly (*Boston Globe*, 14 March 1986) thought the play had an abstract splendor but remained humorless; it was but a series of mystically lighted stage pictures. His final verdict was mixed: although the play made no literal sense, it remained fascinating, stunning the vision and invading the mind—but still it failed because Wilson treated "the reality of death as myth." Furthermore, added Kelly, while the stagecraft was wonderful, there were many moments of confusion, which were not helped by Müller's prologue or the Kyogen epilogue. "For all of Robert Wilson's mix-and-match byplay, for all his sense of adventure, his Euripides is out to lunch." Mel Gussow, critic for the *New York Times* (21 March 1986), was the least satisfied. He had hoped at least for Andrei Serban's *Fragments of a Trilogy*, but found Wilson falling far short of Euripides. But while the play was not emotionally moving, Gussow stated, it was usually astonishing. He enumerated the images he especially liked: towering sarcophagi on one side of the stage; the moth-like Death with his huge wings; Heracles as a caveman. Stage pictures hold one's attention, and these remain in one's mind long after leaving the theater.

Alcestis' theme, death and return, remains foreign to a modern audience, and thus the play stays on the edges of the contemporary repertoire of Greek tragedy productions in today's theaters. On the one hand, if a director remembers that this text was Euripides' substitute for the traditional satyr play, then a comic interpretation might be offered. In this guise, the focus is upon Admetus, who honors hospitality but fails to realize the true implications of Apollo's offer, who is thus surprised when he feels acutely the loss of Alcestis and who only belatedly understands what her sacrifice truly means. But all ends well: the rowdy Heracles turns out to be a powerful guest, Admetus learns what the audience always knew, and the devoted wife is returned so that this couple might continue together to offer the best hospitality in Thessaly. This interpretation may be only tangential to

Euripides' theme, but does permit the play to bring an evening's enjoyment to a modern audience.

Another approach to this play was that taken by Robert Wilson, who by removing it to a surreal world of striking images allowed the ancient mystery of death and rebirth to remain. Many viewers resist this attempt to merge ancient mystery into a contemporary performance, and this resistance is not unreasonable. On the other hand, for the individual who can take delight in a series of strange yet beautiful images, who can seek a meaning in life's mysteries but not feel cheated if they remain unexplained, *Alcestis* in modern form offers a rich theatrical experience. Euripides' earliest extant play can exist in the modern theater either as a surrealistic interpretation of the liminal area of human life, or as a gently comic consideration of a man who must learn what death can mean.

EURIPIDES: *ORESTES*

A play that has had sudden appeal in these later years of the twentieth century is Euripides' *Orestes*. This bitter drama, written in 408 B.C., after which the playwright left his native city and retired to the court of the Macedonian king, reflects his despair and disappointment in Athenian society. Nothing in this tragedy offers any hope; the theme veers far away from the traditional myth, and when Apollo, arriving ex machina at the end, hands out the established roles to these atypical characters, no one can believe the deity brings a resolution. *Orestes*, then, reflects a society without guidance, where traditional values are sullied. To several contemporary directors, this situation seems to echo the modern American world, and hence they have turned to this dark tragedy as a reflection of the current social milieu.

Euripides' play might well be considered a psychological thriller, a play of intrigue, excitement, and comedy, but it has received little critical acclaim: classical scholars often dismiss it on various grounds, most notably because no figure can be admired, and few contemporary directors have considered it a viable text, perhaps because it is so seldom included on the lists of "greats" from antiquity. While it has been staged recently in Greece, productions in this country have been few indeed.

While the first production in English seems to have been that staged at Yale in 1926 to mark the school's 225th commencement, another fifty years passed before *Orestes* appeared in any venue that might be considered commercial. In 1968, Jan Kott staged a "hippie" version of the play at the Durham Theater at the University of California at Berkeley.[27] The text was chosen for its antiwar message: "Get Out of Troy, Now." To be sure the audience would understand that directive, the setting was Washington, and added were such innovations "as the Capitol going up in flames, and film clips of the Vietnam war and of antidraft demonstrations in Oakland."[28]

Orestes himself was portrayed as a hippie in red jeans, while the chorus, carrying placards reading "We're All Murderers," "Helen Is a Whore," and the repeated injunction "Get Out of Troy, Now," were costumed in hippie clothes and love beads.

Washington was chosen as the setting because, according to Kott, "it is appropriate to the madness and violence, both foreign and domestic, that is the theme of the play." He claimed *Orestes* was his favorite Greek play because it is "so appropriate to our times. . . . In this country, the problem of the violence of war is urgent." Critic Robert Windeler (*New York Times*, 17 February 1968) did not say whether he found the play's theme relevant or not, or whether the production was successful. To him the mere fact of an ancient play with a modern message was of sufficient interest to merit a special review.[29]

Twenty-five years later Charles L. Mee Jr. created a modern *Orestes* which played to mixed reviews in both San Diego and New York. In Mee's version the mental torment of Euripides' play was given literal expression when the action was set within an insane asylum; the characters are gathered there because, as Electra notes, "a certain homicidal rage runs in this family." Theme and plot line stay fairly close to the ancient text; such Euripidean lines remain in the script as Helen's unfeeling comment to Electra, "Still unmarried, a girl of your age." To update the classic, Mee amplified and augmented his original with ideas from various modern sources, genres, and ambiances: *Soap Opera Digest*, punk-rock costumes, cross-gender casting, and rusty metal all played a role in his *Orestes*.

For the San Diego production, director Robert Woodruff created, according to Sylvie Drake, "a hospital ward from hell," with bombed-out walls and rusted bedsprings.[30] In New York, under Tina Landau's direction, the show was staged at Penn Yards at 59th Street and 12th Avenue, where a collapsing pier on the Hudson river formed a "starkly beautiful" setting for this story of "civilization's moral decline."[31]

A program note for the performances in San Diego warned that "there are one and a half tons of scenery hanging above your head." Drake noted that there was nearly an equal weight of symbolism in the modern version. Under a huge ceiling sign proclaiming "WE ARE NOT IN DECLINE," an assault on contemporary morality took place, but for Drake too many fronts were attacked while any ritual sense of doom was sacrificed. Perhaps the caption line of the photo accompanying her review best sums up her reaction to this recent version: "Trendy points about political rectitude, dysfunctionality and America's skidding decline."

Mee's adaptation, despite its updating additions, clings very closely to the ancient play. Here, as in the original, avoiding blame is a major theme, and none of the characters is particularly appealing. Several nurses have been added to tend the asylum's patients, but as these serve as needed as a chorus, they are not really new creations. All Euripides' characters are present: Orestes, Electra, Pylades, Helen, Menelaus, even the Phrygian slave and Apollo—the latter as an adolescent who, in the New York production at least, was disposed of "in a way that's very site-specific."[32]

Overall the New York critics gave higher praise than did their West Coast counterparts—but, as we have seen, Greek drama does not play particularly well in California. Greg Evans, writing for *Daily Variety* (8 July 1993),. claimed the choice of set for Mee's *Orestes* was "nothing short of inspiration on the part of producer Anne Hamburger," director of En Garde Arts, who always mounted site-specific shows. Evans gives high marks to all the characters, but returned again to applaud the striking interconnection of ambiance and theme:

> But more impressive than any single characterization is an overall visual style that makes this two-hour, intermissionless comedy-drama [*sic*] a treat. The fall of the House of Atreus is played out against the 300-foot sagging steel sculpture that was once the Penn Yards pier, an apt metaphor for the societal breakdown and moral decay charted by Mee's play.

Tom Brazil, in an article titled "Making Theater in Unlikely Places" (*New York Times*, 27 June 1993), asserted that En Garde Arts "has taken care of" any doubts that the rusting piers of Penn Yards might have been too distant from the classic Greek theater. Here, especially, Anne Hamburger proved well that "old themes may seem new again and timeless" when existing architecture is used for a set and dusk as a curtain.

Orestes' story was popular in 1993. In addition to Mee's adaptation playing on both coasts and the continuing successful tour of *Les Atrides*, another modern version appeared in Los Angeles in April of that year. R. Jeffrey Cohen adapted and directed a play titled *Orestes—I Murdered My Mother*, a retelling that started from Euripides' text and then drew upon television news and interview shows to make the theme current. Reviewer T. H. McCulloh found the text strong but the acting, overall, rather weak. Writing in the *Los Angeles Times* (24 April 1993), he asserted that Cohen's message was clear when he "juxtaposes some recent parricides with a classic Greek one." The best performance in the production at the Burbage Theater was that of Soleil Moon Frye playing Electra who, McCulloh stated, "has the iron core and vocal sinew" to carry off the demands of the role. While it is possible that Joshua Miller and Stephen Cooper did not have the power to give Orestes and Pylades (respectively) sufficient "authority," we can note in their defense that in Euripides' version the two male leads are hardly heroic: they are bullies but not brave knights. Cohen's version has not yet (1994) been staged elsewhere.

In their critical comments about Mee's modern *Orestes*, all reviewers noted both the power and the relevance of the ancient myth. The decline of the House of Atreus into murder and madness emerged as a pertinent metaphor for contemporary America. This story of domestic violence, in

Euripides' *Orestes* of such violence run amok, rings true to an audience assaulted with daily television coverage of real-life examples of intrafamily war. The role of the deities in the later Greek versions of the legend faded in importance, often becoming merely an excuse for murder. Thus the absence of divine sanction for violent action renders the plays even more accessible to the American public of the late twentieth century. The myth of the House of Atreus has a disturbing relevancy for the nation as the end of the century draws near.

NOTES

1. D. Plugge lists seventy-five productions by college theater groups between 1882 and 1936 (see his charts 13–32); he lists the earliest at Notre Dame in 1883. Chapter 2 records the first (and unsuccessful) attempt to bring *Antigone* to the commercial theater in 1845.

2. Review headlines can catch the unwary reader: "Cornell's *Antigone* Interesting Switch on the Ancient Sophocles" (*Daily News*, 19 February 1946), "*Antigone.* A Neo-Greek Cornell" (*Herald Tribune*, 19 February 1946), "Katharine Cornell Acts in New Version of Sophocles' Great Play" (*Life*, 18 March 1946). Only within the body of the review does one learn that this is Lewis Galantiere's translation of Anouilh's version of Sophocles' play.

3. But the production did have political importance. When it was staged at the National Theater in Washington, DC, classics professor Frank Snowden and his students were unable to attend the performance because the theater did not admit blacks. Dr. Snowden wrote a letter to the *Washington Post*, which editorially agreed with his position. When Katharine Cornell learned of the situation, she apologized to Dr. Snowden and promised that she would not perform at the theater again until the whites-only policy was changed. Her stand, like that of Antigone, pointed out how a social policy was wrong. Cornell, unlike the Greek heroine, was successful: segregation ended at the National Theater. (This incident was described by Frank Snowden in his commencement address at the University of Maryland in June 1993. I thank Dr. Judy Hallett for calling it to my attention and for sending me a text of Dr. Snowden's speech.)

4. I noted above the difficulty of explaining *Medea*'s continued popularity, for to the casual observer her actions are less understandable than those of other women of ancient myth. But the recent attention paid to such deeds of fictional female violence as that portrayed in Adrian Lyne's film *Fatal Attraction* or to such actual female vengeance as the Lorena Bobbitt case (1993) or Susan Smith (1994) may offer some clue, albeit a rather frightening one.

5. A full discussion of this performance and of the Living Theatre may be read in Marianthe Colakis, *The Classics in the American Theater of the 1960s and Early 1970s* (Lanham, MD: 1993): 50–56.

6. One suspects that Sullivan was thinking of Anouilh's version here rather Sophocles' play, for the Greek ruler deserves and receives little sympathy in the ancient text. He suffers, and has often been considered "the tragic hero," but he brings his suffering upon himself by deliberate and self-determined choices.

7. This version noted by Gisela Casines in "Greater Miami," in *The Book Lover's Guide to Florida*, ed. Kevin M. McCarthy (Sarasota, FL: 1992): 248–249. Morisseau-Leroy "translated [Sophocles'] play into Creole, juxtaposed Greek religion with voodoo, and pointed to the similarities between Kreon and Duvalier." He was forced into exile in 1959 as a result of this act.

8. Richard L. Coe, writing in the *Washington Post* (18 November 1978), termed the performance both exciting and impressive. Director Walker considered Creon the lead figure, but Coe found the young actress portraying the title character to be the star.

9. A. R. Gurney's recent play, *Another Antigone*, sets the conflict within the academic arena, where student and professor contest their rights. The play has dramatic power, but the disputed issue lacks the significance of the original.

10. There was, for instance, a production in January 1967 at the Sheridan Square, starring Sima Gelbart as Antigone; the show closed after five performances. *Antigone* was a part of P. Roche's *The Sophoclon* by the Classic Stage Company in October 1981; see discussion in Chapter 7. In 1992, Charmed Life Productions, lacking sufficient funds to do Shakespeare in Los Angeles' Farnsworth Park, instead staged Sophocles' *Antigone*. Although their script was the Greek text, the directors wanted to re-create the political atmosphere of Anouilh's version. To this end they used Nazi props, banners, and the German national anthem, while a German youth passed out Nazi propaganda leaflets to the audience.

11. Other short-run productions include that in October 1988 by the Sidewalks of New York, a company devoted exclusively to the classics (opening after *Antigone* a staging of all three versions of the Electra story); that by Blind Parrot Productions of Chicago, which staged a Theban "trilogy" titled *Oedipus Requiem* in March 1989; followed in April 1989 (also in Chicago) by Stage Left Theatre's *Antigone*, a staging by Dennis McCullough that included "interviews on the street, a standup comic and a bar filled with foreign correspondents," according to Lawrence Bommer (*Chicago Tribune*, 28 April 1989).

12. Quoted by Mel Gussow, "The Living Theater Returns to Its Birthplace," *New York Times*, 15 January 1984.

13. Equally unrecognizable to any serious student of Greek tragedy was the 1992 staging on New York's Lower East Side by the Irondale Project, which attempted to connect *Antigone* with the art of clowns. Intending to echo ideas of Brecht and Joseph Campbell, director Jim Niesen cast Creon as a circus ringmaster and Antigone as a stubborn clown, thereby to show the play as "an allegory of public life in an age when politics have become show business." A pie in the face ended the clash between ruler and rebel, but the play ended with a stage piled high with plague-killed corpses. Reviewer Stephen Holden (*New York Times*, 16 February 1992) generously suggested that if the clown metaphor was accepted, other parallels fell into place.

14. Quotation taken from *Performing Arts* (February 1993) for A.C.T.'s production of *Antigone* (6). On the other hand, Perloff's analysis of Antigone as a young woman who must believe in the essential goodness of her family to be able to "survive the horrors of her childhood" is too modern to be attributed to the ancient text.

15. *New York Daily Mirror*, 2 April 1904. All further comments are drawn from the review of this anonymous critic.

16. So called by Dan Sullivan in his review "Sellar's 'Ajax'—More than Games," *Los Angeles Times*, 2 September 1986. All further quotations by Sullivan are from this review.

17. Cast included Aleta Mitchell (Athena), Charles Brown (Odysseus), Brent Jennings (Agamemnon), Ralph Marrero (Menelaus), Lauren Tom (Tecmessa), and Ben Halley Jr. (chorus leader and Messenger).

18. Howie Seago, quoted from an interview with Mike McIntyre, "The Vital Signer: Howie Seago of *Ajax*," *Washington Post*, 18 June 1986. Seago, a performing-arts instructor at the National Institute for the Deaf in Rochester, NY, thinks there are many roles for the deaf actor if a director has imagination: Othello, for instance, "a [black] foreigner in a strange land" could be interpreted as "a deaf person in the land of the hearing."

19. Marianne McDonald, *Ancient Sun, Modern Light. Greek Drama on the Modern Stage* (New York: 1992): 83. Her chapter on this play, "Peter Sellars' *Ajax*: The Obsolescence of Honor" (75–87), offers an excellent interpretation of both the ancient and modern texts. She believes the guiding question of the modern version is one that must be asked in a world lacking heroes: "In this version, we mourn Ajax's death, but can we afford his life?" (76). She concludes that we are to understand at the end of the play, whether Sophocles' or Auletta's, that "it is Ajax's unique truth that blasts the compromising mediocrity of an Odysseus into insignificance" (86). In the Sellars/Auletta staging, Ajax's burial at the end "is a celebration" to which Odysseus, "the political master, the culmination of Aristotle's *politikon zoon* ('political animal') is not invited" (87).

20. Playing at the Kennedy Center at the same time was a production of Herman Wouk's *The Caine Mutiny Court Martial*, directed by Charlton Heston. As Sylviane Gold pointed out in the *Wall Street Journal* (2 July 1986), Ajax and Queeg were indeed strange bedfellows to be "encamped" together, and two directors could not differ more than Heston and Sellars. But Gold noted that there is, after all, a strange similarity, too: both crazed military men "are out to retrieve their honor after being disgraced. . . . Both [are] victims of their own unstable personalities."

21. The play's plot is simple, its meaning deceptive. Apollo rewards Admetus with a gift: he can escape his day of death if he finds a substitute. The mortal accepts the god's offer quickly, then discovers it is not easy to find another to die for him. At last his wife, Alcestis, agrees to go to the grave. Just after her funeral Heracles arrives, learns the situation, and wrests the queen from the hands of Hades; Admetus regains his wife. Euripides offered *Alcestis* as the fourth play in his submissions for the City Dionysia in 438 B.C. Whether this play is to be considered comic or tragic in tone depends upon the critic reviewing it. I tend to think that its theme is too serious to be a genuine satyr play, but one cannot deny that King Admetus is rewarded for the *xenia* (hospitality) he extends to Heracles, and that Alcestis' restoration gives the play a "happy ending." For one interpretation, see my discussion in *Ambiguity and Self-Deception* (Frankfort am Main: 1991): chap. 1; for an opposing one, see Anne P. Burnett's analysis in *Catastrophe Survived: Euripides' Plays of Mixed Reversals* (Oxford: 1971): chap. 2.

22. Of these we might note that in 1922 the Bennett School of Applied Arts inaugurated its new Greek theater with a production of *Alcestis*, with Edith Wynne Matthison playing the title role, and that in 1938 the play was done at Sanders' Theater at Harvard, where so many of the Greek texts received their first airing on

this side of the Atlantic. *Variety's* critic (21 May 1938), signing simply "Norm," called the play, wherein Admetus is one "whom gods have fingered for death . . . a successful surprise." Elliott Norton also reviewed the Harvard production. Noting that the chorus is retired to the background so focus may be on character, he remarked that the play's theme is not easy for the modern mind, but offered an explanation: "In the days of great Greece's beautiful civilization, wives were chattel and only men were of major importance." He thought Michael Linenthal's Admetus tended to dissolve into foot-stamping petulance, but that the well-known actress and author Dorothy Sands playing Alcestis gave a strong performance. For some reason the short play was done in two acts.

23. Robert Wilson's comments are quoted from "The PAJ Casebook: Alcestis," *Performing Arts Journal* 10 (1986): 86–87, assembled with commentary by Elinor Fuchs. The "casebook" includes comments by all involved in this unusual production: the designers of the set, costumes, music, movement, lights, and audio environment, as well as the lead players and the authors of the accompanying pieces.

24. Quoted from Ronn Smith, "Wilson Weaves Classical Magic. *Alcestis* at ART," *Theatre Crafts* 20 (1986): 30.

25. Heiner Müller had been asked by Wilson to write an introductory piece for the Gluck opera *Alceste*, which Wilson was to produce for the Stuttgart Staatsoper; eventually he decided to use Müller's piece (in fragments) for the Cambridge production instead. Although Wilson and Müller did not consult with each other about their texts, Müller's short play matched Wilson's idea in both theme and image. The match was fortuitous, since Müller had written his single-sentence, thirteen-page script to describe a painting done by a student in Sophia.

26. *PAJ* 10 (1986): 82. One might have named other equally significant changes. Most commentators focused upon those.

27. Jan Kott is well known for his book *Eating the Gods*; in theater he attracted attention by staging in London an all-male production of *As You Like It*.

28. Information on this production is from Robert Windeler's review in the *New York Times* (17 February 1968).

29. In the summer of 1970 Euripides' bitter tale opened in New York City in a version by O. Rozakis, staged at the Cubiculo by R. Link. Three years later, in February 1973, the Playwrights Workshop Club played the same version in Bastiano's Studio. Both had short runs that escaped critical attention.

30. Sylvie Drake, "A Wildly Uneven *Orestes* at Mandell Weiss Theatre," *Los Angeles Times*, 14 March 1992; all further quotations by Drake are from this review. A virtually verbatim text also appeared in the *Times* on 13 March, under the title "*Orestes* Message Writ in Capital Letters."

31. Thus did Aileen Jacobson comment on the production in New York City in the summer of 1993, in her review "In a State, on a Set, of Decline," *Newsday*, 2 July 1993.

32. So Jacobson asserts without further revelation; the setting permitted several possibilities. In San Diego, the ex machina Apollo was a televised child.

9

Occasional Productions: Greek Tragedies Rarely Brought to the Boards

As we have noted, the basic repertoire of Greek tragedies granted a chorus for the commercial theater in the United States is rather small. Of the thirty-two extant tragic dramas, only about a dozen have been deemed worthy of modern productions outside of an academic setting. Euripides' powerful *Heracles*, for example, has been performed only once, and that simply a reading (1959). His *Suppliant Women* was staged at Stanford in 1993 and then moved to a commercial venue, but this was a unique event. *Hecuba* also has been mounted rarely; the most recent production was in 1987, although it is in the 1994–1995 schedule of the American Conservatory Theater in San Francisco. Sophocles' *Women of Trachis* played but once (June 1960), and that in Ezra Pound's version; neither *Suppliant Women* nor *Seven against Thebes* by Aeschylus has been staged. Directors have chosen but few of Euripides' eighteen extant dramas; the list of those not produced is only slightly shorter than the list of those chosen.[1]

Several stagings of Greek tragedies reflect a director's dream more than they do contemporary society, but nevertheless they have garnered attention from the drama critics. In this chapter I consider those single plays that still remain vibrant when produced, but that are less indicative of current issues, texts that are staged *ars gratia artis* rather than to make a social statement. Since a show must still turn a box office profit, however, the choice to offer a Greek tragedy must rest ultimately upon the faith of both director and producer in the power of the classical text. Such texts include Aeschylus' *Prometheus Bound*, Sophocles' *Philoctetes* and *Women of Trachis*, and Euripides' *Hecuba* and *Suppliant Women*. Upon these, then, my discussion here is based.

AESCHYLUS: *PROMETHEUS BOUND*

Of all the "hero" plays that are still revived with some frequency on the modern stage, *Prometheus Bound* is the most static, and thus it is surprising that this one piece of an Aeschylean trilogy[2] is still in the repertoire. Virtually all of the action in the play takes place in the words of the Titan and those who visit him: *Prometheus Bound* is a play of verbal action. But it is also a play with a message that continues to inspire: the rebel who stands against the tyrant, even when he knows that his punishment for so doing is assured, still commands attention. We may wonder if this was Aeschylus' intent: was he rather giving a warning against tyranny, an argument against a new ruler's preference for violence over negotiation; in short, was he writing a political play, not a call for rebellion? The ancient dramatist's reasons are lost in time, but there is no question that modern stagings believe we are to see in Prometheus' bold stand a model for action: to dare the better deed and to suffer for one's actions is an ideal instilled in modern thought. Prometheus and Antigone are not too far apart in post-classical interpretations of their characterizations.

During the spring of 1930, several performances of *Prometheus Bound* were staged in New York City as benefits for its opening at the festival to be held at the Theater at Delphi in May of that year.[3] While *Prometheus Bound* was part of the spring season at the University of California at Berkeley in 1956, it was twenty-seven years after the Delphic festival that this play opened in New York City. The 1957 production was a revival of the earlier text, but performed only in English, not modern Greek. Blanche Yurka, quite the darling of the American stage at that time, and Clarence Derwent played the same roles they had created for Delphi, and the costumes were those designed by Eva Sikelianos. James Elliott, a Broadway producer of Greek descent, directed the performance. In 1964, the Group of Ancient Drama performed *Prometheus Bound* at the East River Amphitheater.[4] None of these performances attracted much critical attention. Greek drama languished in the commercial theaters of America during the 1950s, and in the early years of the next decade Aeschylus' static and intellectual play held little appeal.

Then in 1967 Yale University's Drama School staged a production of *Prometheus Bound* in a version created by Robert Lowell, "a very free redaction of Aeschylus' difficult original," according to Walter Kerr (*New York Times*, 11 June 1967; his second review of this play), wherein Lowell "attempted to find in its ancient iconography a thundercloud of overtones that will be as up to the minute as 'God Is Dead.'" While the text was effective, the production was successful because of the fine quality of the acting: Irene Worth as Io, a victim of the new God, and Kenneth Haigh as the Titan who had befriended man in opposition to God both gave memorable performances.

The first half of the play (which had been divided into two acts broken by an intermission) was powerful. There Io, ravaged by a deity both "obscene and real," became through the acting skill of Irene Worth a figure both alive and trapped in myth. Kerr waxed eloquent in his praise of Irene Worth's portrayal of Io. "It is a role," he stated, "that Miss Worth cannot conceivably have expected to play in her time, any more than we can have honestly hoped to see it played in ours." The play would have lacked power without her extraordinary interpretation, he claimed, for "mythological materials are stiff icons to us, wrought of ancient and rusty iron rather than vulnerable flesh," but because of Worth's mesmerizing acting ability, the play had a fierce and modern emotion. Walter Kerr found her acting so powerful that he accorded her two columns of praise.

Kenneth Haigh was equally effective. His talent enabled him to bring life and fire to long, time-sweeping passages of poetry. In the second act, however, critic Kerr found that even Haigh's extraordinary ability could not carry his audience into the Titan's tormented vision: "[The Titan's view] goes on far beyond our capacity to absorb pyramiding images by ear. . . . We are finally bowed under the weight of words that are variations rather than progressions."

The ending Lowell provided for his version did not match the Aeschylean finale. Rather than a final storm, Prometheus "anticipates Olympian twilight" and thus, according to Kerr, the drama faded into an ending rather than into glorious resistance. Overall, however, he deemed the fine-quality acting made the production a success.

Elenore Lester, also writing in the *New York Times* (21 May 1967), was equally impressed. Titling her review (really an interview with author Lowell and director Jonathan Miller) "Prometheus: Hero for Our Time," Lester stated firmly that the "play was a smashing success and that it couldn't possibly make it—on Broadway or off." All agreed that the play's message was important, and that the impossibility of putting such a show on Broadway indicated the lack of intellectual rigor of that venue, not the weakness of the ancient play.[5]

Lester saw in the play what modern audiences tend to see: Prometheus offers "man's cry of pain in a universe ruled by a 'radiant malignant mind.' . . . [He is] an existentialist . . . a humanist and political radical." It was Walter Kerr, however, who seemed to understand the play's political meaning, for he summed it up thusly: "Suddenly we are made intimates . . . of an actual Zeus, bleak, blackened, and in some ways turned pathetic by the coarseness of his absolute authority." Not once did he mention Prometheus as a rebel against tyranny; for him, the play was a tract illustrating the "ravaging [that] comes from any dealing with God."

In the winter of 1985, Richard Schechner returned to the ancient theme for a new offering titled *The Prometheus Project*. In this version, Prometheus has unwittingly contributed to the creation of the atomic bomb, while Io is shown as the prototype of the sexually abused woman. Walter Goodman, writing in the *New York Times* (27 December 1985), found that the production, subtitled "Four Movements and a Coda," was effective in evoking mood, but weak when words were added to the action.

The performance featured many slides of the destruction of Hiroshima watched by a man in a leather jacket, X-rated film clips, a lascivious dance by the show's leading female, and two sequences of repetitive actions, one a dance to remind the audience of Io's running and the other a lengthy binding of Prometheus. The myth was recited at the play's close, enhanced with banal phrases intended to sound large, e.g., "It is the nursery of life itself that is being poisoned."

Goodman's review pointed out what must have been the failing of this modern version: the attempt to link Hiroshima's bombing and sexual abuse. While both are evils, they are not truly equal ones; pornography, rape, and the dropping of an atom bomb are too different to be equated. In Aeschylus' play, both Prometheus and Io are victims of Zeus' overweening power, his brutality or his lack of concern in his interactions with those around him. In Schechner's *Prometheus Project*, there was no common abuser, unless one replaced Zeus with modern society itself. Such a large identification, if intended, would have needed to be explicitly stated.

Prometheus Bound has been twice performed in another venue as well. Although my study concentrates only on Greek tragedies performed in commercial theaters, it seems appropriate at least to mention one of the longest-running festivals of Greek drama production in this country, one that is closer in its setting than any other to the theater of Dionysus in fifth-century B.C. Athens.[6] In Utah, the Classical Greek Theatre Festival has been staging tragedies in Salt Lake City for nearly twenty-five years and draws its cast and crew both from the academy (University of Utah) and the community at large, while it occasionally imports professional players to its ranks. The festival began in 1971 with a production of *Prometheus Bound*; since then the list of plays performed is large, including, among others, *Agamemnon, Philoctetes, Alcestis, Hippolytus, Iphigeneia at Tauris, Helen, Bacchae,* and *Trojan Women*, in addition to the three plays of the "Theban trilogy" as well as a second staging of *Prometheus*. The company plays in Salt Lake in the late summer, then tours Utah and neighboring areas in the following months.

This troupe is both adventurous in interpretation yet conservative in its adherence to the classical tradition. The performances begin early in the morning at a circular clearing on a hillside; the audience sits on the grassy slopes to watch the simply mounted productions. This playing area is peculiarly appropriate: "This is the Place Amphitheatre" is located on what was once an Indian holy spot and thus offers a unique sense of continuity to festival performances. The setting also allows modern audiences to recapture the temporal aspect of the ancient festivals. Tragedies began in the dark light of early morning and reached their climax in broad daylight.

Here, too, the rays of the sun gradually fill the orchestra, reinforcing what we today, familiar with artificially lighted playhouses and the dark endings of Shakespearean tragedies, tend to forget: the moment of truth in Greek tragedy was revealed in brilliant sunlight.[7] In the late Utah summer, the American audience has the rare opportunity to see a Greek tragedy expertly done in a natural setting that vividly recalls the theaters of Greece.

SOPHOCLES: *PHILOCTETES*

The earliest commercial production of Sophocles' late and difficult play seems to have been in the winter of 1959 when the American National Theatre and Academy (ANTA) offered it as part of their matinee series at the Theatre de Lys. It was staged twice: first with Sophocles' text, then in Gide's adaptation.

The idea was "an amusing stunt," asserted John Martin, writing in the *New York Times* (14 January 1959). The first is "one of the noblest of dramas," the second a "witty counterpoint on the same theme." Stephen Porter directed the afternoon's productions, and the same actors played the corresponding roles in both plays; Ellis Rabb played the lead part, Ray MacDonnell portrayed Odysseus, and Claude Woolman acted the role of Neoptolemus. This consistency allowed the changes to be appreciated, while the enthusiasm each actor brought to his role made the performance worthwhile.

As Martin noted, Gide's work was primarily a text, not a script, and in this presentation, Sophocles' play too, a work of "pure theater," became almost as literary as Gide's. Nevertheless Martin had praise for the venture and its result. What he missed, oddly enough, was the sense of ritual that is usually accorded these ancient plays; Porter had emphasized the "realistic values" of the scripts. Nevertheless, since these are works that are seldom, if ever seen, Martin asserted, it is a "privilege all around" to see such grand pieces in performance.

A *Philoktetes* written by George M. Ross was put on as an "experimental" weekend production at the One Sheridan Square Theatre in April 1961. Arthur Gelb (*New York Times*, 25 April 1961) compared the play to Jack Richardson's *The Prodigal*, as both plays are "slanted, contemporary re-examination[s] of a classical Greek theme." Ross' modern version retains an unchanged cast but lacks a chorus. The absence of physical action, onstage or off, was not altered; the play is mainly talk. The theme, "the struggle for power among three vital and disparate men," also remains constant, although the modern Neoptolemus believes neither in the war nor the power of Philoctetes' bow. Greek legend translated into modern terms has ironic possibilities, and these seemed to underlie Ross's decision to return to the ancient theme. Thus he can have the exchange quoted by Gelb: "What will happen, Neoptolemus asks Odysseus, if the Trojans, when threatened with the bow, don't believe it can kill 10,000 men with one arrow. 'Then we will kill 10,000 men with one arrow' is Odysseus' implacable answer."

Philoctetes by Sophocles has remained outside the standard repertoire of Greek tragedies staged in America,[8] but it was given at least one spectacular production, in the summer of 1964, when the Group of Ancient Drama staged the play at the East River Park Amphitheatre, using a translation by Robert Torrance and under the able direction of Anthony Keller. "With this performance," writes Albert Ashforth in the *New York Times* (19 August 1964), "the Group of Ancient Drama . . . has made a substantial step toward the establishment of a solid repertory of Greek classics."

Ashforth begins his review by stating, "Neither human nature nor the dilemmas of mankind have changed very much in the last 23 centuries." While this observation has certainly become the cliché for describing Greek drama when performed, it is noteworthy that the critic found it to be true about this particular play. *Philoctetes* might be considered Sophocles' most Euripidean, and hence most bitter, text, for its action is based upon deceit and the abuse of men's better emotions. Its message of political expediency makes it seem to echo so accurately the issues of the modern world.

Ashforth enjoyed the ambiance of this production: a starless sky and the "occasional sound of a ship's horn from the river" added to the evening's performance. He did not, perhaps, fully understand the play's meaning, since he saw its action "chiefly concerned with [Odysseus'] efforts to wrest the magic bow of Heracles away from Philoctetes"; the text makes it clear that both bow *and man* must be persuaded to return to Troy, to assist the very men who had put Philoctetes into exile some nine years previously. This critic determined that all three characters were vigorously acted, and gave the staging high praise. We may overlook the (unintentional?) irony of his rather inappropriate final remark: "But it is Richard Kuss as Philoctetes who walked off with most of the acting honors."

Julius Novick, writing in the *Village Voice* the following week (27 August 1964), also remarked upon the modern relevance of this play, noting that with its myth suffused by realpolitik, *Philoctetes* is perhaps better suited than any other surviving Greek play for a modern, realistically detailed production. Novick wondered why this play had no tradition of performance in English and suggested two possibilities: it needs either a stately ritualistic style or one that seeks immediacy by modern theatrical conventions. To his mind, however, the production by the Group of Ancient Drama was not successful because it failed to be faithful to either style. He found nothing to praise in the modern version: directing, acting, music, and dance of the chorus all received Novick's ire. The only aspect he could enjoy about the evening at the East River Amphitheatre was the ambiance: a pleasant summer evening and "the occasional relief afforded by an airplane overhead or the hooting of a tugboat horn on the river." Novick recognized the possibilities inherent in Sophocles' play, and was disappointed not to find these well presented.

The social issues of *Philoctetes* might indeed have relevance to the modern world, i.e., what to do with those members of society whose illness or infirmities annoy those around them: how are those with AIDS to be treated; where should the aged be placed? But the play has not attracted contemporary directors, either because there are only three characters and their speeches are long, or they have not understood the significance of Sophocles' text for a modern audience. I predict, however, that with its issues defined as above, this play will be offered more frequently in the last years of the twentieth century.

What of those ancient texts that have seldom been granted modern staging? The leading role of the chorus might explain why Aeschylus' *Seven Against Thebes or Suppliants* has been neglected, while the obscure myth gives a reason for leaving Euripides' *Children of Heracles* on the shelf. The neglect of the latter playwright's *Suppliants*, *Andromache*, or *Phoenician Women* is less easily explained, although again the lack of action and less familiar versions of well-known myths offer some clues. But the fact that Euripides' *Ion*, *Helen*, and *Heracles*, or Sophocles' *Women of Trachis* have been rarely if ever performed defies easy explanation. *Ion* is filled with exciting action based on mistaken identity, while the hero's devotion to his deity is an accessible idea. Helen of Sparta, or more commonly "of Troy," is the most famous woman from the ancient world; even if Euripides' play treats an alternative version of her myth, her fame and beauty so transcend time that a simple program note could explain the Egyptian setting. Nor do the humor and suspense of this light tragedy mask its serious considerations: what is the basis of knowledge? How can one determine truth versus illusion?[9] Heracles, the hero hated and maddened by Hera, but who in Euripides' drama takes responsibility for the hell he himself creates, offers a paradigm that is worthy of emulation. The more common version of this hero's myth, that told by Sophocles in his *Women of Trachis*, might at first glance seem foreign to the modern psyche, but Deianeira's doomed attempt to save her marriage could arouse pity and fear in any modern viewer.

Perhaps these plays, despite their psychological significance, have not been selected by contemporary directors simply because they are not familiar; they are not the ones commonly read in schools. When a Greek play is chosen for production, the director and his dramaturge face the familiar problems we have already seen: a text that even in the most current translation is still not common speech, fairly static onstage action, that ever-present chorus, and the traditional audience expectation that it is more tedious to sit through a Greek classic than a new musical. Thus to have to explain at length the play's story line as well as arouse audience interest in an unfamiliar ancient text might seem a task too arduous to undertake. To make a statement via a familiar Greek text is easier than to do this through a lesser known drama. We can only hope that as the popularity of Greek tragedy increases there will be directors who dare to stage *Ion, Helen, Heracles,* and *Women of Trachis.* Since it is within recent years that *Ajax, Alcestis,* and, most surprisingly, *Persians* have been brought to the boards, perhaps there is hope for the heretofore neglected scripts.

SOPHOCLES: *WOMEN OF TRACHIS*

Women of Trachis has been staged once in the commercial theater, in Ezra Pound's version and sharing the bill with an avant-garde one-act titled *The Marrying Maiden.* In June 1960, in an evening of drama titled "The Theatre of Chance," Judith Malina combined the very new and the very old at the Living Theatre Repertory; Malina directed *The Marrying Maiden,* Julian Beck, *Women of Trachis.* Just why these two scripts were offered together is not clear. Brooks Atkinson (*New York Times,* 23 June 1960) declared that the *first play meant nothing, despite Malina's profes*sional directing and the attempt of all involved "to make it seem like something that would be intelligible to a theatre-goer who had never learned any language." Of Pound's Sophocles Atkinson said little. He found it conventional, poor in language, but well acted in "the traditional style of classical acting" by Judith Malina. Without further knowledge of Jackson MacLow's ephemeral text we cannot know why it was linked to the story of Heracles' death at the hands of his wife, but perhaps a clue lies in the title of the evening's bill. The robe sent by Deianeira (called by Pound Daysair) was not intended as a deadly gift: the queen believed the Centaur's potion to be a love philtre, not a fiery poison. Chance ruled the fate of these two figures of ancient myth, for neither could know that Heracles' arrows, poisoned by the Lernaean Hydra's blood, would many years later indirectly cause the hero's death.[10]

EURIPIDES: *ION*

Another play holding limited billing on the commercial boards is Euripides' *Ion.* This action-packed play should appeal to the modern audience: the exposed babe found and reared, then reunited at last to his proper home and destiny. Perhaps because it is similar to more contemporary texts and has a "happy ending," directors wishing to do Greek tragedy find it less appealing; they want their show to arouse truly tragic emotions. *Ion,* like *Helen* and *Iphigeneia at Tauris,* is often described as a "romance," a "tragi-comedy," or even a "melodrama," and as such does not fit the bill for those wishing to do an ancient drama. Thus *Ion* has been seen only in two readings, both in 1954. At the first, it was linked to Eliot's *The Confidential*

Clerk in a reading done by "Chapter One," the New York chapter of the American National Theatre and Academy (29 March). The second was a benefit held for ANTA in Westport, Connecticut (24 May), notable for starring Clarence Derwent as Xuthus, Blanche Yurka as both Pythia and Athena, and Stuart Vaughan in the title role.

A version of the story had been offered as early as 1881 by Mary Anderson at the Fifth-Avenue Theatre, but the play was a complete reworking of Euripides' text by a playwright almost forgotten one hundred years ago, surely forgotten today, Sir Thomas Noon Talfourd. The reviewer of the *New York Times* (4 January 1881) describes Miss Anderson's "revivals" at some length. The actress offered two shows in repertory during her winter engagement, but was well known for her portrayals in other long-neglected plays.[11] According to this critic, the modern *Ion*, a play "looked forward to with uncommon interest, for [it] is unknown to the present generation of theatre-goers," was more true to the spirit of Greek tragedy than to Euripides' drama.

But it seems to us remarkable that a Greek tragic poet should have produced in his *Ion* a play which is a melodrama in the modern sense of the term; while the spirit and purpose of the modern work are tragic in a truly Greek sense. Euripides's play is one of plot and situations, and deals wholly with the relations between Ion and his royal parents; Talfourd's play . . . pictures Ion as an instrument of fate, destined to inevitable death and meeting death with stoical resignation. The Greek play ends happily, in the manner of our melodrama; the English play comes to a tragic and pathetic close.

Here the reviewer's expectations of tragedy are more interesting than the performance itself; conventional beliefs have become the standard by which a Greek play is judged—whatever the reality of the ancient text. One final note on this performance is that Mary Anderson herself played Ion in an "astonishing" metamorphosis into the manliness of the temple youth.

EURIPIDES: *HECUBA*

For the 1994–1995 season the American Conservatory Theater in San Francisco has Euripides' *Hecuba* on the schedule.[12] Director Carey Perloff believes it is no accident that Greek drama is now more than ever appearing on the contemporary stage, for directors find in the ancient texts ways to explain crucial issues of the modern world: political turmoil, the role of women in a patriarchal society, the loss of spirituality, and the moral ambiguity in both politics and society.[13] *Hecuba*, she declares, is about a defiant woman "who takes on the prevailing political establishment to regain or reassert the dignity of [her] own family and [her] own individuality." Hecuba shares this theme with Antigone, declares Perloff, only the latter is young, the queen of Troy old.

To date the only performance in America,[14] however, was one that used the text to assert a strident political message. In the winter of 1987, the Powerhouse Theater of Santa Monica presented the play with a Middle Eastern twist. Director Lamis Khalaf stated in a program note her intent in this updated version of Euripides' play:

Suppose that the Greeks are Israelis, that the Trojans are Palestinians, that the Thracians are one of the clashing political factions in Lebanon. . . . Suppose that the gods are the super powers (Europe—early in the century, the United States and the Soviet Union—now). . . . Now watch and hear the story that Euripides tells, the story of HECUBA.

Khalaf did not alter the text, but tried to alter audience understanding of ancient Greek ideas. She admitted that by aligning the Trojans with the Palestinians, the people of her heritage, she may herself have fallen victim to unintended support of terrorist activities. "I am not advocating terrorism," she asserted, "but when people are driven to the edge, they may turn to violence." So Hecuba's actions are understandable within Khalaf's interpretation of the play. Euripides had portrayed her as a woman driven to violence by the overwhelming wrongs done to her; when Hecuba cannot win by reason, she stoops to an act that perpetuates the cycle of violence she hated and wished to end. Euripides' skill lay in keeping audience sympathy with the ruined queen.

Some theater critics approved of Khalaf's modern version. Jackie Horwitz proclaimed the updating brilliant. In telling the story for her readers, Horwitz wrote (*Santa Monica Evening Outlook*, 16 January 1987) that Hecuba realized she "had become a victim of a senseless war whose senselessness caused men with power to become coldly pragmatic and propelled by narrow self-interest," and thus could only sink to a bloody act of revenge. Horwitz continued by praising this production as "superb in every way," and she singled out each actor for lauded recognition. Susan Nazami as Hecuba was especially fine, in Horwitz's opinion; her "bent posture and tortured face screamed out the burden of her tragedy."

Sylvie Drake also found much to praise here, although her words were somewhat qualified. The conception was well-thought out, Drake declared (*Los Angeles Times*, 13 January 1987), and Khalaf almost made the whole process work. Her political views served an artistic purpose: Hecuba "is a symbol of the dispossessed anywhere, crushed by warring defenders of territories, while the silent superpowers look on." It worked better in concept than in actuality, according to Drake, who found the acting tepid, with the male figures being particularly weak.

The chorus of Trojan women also lacked power in Drake's opinion, with perhaps too much "local color" and not enough evocation of the ancient tragedy. Nevertheless, this critic's summation was that the play's closing image was "a visual assault" whose impact made the show worth seeing:

"all of the participants in this internecine tapestry of political mischief-making helplessly strung out on a twisting cordon of shroud the color of fresh blood."

No show pleases everyone, and Richard Stayton found nothing to like. In his review in the *Los Angeles Herald Examiner* (14 January 1987), titled "New Twist Turns *Hecuba* into a Heck of a Mess," Stayton railed against the writhing that he thought was not just overdone but excessive. He found the symbolism offensive; he mocked Khalaf's suppositions: "Suppose that these noble sentiments add up to staged boredom. Suppose that correct political attitudes don't necessarily equal good theater. Suppose [the director] has trouble distinguishing between psychodrama, the tragic-in-life and the tragic on stage." Whether or not one approves of such one-to-one symbolism as Khalaf introduced into her *Hecuba*, the attempt should be recognized, for it is yet another way of showing how the message of the ancient dramas has vitality, although perhaps a more subtle presentation would have had a more powerful effect. Euripides' play is worthy of staging, whether or not it is updated, as an example of the effects of political violence upon good people. Euripides doubted Sophocles' contention that under stress human action becomes brave and noble; he posited as more valid the idea that when pushed to the limit men and women pursue the baser path. But the poet did recognize shining exceptions. Thus within the same few years as writing *Hecuba* Euripides penned his *Heracles*.

EURIPIDES: *HERACLES*

The penultimate "single" performance play tells the story of the most popular hero of ancient Greece, Heracles. This great figure possesses a full gamut of characterizations in extant Greek drama, with roles in tragedy, comedy, and satyr play (or its fourth-place substitute). In recompense for Admetus' kindness Heracles rescues Alcestis literally from the tomb in Euripides' drama titled from the saved (and saving queen). In Aristophanes' late comedy *Frogs*, Dionysus dons the garb of Heracles when he descends to the Realm of the Dead, where he is greeted with anger or joy by the area's various denizens. As we have seen, the hero appears in his final moments in Sophocles' *Women of Trachis*, where his wife innocently causes her husband's death. Deified, he enters ex machina to bring resolution to *Philoctetes*, ordering the title character, as inheritor of the great bow, to return to Troy to win victory for the Greeks, healing and honor for himself.

Euripides' version of Heracles' legend is the most tragic, for the playwright placed the hero's madness immediately after he completed his famous labors. In *Heracles*, Hera drives mad her husband's bastard son, and in his unconscious frenzy he slays his wife and several children.[15] Awakening to realize what he has wrought, Heracles must choose to live with the terrible truth and to accept responsibility for actions done within the grip of divine anger.

Despite the power of this unusual version of the myth, I can find record of only one production of this drama in what may only loosely be termed a commercial venue. On 20 February 1959, a reading was done in William Arrowsmith's translation by the group known as Qwirk Productions.[16]

For the most part the lines were delivered well, according to Michael Smith, who reviewed the performance in the *Village Voice* (25 February 1959). He found that about two-thirds of the production was alive and gripping, that James Noble's Heracles had a quiet strength, and that Geraldine Lust's direction made the evening rewarding in spite of certain "problems." The problems to which Smith referred lay (in his opinion) in the very text itself: "Then the actors seemed to realize—correctly—that this is not a very good play. . . . As in *J.B.* the suffering is motivated solely on a cosmic plane and simple reiteration of the fact that men get the short end of the stick is not very interesting." Smith claimed that Euripides' play fails because there is no interaction of man and fate. He failed to understand that the hero was indeed interacting with the destiny designed for him, that when he took responsibility for actions done while mad and chose to go on living, he had made a bold statement in the face of cosmic suffering.

But we have no idea how Euripides' play might have fared in more recent years, for the 1959 Qwirk production stands alone. On the other hand, the misuse of power by modern man was examined several years later by Archibald MacLeish in his play titled *Herakles*. In the early 1960s new military technology was disturbing many American citizens, and their fears and concerns were given expression by contemporary playwrights turning to ancient legends to make their message meaningful. Whether it was Heracles recast as a nuclear scientist or Odysseus portrayed as a man without scruples, the playwrights focused upon the moral question of the ability to act versus the right to do so. Sophocles portrayed Odysseus as the word-turning politician so dangerous in the Athenian democracy in the closing years of the fifth century B.C. and the Peloponnesian War. MacLeish created his figure appropriate to the early years of the 1960s.

Archibald MacLeish's *Herakles* was performed in 1965 in Ann Arbor by the University of Michigan's Repertory Company, starring Rosemary Harris as Megara and Sidney Walker as the nuclear scientist. Although this was a university production, reviews of the play ran in numerous magazines and newspapers, from *Variety* and *Life* to the *New York Times Book Review* and the *Christian Science Monitor*. This interest rested both on the fame of MacLeish himself and the desire of the critics (and hence their public) to see the ancient stories performed, whether in their original form or in a modern retelling. Interestingly enough, most of the critics did not like MacLeish's script, claiming preference for Euripides' text, even though the latter is not performed.

Tom Prideaux of *Life* (3 December 1965) proclaimed that the modern play was weak, but that "Euripides' play is suspenseful and tragic." The reviewer of *Variety* (10 November 1965) complained that MacLeish's play was too complex to play well, so that despite Harris' superlative performance as Megara the show was not successful. Only Richard Cattani, writing in the *Christian Science Monitor* (13 November 1965), praised both the performance and the play: "Heracles presses us to consider the values of decency and family life in an affluent and atomic age where labors of Heraclean magnitude can so easily entice us to feats of mock-godly grandeur."[17]

EURIPIDES: *SUPPLIANT WOMEN*

In the winter of 1993, Rush Rehm directed a production of Euripides' *Suppliant Women* at Stanford University, and the show was brought to Washington during the summer as part of the "Democracy 2000" celebration. This play, performed at the City Dionysia in Athens in 423 B.C., takes its name from the chorus, and its theme from the Theban cycle. The women of Thebes plead the same case as Antigone does in her play: they beg Creon to let their sons be buried, sons who died in the battle when Polyneices attacked Eteocles at the seven gates of Thebes. When Creon remains adamant, they address their pleas to Theseus, king of Athens. He is finally touched by the passionate appeal of Aethra and orders the dead to be honored. Thus the women, unlike Antigone, achieve their purpose and live.

Rehm selected this play for the very reason that it had never been performed in this country, and because it, like so many Greek tragedies, uses women as the moral force to illustrate a society's conscience. In a preshow interview with Judith Green (*San Jose Mercury News*, 14 February 1993), Rehm described his understanding of Euripides' text:

Suppliant Women deals with the exercise of conscience in a system wherein the majority rules. . . . [The women] are not going on an odyssey of discovery, like Oedipus. . . . Their desire is human and universal: the dead deserve burial. One of the first signs of civilization is that people took care of their dead. It's an essential defining thing about a domestic community.

The performance, done as a single eighty-five-minute piece in a translation by Stephen Scully and Rosanna Warren, used a chorus of eight women in the title role. Masks were used to illustrate the antiquity of the play, and constantly changing projected slides formed a backdrop that set the play both in modern times and timelessness. Finally, the ritual movements of supplication, a traditional and essential aspect of Greek life, defined the choreography of the women.

Reviews of the performance were mostly laudatory. Judith Green, after seeing the performance, asserted it deserved kudos. While she spent much of her review (*San Jose Mercury News*, 20 February 1993) describing the play itself and technical aspects of the production, she gave strong approbation to both the professional actors playing the key roles and the Stanford students portraying the suppliants and the lesser characters. Robert Hurwitt, writing in the *San Francisco Examiner* (19 February 1993), praised it as a striking presentation, acclaiming especially the translation, set, music, and stunning staging of Evadne's suicide. He was less pleased with the "undulating choreography" and the final filmed image of Athena, which he found at odds with the fine acting of the show's leading characters, whose style underlined the emotional quality of their words. Hurwitt expressed no surprise that the show is seldom performed, for he found it, despite the fine presentation, too static to be fully enjoyable.

Steven Winn, however, had no reservations: Euripides' tragedy was reborn through the spectacle and ritual that Rehm created for the production. Writing in the *San Francisco Chronicle* (18 February 1993), Winn praised all aspects of the performance: direction, acting, set, and music earned carefully considered approval. L. Peter Callender as Adrastos gave, in Winn's opinion, the show's finest performance, but he had high praise as well for Kathleen Turco-Lyon's Aethra (and Evadne) and Mark Capri's Theseus. Winn, like Hurwitt, found Rehm's frontal blocking of the main characters assertive and evocative, and like Hurwitt again, he found Evadne's suicide an effective "knockout visual punch." On the other hand, he thought the final filming of Athena ex machina an extraordinary and powerful image. Winn summed up, "*Suppliant Women* musters theatricality to match Euripides' woeful tragedy about the cost of war." The play is seldom staged, although it shares the message of both *Antigone* and *Trojan Woman*.[18] Rush Rehm is to be applauded for bringing this too-long neglected Euripidean tragedy to the boards.

These neglected plays run the full gamut of dramatic and social interpretations. *Hecuba*, *Suppliant Women*, and, to a lesser extent, *Prometheus Bound* offer a political message pertinent to contemporary society. *Women of Trachis* and *Philoctetes* portray individuals trying to achieve a personal or social goal. In the former Deianeira fails in her intent; in the latter Neoptolemus can win only with the aid of Heracles ex machina. In *Heracles*, Euripides compels his audience to look within their own psyche and find strength there, for the external forces, in this play divinities, cannot be trusted or even admired. For the modern audience, *Ion* alone offers perhaps little more than another telling of the lost-child restored. Yet as the political significance of the play for ancient Athens was great, knowledge of its historical importance can add further meaning to present enjoyment of the action-filled drama. Each of these neglected plays deserves to be granted a chorus more often; all present issues of concern to the contemporary American audience. We may hope the repertoire of Greek tragedies performed will expand during the opening years of the next century.

NOTES

1. Beyond the academic walls the American audience has not seen *Children of Heracles, Seven Against Thebes, Phoenician Women,* or *Andromache.* One experimental theater production of *Ion* was done in 1954, of *Heracles* in 1959, of *Hecuba* in 1987; a single staging of Euripides' *Suppliants* in 1993 played both in California and in Washington, DC. These productions are discussed below.

2. While it is clear that this is but one "act" of a three-piece set, there is no consensus as to which "act" it is. Most scholars place it first, followed by *Prometheus Unbound,* with the trilogy closed by *Prometheus Pyrphoros (Firebringer)*; see D. J. Conacher, *Aeschylus; Prometheus Bound. A Literary Commentary* (Toronto: 1980): 98–119. Mark Griffith, however, suggests that *Firebringer* may have been first; see his discussion in *The Authenticity of Prometheus Bound* (Cambridge: 1977): 15.

3. The performance at Delphi was to be part of a festival inaugurating the "Delphic Dream" of Angelos and Eva Palmer Sikelianos. There, in costumes designed by Eva Sikelianos and to Byzantine music performed by the Athens Symphony Orchestra, the actors read their lines in both English and modern Greek. Neither reviewers nor audience were pleased with the dual languages or that the lines were read, not spoken.

4. In 1970 this group offered an altered version. Titling the new text *Black Titan,* they gave a single performance on 21 April in honor of Martin Luther King Jr. Unfortunately no reviews remain.

5. In Lester's review, Miller is quoted as predicting "in no uncertain terms that Walter Kerr would pan the play." It would seem that his prediction, this time, was inaccurate.

6. As the company's promotional information says, "The Utah Classical Greek Theatre Festival is unique in its annual presentation of a Greek tragedy in a modern American translation for a community audience." The term "festival" is used to indicate that other events are offered in connection with each show, e.g., pre-play lectures, post-show symposia, and photo exhibits.

7. Comedies were played in the afternoons (at least by the late fifth century B.C.) and ended in torchlit festivals; this may have been for practical reasons as well as thematic ones. Exceptions always exist, of course: the final torches of *Oresteia* flared in the late-morning sunshine.

8. David Grene's translation was performed at Union Theological Seminary by the Program in Religious Drama in a single performance on 3 December 1963. While not a production on a "commercial" stage, it was included in Henry Hewes, ed., *The Best Plays of 1963–1964* (New York: 1965): 368.

9. That is, they should not obscure its serious ideas. But as we have seen, when *Helen* has comprised part of the epic versions of the House of Atreus legend (*The Greeks,* for example), the text has been played for laughs more than message.

10. Heracles had dipped his arrows in the blood of the dying hydra of Lerna to poison them. When he shot the Centaur Nessus for attempting to rape Deianeira, the dying Centaur gathered the blood from his wound and gave it to the queen, telling her it was a magic potion that would ensure her husband would not love another woman. When Heracles returned from war with Iole as his concubine, his wife anointed a robe with the blood and sent it to him as a "welcome home" gift. The robe at once caught fire and devoured the flesh of the great hero. He would not

love another woman, and, as an obscure prophecy foretold, he had been killed by one already dead.

11. At this time she played Sheridan Knowles' *Love* along with Talfourd's *Ion*; in other years she had performed in *Evadne, Ingomar,* and *Fazio,* scripts the 1881 reviewer claimed were "familiar to our audiences." In his *Ion* Talfourd changed not only the theme but also the names of the characters: here Ion nearly kills his father, Adrastus, before the recognition; the boy's mother is not, apparently, in the play at all.

12. In the 1994–1995 season, A.C.T. will perform *Hecuba* at the Yerba Buena Gardens, a larger space appealing to director Carey Perloff. The play had been scheduled twice before but withdrawn each time for various reasons. I quote here the director's words about her intent, as the performance lies in the future.

13. Carey Perloff, "Notes from the Director," *Performing Arts,* February 1993, 6. Perloff illustrated each of these themes with performance examples; I have paraphrased her ideas here.

14. *Hecuba* was performed in London in 1992 by the Gate Theatre, in a performance acclaimed by Jeremy Kingston (*Times,* 8 September 1992) as able both to illustrate Euripides' distaste for political slaughter and to keep sympathy with Hecuba.

15. It was Euripides' innovation to place the murders after the *athloi* (labors), thus making the play a more powerful indictment of harsh divinity. Furthermore, the hero is fascinating in his self-awareness and self-acceptance.

16. Qwirk Productions does a Greek play nearly every year, but they work so far Off Off Broadway that their shows receive little critical attention. As they do not respond to requests for information, I am sorry to say that I have not been able to include any discussion of their productions in my study.

17. In MacLeish's drama the central question is the morality of power, while the issue of taking responsibility for the use of that power parallels the Euripidean theme. For a discussion of the modern play, see Colakis, *Classics*: 30–34, and my article "Herakles in a Technological World: An Ancient Myth Transformed" in *Classical and Modern Literature* 5 (1984): 33–38.

18. Oddly enough, and a detail the drama critics eagerly pointed out, Rehm's *Suppliants* opened the same week as A.C.T.'s *Antigone,* two plays that shared setting and theme. Running at the same time at San Francisco State's Theatre Arts Department in Noh Space was Theatre of Yugen's revival of Suzuki's *Trojan Women.* Robert Hurwitt (*San Francisco Examiner,* 19 February 1993) thought this play more powerful in theme but less successful in performance than Rehm's *Suppliants.* In a production that lacked emotional power, the finest moment, he stated, was "the horrific silent scream of the Buddhist god of compassion, Jizo, that brings [the play] to an end." Euripides, of course, had no such deity, no such scream, to close his text.

10

Conclusion

The texts of the ancient Greek plays have been performed on the American commercial stage with surprising frequency during the last century. During the past two decades, the production of these dramas has been ever more frequent; despite our culture's obvious devotion to the new, directors in contemporary theaters have turned to the oldest extant scripts of our Western heritage, seeking through these to address issues that still touch the human soul. As we have seen, however, only some of the possible plays have been selected, and it is now time to consider why this is so, and to define in summary how the Greek plays speak to modern society.

When Sophocles' *Oedipus Tyrannus* was first performed in 1882, it was attacked as having an immoral theme, that the actions condoned (if not actually seen onstage) would have been banned from the stage were the script not one of the "classics." In the early decades of the twentieth century, this play became one respected not only for the classroom but also for the theater. The American audience came to realize the events described in Sophocles' play have little to do with the drama's meaning, that the power of this first and, to some minds, greatest, detective story lies in Oedipus' relentless quest for the truth, a truth that brings him to realize his own identity. Post-Freudian society understood the value of facing the darkest fears of the psyche, even if these are also the strongest taboos of civilization; healing could come through recognition. When Laurence Olivier gave his famous wail of understanding (1946), he initiated this interpretation of Sophocles' play. As the years unrolled, Oedipus' quest took on even further meaning; the play came to mean not only a quest for self-identity, but it also offered an example of social responsibility: the Theban king's knowledge could heal both his own ignorance and the ills of his city. Oedipus became the scapegoat and thus the savior of his society.

The latter interpretation arose from the anthropological interests that came to popularity in the 1960s and 1970s. In tune with this new attention to the early rituals of society, the directors of Greek drama attempted to emphasize in their staging the more primitive elements that could be discovered in the texts. If these were not obvious, they were added; thus the Burgess-Langham *Oedipus* at the Guthrie in 1972 began with a new prologue showing human sacrifice. After this desperate attempt, the cure would then lie in the hands of the king. Oedipus as savior involved social responsibility as well as self-recognition. After nearly a century of production, *Oedipus Tyrannus* had attained success in the American commercial theater. Far from representing a moral failure, as it did in 1882, in the later years of the 1900s the Theban king's search was an exemplar of moral victory.

Although Sophocles' play is arguably the most familiar drama from ancient Greece, it has not appeared recently on the commercial stage, and we might ponder why this is so. A simple answer might be that it is too well known; it is not a play that can be done in modern dress, and its primitive elements have been played too often. More contemporary directors have been turning to less well-known plays: *Ajax*, *Hecuba*, and *Persians* are the plays of recent years. It has long been recognized that the legend of Oedipus is one that cannot be retold; a modern playwright has difficulty putting a new spin on this story, so there are few, if any, modern versions of this myth.[1] But I think the lack of interest in this play rests on a deeper foundation. *Oedipus Tyrannus* is now interpreted as a play of social and personal responsibility, and these are not popular traits in contemporary American culture. Self-knowledge as a virtue no longer holds pride of place in the current national psyche. On the other hand, if Sophocles' play is reconsidered as a drama that displays the ultimate victim, an innocent plaything doomed by the misdeeds of his parents and the inscrutable plans of the gods, I predict it will return to the stage. While I cannot argue that Sophocles intended *his* audience to understand his play thusly, neither could he have foreseen that the audiences of 1882 would condemn its morality.

The same lack of interest in social ills underlies, I think, the lesser appeal of *Antigone*, although the 1994 staging of this play by A.C.T. in San Francisco reveals the text still has meaning. However Carey Perloff's understanding of the role differs from that of Katharine Cornell in 1946 or John Hirsch, who directed the 1971 performance at the Vivian Beaumont at Lincoln Center. In 1946 the world was recovering from the madness of a political tyrant, and *Antigone*, in Anouilh's version, addressed how an individual might stand against such rulers. But, as we have seen, the play's message fell on deaf ears in this country; postwar America did not care for this theme. Although Cornell gave a fine performance, critical reception was cool. By

1971, however, the United States had seen and approved of political protest, and *Antigone* at the Vivian Beaumont was hailed as both timeless and immediate, a play whose plot and theme seemed torn from the daily headlines.

Twenty-three years later, A.C.T.'s Perloff held a different view. She saw in Antigone's character a defiant young woman, yes, but also one who had to believe in her image of her family to survive the horrors of her childhood.[2] Whereas in earlier years Antigone was believed to offer a model for public action by her stand against the state, this was not the primary concept underlying the most recent production of *Antigone*. In 1994, Antigone had become a victim of her past and her society, and her defiance was as much to prove her self-worth as to prove Creon's tyranny wrong.

The second play of the "Theban trilogy" has never caught on in the American theater. Actors have not sought out the role of the aged king with the same zeal that drew actresses to portray Antigone or, more especially, Electra or Medea. The most popular contemporary version of *Oedipus at Colonus* has been Lee Breuer's *Gospel at Colonus*, wherein the king's final moments are retold as a Pentecostal gospel service. Although *Oedipus at Colonus* earned strong reviews on the rare occasions when it was performed, Sophocles' last play remains in the margins of the current repertoire of Greek drama in this country. Although this script confirms Oedipus as an unintending actor, an innocent victim of unfeeling gods, the final transfiguration does not seem to play well on the modern stage. But perhaps the text will be revisited in the near future, for Sophocles' final interpretation of the Theban king should touch some chord in the contemporary American psyche.

Protest against military action, however, has remained a popular theme throughout the century. From the first staging of Euripides' *Trojan Women* in 1915 to Peter Sellar's production of Sophocles' *Ajax* in 1986, the plays that point out the suffering of war continue to appeal. There is no mystery here: the horrors of human conflict and the pain of its victims continue unabated, while the words of those who speak out against it are usually spoken in vain. In the production history of *Trojan Women*, the only time the tragedy lacked appeal was during the "happy days" of the 1950s. At all other moments when the play appeared on the American stage, the critics unanimously proclaimed that Euripides understood and expressed the vanities of war.

Ajax, while it is a play that shows how an individual can suffer at the hands of the "military establishment," and thus illustrates the victimization of the hero, also portrays how the maddened man feels guilt for his deeds and ends his life to avoid further humiliation. As I suggested above in regard to *Oedipus*, this is not a popular theme in modern America. As there have been no productions of Euripides' *Heracles*, another play in which the hero takes responsibility for his actions done in madness (even if sent by a god), so *Ajax* has been staged only once. As a play that speaks against the military establishment, it has appeal; as a text that celebrates personal responsibility, it does not. The tragic grandeur of Oedipus, Heracles, or Ajax, victims of uncaring gods but facing their destinies with courage, cannot shine through that basic issue of personal responsibility.

Revenge is a theme that continues to hold appeal on the contemporary American stage. *Medea* and stories from the House of Atreus have been "granted a chorus" throughout the period of this study. In the early years of the century, Euripides' *Medea* and Sophocles' *Electra* were chosen as vehicles by an actress wishing to play a role that tested her dramatic ability. Thus although the reviewers at Margaret Anglin's first performance of *Electra* took time to note that its theme of revenge was alien to modern thought, they were able to focus upon the power she gave to the role, especially to the scene with the urn she believes holds her brother's ashes.

For *Medea* the lure of the role itself has remained the motivating factor; the theme of Euripides' text has not seemed to trouble either those onstage or those in the audience overly much. While the drama critics at the earliest performances, those of Margaret Anglin and Blanche Yurka, were somewhat put off by the heroine's violent retaliation, they chalked up her fury to her barbarian nature: Medea may be the heroine of a Greek play, but she is a foreigner. In more recent times, directors have made an attempt to focus upon Medea as victim of chauvinist men; Jason is easily recognized even by those who do not consider themselves feminists. Medea's act of revenge thus springs from this victimization.[3] Once again, when the ancient text can be interpreted on the personal, rather than the social level, then it plays well on the modern stage. Sophocles' *Philoctetes*, for example, has seldom been offered, because although the hero is clearly a victim and exiled through no fault of his own, his healing and his glory depend upon his return to society, the very society that wronged him. Philoctetes is allowed no personal revenge against those responsible for his suffering, while Medea takes the ultimate revenge and is exalted for taking it.

Revenge at the hands of a god, on the other hand, is another matter, and so Euripides' *The Bacchae*, a play in which a god calmly destroys a mortal who has denied him, has a fairly brief, albeit colorful, performance history. The popularity of the play, which both arose and peaked in the 1960s, rested on what we might consider a misinterpretation of its text: the celebration of nature and free love. Dionysus' demand for recognition and his punishment of Pentheus and Agave who denied him were secondary themes at that time. In the most recent successful staging of *The Bacchae*, that at the Guthrie in 1988, the emphasis was on the balance that one should try to achieve in life, and this is surely one theme of Euripides' play. Unnoticed to date by contemporary directors, however, is the option of interpreting the conflict of Pentheus and Dionysus as that between state and church, between political and religious demands. This ancient play illustrates so well the futility of trying to oppose religious belief with military power that

I would have guessed it to be a text extremely relevant to the times. But as no such conflicts are currently within our national borders, perhaps that interpretation of the Greek play appears less relevant at the moment, just as Anouilh's *Antigone* did not have the same urgency for the American audience in 1946 as it did for those in French theaters just three years earlier.

Let us return now to *Electra* and the other plays arising from the House of Atreus legend, all but one based on the theme of revenge. The performance history of Sophocles' *Electra* begins early, and the play continues to be performed regularly. The other texts based on this myth, *Oresteia*, *Orestes*, and *Iphigeneia at Aulis*, however, did not appear on the American stage until midway in the twentieth century. The first full productions of Aeschylus' *Oresteia*, for instance, were at Ypsilanti, Michigan, in summer 1966, and at the Guthrie Theater in the fall of that year. A separate staging of Euripides' *Orestes* first took place two years later, while his *Iphigeneia at Aulis*, apart from the performance in 1921 when Margaret Anglin played Clytemnestra, was not "granted a chorus" until 1967. In recent years, however, it is these plays that have held pride of place among Greek dramas in the commercial theaters of the United States.

In 1977 Andrei Serban offered his version of *Agamemnon*. He was interested in the play as ritual, as a vehicle for displaying his belief that emotion could be carried by sound and motion, not primarily by words. I would characterize Serban's show as out of the mainstream of Greek tragedy production, one more interested in theatricality, perhaps even *ars gratia artis*, than illustrative of ideas prevalent in America during the 1970s, although his emphasis on the play's violence was right on target.

With the dawn of the 1980s plays from the House of Atreus myth moved into the spotlight. First to appear was the Barton-Cavander epic ten-play presentation *The Greeks*. This collage of ancient texts was, perhaps, as much a theatrical trick as was Serban's, but here the intent was to present the entire myth as a sequential package, so that audiences could see the growing power of the curse and the revenge, how the wrongs of one generation spread into and infected the next. By placing *Iphigeneia at Aulis* as the prologue, Agamemnon's guilt was brought to the fore; he did not die for Clytemnestra's whim; her revenge was aptly motivated by the king's wanton actions done in his desire for glory. This massive production was imported—and shortened—from the London stage,[4] and toured the United States; by the time it reached the West Coast, the plays had become so altered that one critic suggested the show be retitled *The Greeks Go to Hollywood*.

It can be no accident that the opening years of the 1990s have seen three productions of the full *Oresteia*, plus a very popular interpretation of *Orestes* alone. In 1992 Ariane Mnouchkine brought to America her Théâtre du Soleil's epic staging of the trilogy, plus *Iphigeneia at Aulis*, and the performance won instant (if at times exhausted!) acclaim. In the same year the

Guthrie staged its three-part version of the story, this time focusing on Clytemnestra, while in 1994 Tim Robbins' Actors' Gang Theater also offered a House of Atreus trilogy; neither included *Eumenides*. Mnouchkine's *Les Atrides* makes the myth both timeless and multicultural, but the emphasis is on the importance of women in civilization, on the part they play in this great legend and thus in the collective consciousness of contemporary society. The Guthrie's trilogy (*Iphigeneia at Aulis, Agamemnon,* and Sophocles' *Electra*) also focused on the women, but on Clytemnestra's proper action in taking revenge against the man who had wronged her (and her daughter); this was to be a feminist portrayal of Aeschylus' text. The suffering of women and their condoned personal revenge is the interpretation currently given to the play that in Aeschylus' day celebrated the institution of civic justice and the closing of vendetta law.

Tim Robbins' trilogy (*Agamemnon*, Sophocles' *Electra*, and *Orestes*) was set in the modern world, with no attempt to evoke the ancient palaces. The scripts were also new: Charles Mee was author of the first and last, Ellen McLaughlin adapted Sophocles' text. Critics hailed the relevance of the play(s), since domestic violence run amok rang true for the American audiences of the 1990s. The insane asylum that was the setting for *Orestes* was also proclaimed as an appropriate metaphor for the times: in the ruins of the House of Atreus lies the deterioration, if not the collapse, of modern society.

Greek plays of revenge and ruin are thought to reflect the temper of the times in the contemporary commercial theater. It is certainly no accident that performances of *Medea* and stories from the House of Atreus are currently popular on the American stage. In earlier years of our century, these dramas were considered illustrative of the higher aspects of the soul. Today these plays are understood to illuminate the negative qualities of the human psyche. Such wide discrepancies are not new: the ancient playwrights also found different meanings in the myths. At the midpoint of fifth-century B.C. Athens, Aeschylus was celebrating the liberation of his democratic society from the dangers of vendetta justice, the creation of a jury court system that would deny the validity of personal revenge, and used the House of Atreus legend as the foundation for his ideas. Fifty years later, Euripides put a different spin on this myth. He still denied the validity of personal revenge, but showed in his *Orestes* that the stain of murder can drive a man and those associated with him into madness. He thought that Athens of 408 B.C. was a society sick with its political and military problems; he could only hope that his despair might be translated into positive action. Charles Mee's updated version of Euripides' play is thus on target when it is set within an insane asylum, and although its images are drawn from popular culture, we can hope, perhaps, that his play will be viewed as a warning, not a celebration, and that its message will have more power than did the Greek playwright's in his own day.

In ancient Athens, the playwright's texts reflected the current political scene and dealt with contemporary social issues. As I have shown in this study, performances of Greek tragedy in contemporary America also respond to social conditions, while the interpretations of the myth vary with the concerns of society. As Aeschylus used the House of Atreus myth to celebrate the deeds of his city-state in 458 B.C., Euripides turned to the same tale in 408 B.C. to condemn its actions. In twentieth-century America, Oedipus' story illustrated a man's quest for self-knowledge when staged in the first half of the era, his responsibility to his society as its scapegoat in later years. Euripides' *Bacchae* reflected current emphasis on free love when staged in the 1960s, responded to a quest for balance in the 1980s. Only *Trojan Women* has remained constant in its message. From the day when Euripides penned it in 415 B.C. to the present time, the suffering he portrayed of war's innocent victims has spoken to audiences in nearly every decade of the past century, for the pain of military conflict is apparently neverending.

Ideas of morality, the right of political protest, the quest for self-identity, the validity of revenge, the nature of sacrifice and the need for it: the Greek tragedies address all these issues. Concepts about these issues, however, constantly change with a society's altering circumstances. But in the unchanging texts of the ancient Greek playwrights, twentieth-century directors and producers find a meaning that has validity, a message they can interpret for their audience, for their own society. From our knowledge of the Greek plays, whether we finally approve of a particular presentation or think it misses the mark, we can recognize its intent. The dramas of the Athenian playwrights address timeless issues of society and the human psyche. During the past century these unchanging texts have been brought continuously to the American stage, and, I fearlessly predict, Greek tragedies will continue to be "granted a chorus" for the contemporary theaters of our nation.

NOTES

1. While the House of Atreus myth has been retold by many playwrights (O'Neill, Giraudoux, Sartre, Eliot, Mee), for the Oedipus story one can cite primarily Cocteau's *Infernal Machine*, and perhaps the obscure *Oedipus and the Sphinx* by Hofmannsthal. The lack of modern Oedipus plays is discussed by G. Karl Galinsky in *The Herakles Theme: The Adaptations of the Hero in Literature from Homer to the Twentieth Century* (Totowa, NJ: 1972): 1–2; ancient myth on the modern stage is discussed by Hugh Dickinson, *Myth on the Modern Stage* (Urbana, IL: 1969), and Angela Belli, *Ancient Greek Myths and Modern Drama: A Study in Continuity* (New York: 1969).

A recent attempt to stage *Oedipus* as a parable of beleaguered Washington, DC, Mayor Marion Barry failed because, as critics pointed out, Barry did not take any responsibility for his alleged wrongs, and certainly did not leave as a scapegoat, voluntary or otherwise, for his society. I must note, however, that unlike Oedipus, Barry was voted back into power in 1994.

2. Perloff chose the text for practical as well as philosophical reasons. She saw it as appropriate in message after the Los Angeles riots (1993), and after viewing the ruins of the Geary Theater as a result of the 1989 San Francisco earthquake, she immediately wanted to set a Greek show in this space where "theatrical order had been violated." Carey Perloff, "Notes from the Director," *Performing Arts* (February 1993): 6–8.

3. Classical scholars, on the other hand, have looked to Jason's violation of his oath as the source of Medea's anger; see Anne Pippin Burnett, "Medea and the Tragedy of Revenge," *Classical Philology* 68 (1973): 1–24. Again, when Jason wronged the granddaughter of the sun he earned inevitable punishment—this time at the hands of the woman he scorned; no other deity was required. There is much debate about the ultimate divinity of Medea; see (among others) Andrei Rivier, *Essai sur le Tragique* (Paris: 1975): chap. 2, and Pietro Pucci, *The Violence of Pity in Euripides' Medea* (Ithaca, NY: 1980).

4. It cannot be denied that much of the interest in the massive productions of Greek drama in America reflects the personal interests of key directors of the British theater, e.g., Peter Hall, Peter Stein, and Tony Harrison. Reasons for the appeal of the Greek plays to these men are most recently discussed by Fiona Macintosh, "Tragedy in Performance: Nineteenth and Twentieth Century Productions," in *The Cambridge Companion to Greek Tragedy*, ed. P. E. Easterling (forthcoming).

Selected Bibliography

Most information about the production of Greek tragedy in the United States has been gleaned from reviews in newspapers and magazines, production advertisements, and program notes. In addition to these, I have consulted the books and articles listed below.

Alexander, Doris M. "Oedipus in Victorian New York." *American Quarterly* 12 (1960): 417–421.

Barton, John, and Kenneth Cavander. *The Greeks. Ten Greek Plays Given as a Trilogy.* London: Heinemann, 1981.

Belli, Angela. *Ancient Myths and Modern Drama. A Study in Continuity.* New York: Columbia University Press, 1969.

Bieber, Margarete. *The History of the Greek and Roman Theatre.* Princeton, NJ: Princeton University Press, 1961.

Browne, Maurice. *Too Late to Lament.* Bloomington: Indiana University Press, 1956.

Burgess, Anthony. *Sophocles' Oedipus the King.* Minneapolis: University of Minnesota Press, 1972.

Burnett, Anne Pippin. "Medea and the Tragedy of Revenge." *Classical Philology* 68 (1973): 1–24.

Chopcian, Kendra Alice. "An Analysis of Maurice Browne's Directing Theories and Practices with the Chicago Little Theatre." Ph.D. diss., University of Michigan, 1989.

Colakis, Marianthe. *The Classics in the American Theater of the 1960s and Early 1970s.* Lanham, MD: University Press of America, 1993.

Dickinson, Hugh. *Myth on the Modern Stage.* Urbana: University of Illinois Press, 1969.

Edwards, Paul. " 'Putting on the Greeks': Euripidean Tragedy and the Twentieth Century American Theatre." Ph.D. diss., University of Colorado, 1987.

Eliot, T. S. *On Poetry and Poets.* London: Faber and Faber, 1957.

Engel, Lehman. *The Critics*. New York: Macmillan, 1976.

Fairclough, H. Rushton. *Antigone. An Account of the Presentation of the Antigone of Sophocles. As Performed (in Greek) at Stanford University in 1902*. San Francisco: Paul Elder, 1903.

Ford, James E. "The Rebirth of Greek Tragedy and the Decline of the Humanities." *Georgia Review* 34 (1980): 545–555.

Gagey, Edmond M. *The San Francisco Stage. A History*. New York: Columbia University Press, 1950.

Gagnon, Pauline. "The Development and Achievement of La Mama under the Artistic Direction of Ellen Stewart." Ph.D. diss., University of Michigan, 1987.

Goodman, Dean. *San Francisco Stages. A Concise History, 1849–1986*. San Francisco: Micro Pro Litra Press, 1986.

Guthrie, Tyrone. *In Various Directions. A View of the Theatre*. New York: Macmillan, 1965.

Haines, D. D. "Greek Plays in America." *Classical Journal* 6 (1910): 24–39.

Knox, Bernard. Review of *Agamemnon. New York Review of Books*, 14 July 1977. Reprinted in *Word and Action. Essays on the Ancient Theatre*, 70–78. Baltimore: Johns Hopkins University Press, 1979.

Lewin, John. *The House of Atreus*. Minneapolis: University of Minnesota Press, 1966.

Macintosh, Fiona. "Tragedy in Performance: Nineteenth and Twentieth Century Productions." In *The Cambridge Companion to Greek Tragedy*, edited by P. E. Easterling. Cambridge: forthcoming.

Moses, Montrose J., and John Mason Brown, eds. *The American Stage as Seen by Its Critics, 1752–1934*. New York: Cooper Square Publishers, 1967.

Norman, Henry. *An Account of the Harvard Greek Play*. Boston: James Osgood and Company, 1882.

Parke, H. W. *Festivals of the Athenians*. Ithaca, NY: Cornell University Press, 1977.

Perloff, Carey. "Notes from the Director." *Performing Arts*, February 1993, 6–8.

Plugge, Domis E. *The History of Greek Play Production in American Colleges and Universities 1881–1936*. New York: Columbia Teachers College, 1938.

Pucci, Pietro. *The Violence of Pity in Eurpides' Medea*. Ithaca, NY: Cornell University Press, 1980.

Rivier, Andrei. *Essai sur le Tragique*. Paris: Boccard, 1975.

Rogers, Priscilla. "Greek Tragedy in the New York Theatre: A History and Interpretation." Ph.D. diss., University of Michigan, 1986.

Ryzuk, Mary S. "The Circle Repertory Company. The First Fifteen Years." Ph.D. diss., City University of New York, 1986.

Taplin, Oliver. *Greek Tragedy in Action*. Berkeley: University of California Press, 1978.

Walcott, Peter. *Greek Drama in Its Theatrical and Social Context*. Cardiff: University of Wales, 1976.

Walton, J. Michael. *Greek Theatre Production*. Westport, CT: Greenwood Press, 1980.

Wilk, John R. *The Creation of an Ensemble. The First Years of the American Conservatory Theater*. Carbondale: Southern Illinois University Press, 1986.

Index

About the Author

KARELISA V. HARTIGAN is Professor of Classics at the University of Florida. She is the author of several books including *Ambiguity and Self-Deception: The Apollo and Artemis Plays of Euripides*.

Recent Titles in
Contributions in Drama and Theatre Studies

ISBN 0-313-29283-3

HARDCOVER BAR CODE